W9-ABQ-096

NEHRU: THE YEARS OF POWER

OTHER NONFICTION BY VINCENT SHEEAN

Nehru: The Years of Power
Orpheus at Eighty
First and Last Love
Lead, Kindly Light
This House against This House
Between the Thunder and the Sun
Not Peace but a Sword
Personal History

Vincent Sheean

DS481
N35
S48

NEHRU:

The Years of Power

RANDOM HOUSE : NEW YORK

NOV 1960

64744

FIRST PRINTING

© Copyright, 1960, by Vincent Sheean
All rights reserved under International and Pan-American Copyright Conventions.
Published in New York by Random House, Inc., and simultaneously in Toronto, Canada, by Random House of Canada, Limited.
Library of Congress Catalog Card Number: 59-10828
Manufactured in the United States of America by H. Wolff, New York

TO UNNI NAYAR

Lieutenant Colonel in the Indian Army,
killed in Korea on August 12, 1950:
truest of friends, bravest of men,
he taught me something about India.

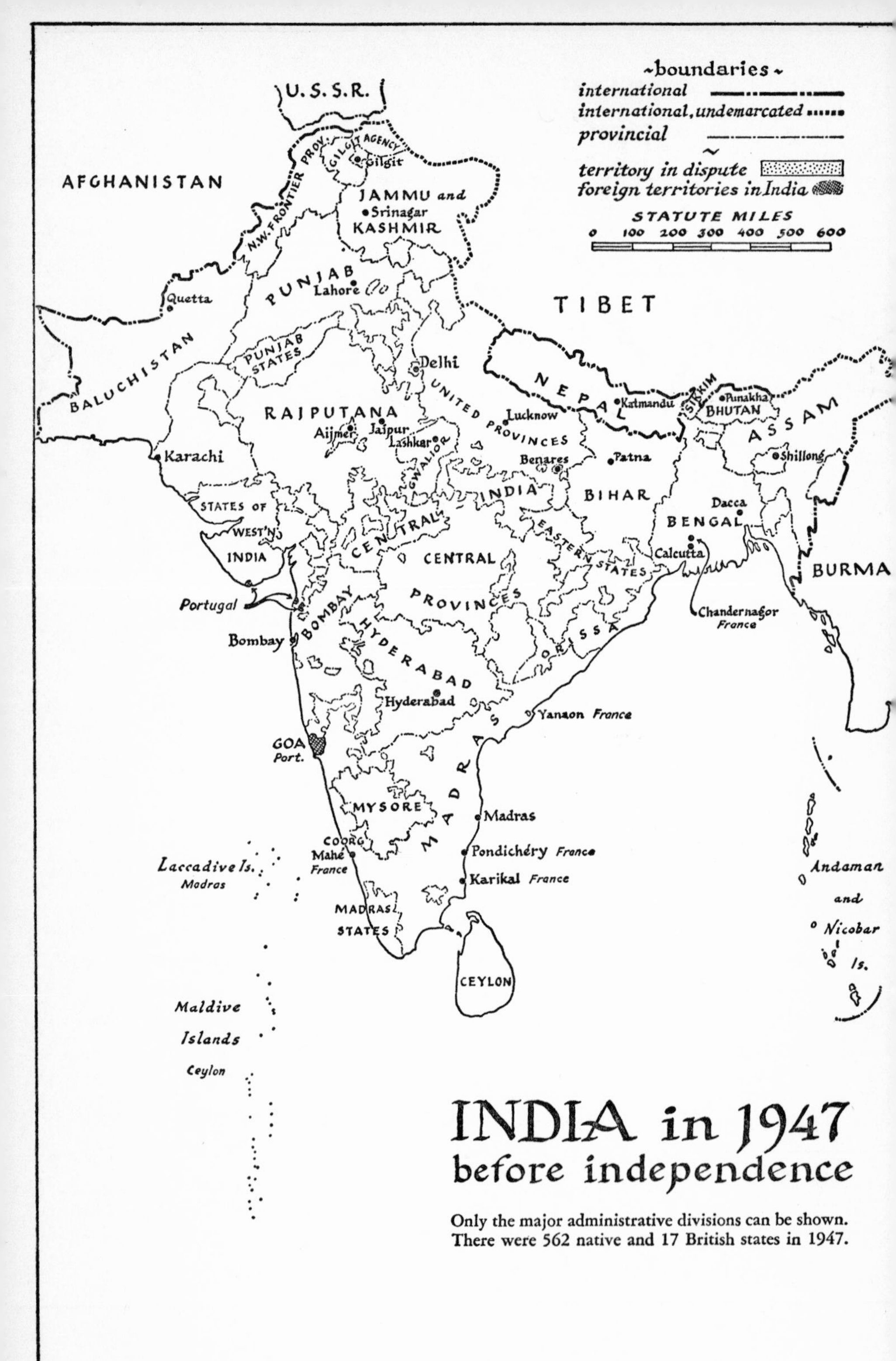

INDIA in 1947 before independence

Only the major administrative divisions can be shown. There were 562 native and 17 British states in 1947.

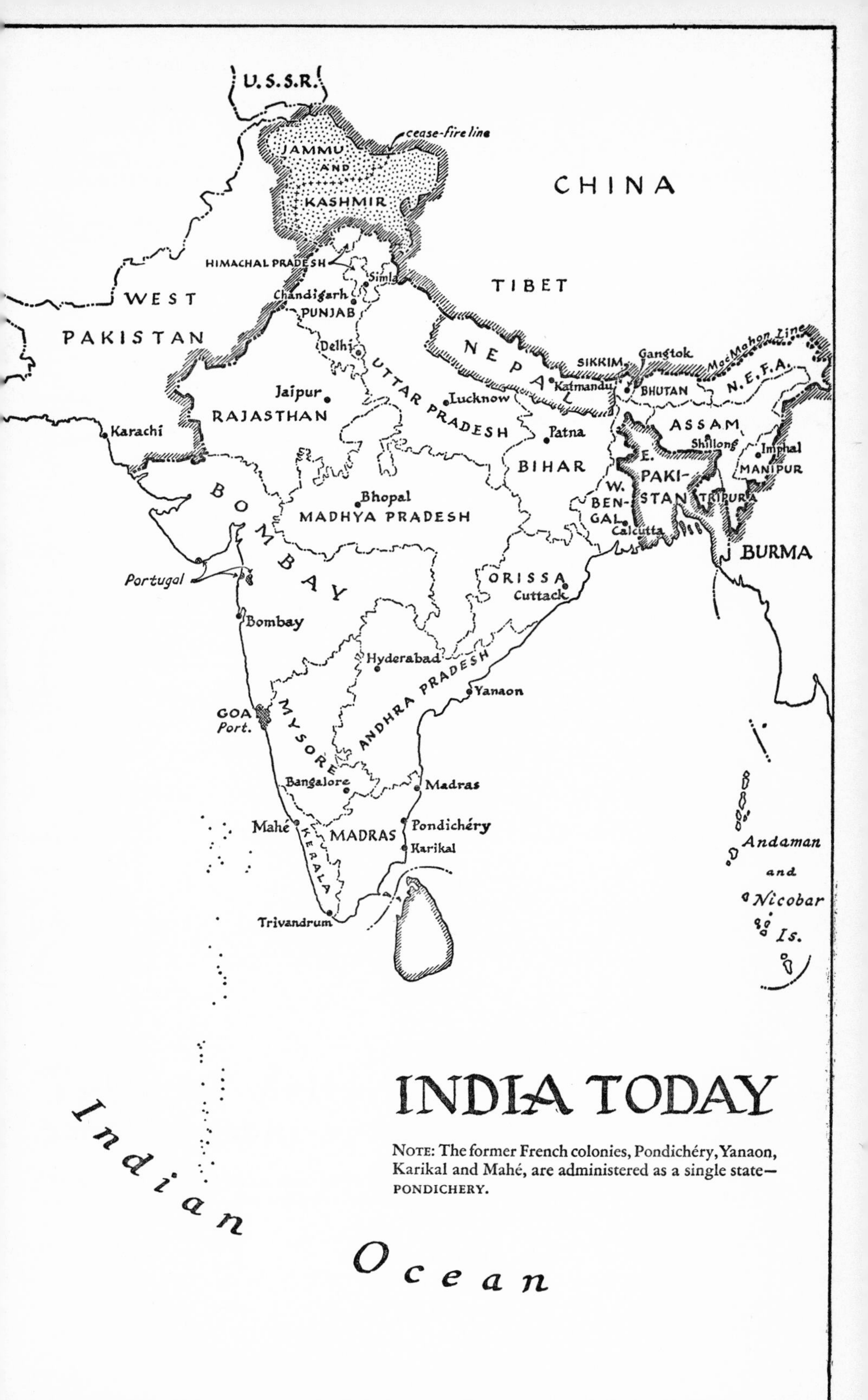

INDIA TODAY

NOTE: The former French colonies, Pondichéry, Yanaon, Karikal and Mahé, are administered as a single state—PONDICHERY.

I *Dawn in a Garden*

EVERY YEAR on the thirtieth of January some men and women come together just before dawn in a garden in Delhi. They do not speak to each other; they come like ghosts across the silent and grassy darkness to the place appointed. There are never more than twenty to thirty such persons, and rather less than more. They sit on the ground in rows while one or two among them chant softly the old prayers and songs of a time none can remember. A good many of the figures that come and go are dressed in white, which gives them a wraithlike luminosity in the dark hush of the hour.

The spot before which they make this gathering is the place where Mahatma Gandhi was killed on January 30, 1948. It is against the back wall of a garden belonging to Mr. G. D. Birla, a rich man, in whose house (or in a wing of whose house) the Mahatma had taken refuge during the weeks before his death. This rear end of the garden is a raised place, a terrace, with a small summer house on one side, and in that summer house or pavilion the Mahatma used to hold his evening prayer meeting while he was there, with the public—whatever public chose to come—seated on the lawn before him. He was on his way from the house to this terrace for the evening prayers, and had in fact mounted the four steps which led to it, when a demented Brahmin with notions of Hindu supremacy shot and killed him.

The steps are not there any more. Neither is the low wall of stones on which I collapsed when I heard those shots in 1948. Mr. Birla, who owns this house and garden, has altered as much of the terrace as possible; we can only suppose it was to obviate the possibility of having a shrine imposed upon him. There is a hedge now where once was a wall, and in many curious, tiny ways the aspect of the place has changed. This garden is private property—a sacred thing in itself—and at one time Mr. Birla had to protest publicly against a wave of popular feeling which wanted to turn it into a national shrine. He said that he had allowed the Mahatma "and his liberal friends" to come there when they pleased, which they did in numbers which, he implied, were not always convenient to him, but it was still his and he meant to keep it. Thus it has remained.

Now a whole decade has passed since that soft and shining January evening when the Mahatma walked to his death through the roses. His punctuality, a lifelong rule, was impaired that evening by a long talk with Vallabhbhai Patel; he did not start his walk from the house to the terrace until almost a quarter past five. I glanced at my watch and it was twelve minutes past five, which was twelve minutes of tardiness and almost without precedent for Gandhi. At seventeen minutes past five he was murdered. There are innumerable men and women throughout the world who will never forget the day or the hour. Those who meet at dawn in the garden on this anniversary are few in number, a handful of close friends and followers. They have, in several of these years, admitted among them a foreigner who, although ignorant of the prayers and chants, was there on the mournful day itself and remembers and returns.

Such a gathering, in silence and darkness, would be extremely rare and perhaps impossible in any other country. In India it has very nearly a secret quality, if we may impute secrecy to something everybody knows. That is, there are never any crowds or any curious here in this garden; there are, above all, no photographers. Although the crowds and the curious are to be seen later in the day, and the photographers, too, those who come to the garden in the hour before dawn are of another kind, the bereft for a decade, bereft forever. They are not numerous but they range widely, as widely as Gandhi's own interests and good will. There is the first President of the Republic of India, Dr.

Prasad, stooped in sorrow, absorbed in it as in the shawls into which his head droops. There is an untouchable; here is a village worker; there is a faithful friend who still carries out the work he did when the Mahatma was alive. Among them, whitest of the white shadows, there passes the memorable apparition of Jawaharlal Nehru, silent and intent, to whom nobody speaks, for once: here all are equal and none has anything to ask of another.

As the darkness begins to lift they dissolve and vanish. The whole thing has taken only a few minutes, ten at the most, and although it is an annual occurrence it has never yet been disturbed by an untoward sight or sound. The great crowds assemble later on, down by the river, where superbly simple lawns surround the cremation platform of the Mahatma. There are crowds in many other places, too, and in many cities, for this is a day of national mourning: it has received the name of the Day of the Martyrs and commemorates not only Gandhi but any and all who died, like him, for this people. A very large number of persons remain indoors all day, fasting and praying, on January 30th, but a multitude assembles in public wherever there is a reason for doing so. At the Rajghat—the cremation platform—after the sun has risen, there are chants and songs which include the entire *Bhagavad Gita*, and the sonorities of Sanskrit poetry rise over a pyramid of flowers to the morning light. The cabinet ministers spin publicly for one hour, after this, and there are other commemorative ceremonies, including a mass meeting later in the day at which it has become the custom for the Prime Minister, Jawaharlal Nehru, to make an important speech of some length.

These are the public observances of a nation's emotional unity at great moments. They are right and proper, for there has scarcely ever been a more tragic birth than that of the Indian Union, partitioned and drenched in blood at the moment it came into being, and then robbed of its guiding star. To remember these things—just to remember them—is in itself a form of thought, and on January 30th there can be very few adult Indians who fail to do so. Whether this could be said the day before or the day after is another question. If January 30th were to become a day of ceremonial mourning, like certain fixed days in Siam or Cambodia or imperial China, it would lose its present significance. So long as many or most Indians actually remember Gandhi, as they do now, that danger cannot arise, and the day is, in a very full sense, a day of solemn recollection. It is a day on which those who only saw the Mahatma once, at a great distance, take pride in telling of that once, and in every detail. They may not feel inclined to dwell upon it before or afterward, but once a year is perhaps—at this stage in history—more than most nations have to give to the unifying power of a great memory.

When we encounter the inevitable question concerning India's fidelity to the teachings of the Mahatma we touch upon a vast and highly controversial subject of debate. The question is incessantly asked in India, in public and in private, in parliament and in the press. Is thus-and-so in accordance with the Mahatma's teaching? Would the Mahatma approve of this or that man or law or policy? "What would Gandhi say?" To a lesser degree the same questions are asked in other countries as well, but generally in a form tempered by international courtesy. In India itself, where discussion is extremely free and the press seems to be about the freest in the world, no such limits are put upon expression, and we can read, every single morning, the most wholesale accusations against the ruling party and government, Gandhi's heirs.

This is not the place to answer that overriding question: in one sense it is the subject of this book and it will be long before we can get through all the considerations it involves. But here, at the outset, it should be stated very plainly, for the benefit of those who have forgotten, that India as a whole *never* accepted Gandhi's teaching. He taught an extremely wide variety of ethical precepts, ranging from hygiene and sexual continence to nationalism, internationalism, the universality of religions, the efficacy of prayer and the necessity of constant effort for the material welfare of the people. Nonviolence was a vital element in his teaching at all times but was subject to notable reservations: he always admitted the right of self-defense, for example, and on some occasions his dislike for cowardice led him into praise for this form of violence as a relative good. The whole body of Gandhi's teaching was accepted only by those immediate followers who made up his Ashram, his own particular community, bound by vows of chastity and poverty not unlike those of the Franciscans. They were never numerous when weighed against the hundreds of millions of Indians. The world at large saw all India aroused in 1921, again in 1930, again in 1941, by Gandhi's irresistible appeal to the masses in the national struggle. What the world at large never saw, apparently, was that these tremendous upheavals were of a purely national character even when Gandhi's peculiar genius gave them a religious coloration. In other words, at the high moments of the Indian revolution there were many millions who followed Gandhi in that respect —toward unity and independence—without for one single moment accepting his ethical and philosophical doctrines. This needs to be made very plain lest we fall into the serious error of supposing that the Mahatma ever, at any time, prevailed over the fundamental nature of mankind, even in India.

How could it have been otherwise? The "irascible and concupiscible appetites," as St. Thomas Aquinas called them, are so strong and deep in man that no sage of any country has overcome them for long at a time. Even Gandhi's insistence upon ethical disciplines was tempered by an unfailing forbearance, or even comprehension for those who proved unable to carry them out fully. His usual method consisted in taking the burden of such frailties upon himself, on the theory that if he had made his principles clearer his followers could not have violated them. Thus his whole life was dotted with episodes which seem weirdly unnecessary to most modern minds—suspending all activity to fast and pray, for example, because a boy and girl in his Ashram had fallen in love and taken the way of nature. The theory that such lapses—for they were lapses from vows freely taken—were his own fault is here superimposed upon the fundamental Indian philosophical concept of the One and the Many, in which the sin, as he saw it, was his own because his soul and theirs were one. Gandhi never indulged in metaphysical doctrine or speculation—he was too busy—but by countless inferences and implications throughout his spoken and written work we can see that he was Hindu to the depths of his being, taking for granted an entire series of concepts which a Western mind has to learn as one learns a foreign language or a multiplication table.

Karma, the merit or demerit of past lives, and the journey of the soul through many such lives toward its union with the over-soul, which is origin and destination alike, are such concepts. He seldom discussed them but their animating power ran through all his work. How could he be too severe with the sinner when the sin was in part his own? How could he condemn a man whose soul was partly his?

Furthermore, some of the closest associates and followers of Mahatma Gandhi were impervious to a great part of his teaching. I have already said that this teaching was *never* accepted by the masses, who did not understand it except instinctually; they reverenced the teacher to the point of idolatry without absorbing the lesson. What is more significant to political history, and also considerably more unusual, is that men and women who were close to Gandhi through most of their adult lives were like the vast, illiterate masses in separating the teacher from what he taught. In so doing, they kept their independence of judgment against one of the most powerful human spirits that ever attempted to influence others. First among these, as history has already amply recorded, is Jawaharlal Nehru, but since his problems in this respect are the theme of our study, it might be well to mention others first.

One, certainly, was Sarojini Naidu, one of the most remarkable women of the Indian national movement, a poet and orator, courageous far beyond ordinary definitions of courage, who gave Gandhi and the Congress Party more than twenty-five years of devotion. Mrs. Naidu learned much from Gandhi, and said so; he was her master, as she declared in the memorable broadcast she made after his death; in the realm of ideas she was humble before him. "He taught us to be just," she said to me once, "when it is so much easier to be generous." Mrs. Naidu as President of the Congress (1930), after Gandhi and others had gone to jail, succeeded in obtaining a degree of nonviolence, sheer physical sacrifice of volunteers before the brutality of the police, which was the wonder of the world. The movement had no more eloquent speaker, Gandhi no more devoted friend. Yet Mrs. Naidu rejected a huge part of the Gandhian discipline, first and last. When I asked her if she had ever tried to follow Gandhi's rules in diet, she laughed at me. "Good heavens," she said.

"All that grass and goats' milk? Never, never, never!" It was the same with "disciplinary resolutions," as he called them, vows and the like. It would have been the same with nonviolence itself, the unique center of the Gandhian system, I have often suspected, if it had not proved to be ideally suited to the conditions of an unarmed mass against British power. This truly great woman was certainly capable of wrath, but for the whole last part of her life she subdued her stormy nature to the overruling principle of nonviolence. In what she accepted and what she rejected of the Mahatma's system she was not only supremely and independently herself (which he freely recognized) but was representative of an entire category of well-to-do intellectuals in the Indian revolution. An extremely witty and downright woman of the world, with a command of the English language seldom equaled anywhere, she was as different as possible (in silks and jewels, too, as was the fashion of the time) from the little black man in homespun, seated on the floor to eat his curds and whey, whom she called upon in London in 1914. From that time onward she was his ally and soon to be his follower, but she remained herself to the end.

Another was the Maulana—or teacher—Abul Kalam Azad, the Islamic divine whose death early in 1958 was an irreparable loss to India. He, too, was Gandhi's ally and follower from an early period, but without any surrender to the ethical system or the disciplinary rule. Just as he remained Muslim through and through, so he remained himself in other ways, with an independence of mind which did not fail him even in old age. Azad (we used to call him "Maulana Sahib," as Gandhi did) was the only person I have ever heard of who dared to smoke cigarettes in the Mahatma's presence. He always did, because it was his habit and he saw no ethical reason for abstaining from it. Gandhi was fond of his little jokes and repeated them often: "Still smoking opium, I see?" he would say to the Maulana. The imperturbable Maulana continued to smoke for the thirty years of their friendship. The one essential condition of the Gandhian revolution, nonviolence, he did accept, but largely because of its historical correctness in Indian conditions. It is not a principle of the Islamic religion, but the Maulana reconciled it to the law of the Prophet by emphasizing the rarity of violence in the Koran and its religious nature. (Long prayer and fasting preceded the "holy war," and the Prophet, Upon Whom Be Peace, was not *a priori* violent.)

A considerable number of other close associates of Gandhi in his national or public work were similarly independent in their various ways. They rejected his ethics as being too extreme; they were bewildered by his religious mysticism; they could not understand how he came to some of his decisions. Much of what he said and did seemed to them irrational, related to theories of "inspiration" which could at times resemble whimsicality, and difficult to interpret according to the views of modern social and natural science. Yet these, too, saw in him the only possible leader and teacher for the Indian national movement for two reasons which, however exasperating, were pragmatic imperatives: first, the Indian masses for thirty years would follow nobody else, and, second, Gandhi's courses of action generally turned out to be right in their results. The soreness of bewilderment which this attitude engendered among such associates has been expressed by Jawaharlal Nehru in his autobiography (1936), although with it he also fully expresses the love and devotion which the Mahatma evoked.

For Nehru, certainly, is the most conspicuous example of the non-Gandhian Gandhian. He never at any time adopted the monastic rules or the religious basis of the Mahatma's life. He was influenced, and deeply, but when he disagreed with Gandhi he said so without regard to the consequences. He led the whole younger wing of the Congress Party in open revolt against the Mahatma in 1929, and carried the vote by a majority which compelled Gandhi, against his better judgment, to make independence the object of the national movement. (Gandhi went home and wrote the "independence pledge" of January 16, 1930, but it was Nehru's idea.) On other and less momentous occasions Nehru asserted his natural independence of mind, without for one moment impairing the flow of confidence and affection that subsisted between them. History affords very few examples of a lifelong association in public work which can be compared to this one, but the point we wish to make here is that it did not involve domination or subjugation: if it were the relation of father and son it was exercised in much greater liberty than is usual in human affairs. Gandhi, it is true, often called Nehru his "heir," but on almost every such occasion he prefaced the noun by the adjective "political." He knew that there were great areas of his own inner pilgrimage into which Nehru would never follow him. It is true that Mr. Nehru wears homespun and probably knows most of the *Gita* (anyhow the second chapter) by heart; on his return from England in his youth he adopted vegetarianism because it is the habit of the majority in India; he conforms to the customs of his own country and never gives offense to its religions; but the shape of his mind is not determined by custom or habit. When he pressed the button which opened a great power dam in the Damodar Valley, not so long ago, he said: "These are our temples." It is utterly impossible to imagine Gandhi either thinking or saying such words.

We return, therefore, to the inevitable question (India's fidelity to Gandhi) with two points which should serve as reminders of historic fact: first, that India never was wholly Gandhian, and second, that many of Gandhi's nearest and dearest were at variance with him in important respects. The whole body of his teaching was accepted by very few of those who followed him to victory in the Indian national revolution. So much for the past: and in the present . . . ?

There will be opportunities in the course of this book to see many aspects of Indian life ten years after the martyrdom of Gandhi. For the moment two generalizations ought to be made for the sake of guidance through the labyrinth. That Gandhi is keenly, deeply remembered is one. That he is widely and thoughtlessly forgotten is the other.

And again, how could it be otherwise? He must be keenly and deeply remembered because there is no living Indian adult whose life was not affected by him in countless ways. He must be widely and thoughtlessly forgotten because he has been gone for eleven years, and citizens of the Indian Union no longer have that constant, gentle admonition in their ears. Every word Gandhi said at his evening prayer meetings was recorded and broadcast to all India every day two or three times; his words were printed in every newspaper; it was impossible for any Indian, during his lifetime, to escape his influence. All this has passed with his own life, and for an ordinary Indian to consult texts of the past as guidance in the present would be contrary to the nature of most human beings. Besides, what Gandhi said in a certain situation in 1936 or 1946 may have little or no application either to a certain situation in 1960 or to what he himself would have said in 1960. He changed his views, in all but a few simple, great principles, according to the development of time and circumstance. His words have now become texts and, as texts, they are not often consulted except by experts. Most of all, the power of the man, his extraordinary magnetism, his ability to convince or beguile even his adversaries, the strange ecstasy he brought into being among vast crowds, the devotion that flamed in his presence—all this departed with his life. Small wonder that in daily existence he is, by many or most, quite thoughtlessly forgotten. When he is universally remembered is on this day, January 30th, the Day of Martyrs, when India remembers and thinks.

But in times of crisis or emotion, of decision or fatality public or private, even the most ordinary Indian tends to consult him, the lost father, and guess what he might do or say. This is why that irksome question is so constantly put forward in the press and elsewhere, and why, from time to time, men are judged by what other men think Gandhian standards might require. While he was alive Gandhi could speak for himself; now there are three hundred and sixty millions who speak for him, and (it sometimes seems) no two of them say the same thing. That is the penalty of his greatness, which was bound up with his life on earth and went into a different dimension at his death. Nietzsche thought that the only Christian died on the cross; we may equally say that the only complete Gandhian perished by the assassin's bullets on January 30, 1948.

Sporadic recollection is not a living presence, and the memory which is institutionalized or fixed upon a single day in the year is not a continuing guide. They may often turn into hollow sentimentality or crocodile tears. A man can scarcely be elected to public office in India unless he pays his due tribute to Gandhi on the required occasions and on such other occasions as he can manufacture. Much of this has become a political routine or device. Office-holding and office-seeking based upon the sanctity of the dead father, claiming, as it were, an inherited halo, are common enough in India—so common that the people are beginning to wonder if it is a valid system of choice. The growing strength of the Communist electorate in great cities and depressed areas is all at the expense of the Congress Party and its candidates in their Gandhi caps and homespun: it is not that the people have rejected Gandhi, which they will never do, but that he is no longer with them. In his absence the white-capped officeholders have come to seem, in a good many places and local situations, like vain shows and whited sepulchres.

In this combination of remembering and forgetting, of thinking and of thoughtlessness, nothing can be fixed or constant. Nobody can predict the results of an election in India with any accuracy. There are powerful tides beneath the surface; Gandhi still governs in many vital respects, but for how long? The actual cabinet of ministers, as well as a big majority in parliament, consists of his followers, that is, of members of the Congress Party, but even among them the degree to which his word is still gospel varies widely. I have talked to some ministers of importance who say they can hear his voice in their ears, in moments of decision: they consult him, dead, as they consulted him in life, and when they have made up their minds what to do they hear the verdict in his familiar whisper. This sounds to me like an unconscious form of self-justification and reassurance: when you know what you intend to do anyhow, it must be immensely gratifying to receive this august authority from beyond our vale of tears. Needless to say, Mr. Nehru has never had such an experience—he is not one to hear voices—but there are some men known to me who have not only heard Mahatma's voice but have actually seen him, in their moments of concentration, during the past decade. The reality of such voices and visions need never be questioned, since they exist in the mind and are not subject to ordinary tests, but it does sound (to me, anyhow) as if Gandhiji's spiritual heritage had become a convenience. The hitch is this: what X may hear or see can quite easily be contradicted by what Y hears or sees, so that an unprejudiced third party, such as Z, has no means of guessing which is right or if both are wrong. In short, the power of a legend which is both political and religious is outside our measurement, and in some cases may become obsessive. Thus we have a number of men in India who honestly do believe that when they speak or act in public matters they are carrying out Gandhi's wishes although they could not possibly prove it.

Nehru makes no such claim. He quite truly says that Gandhiji adjusted his thinking, throughout his life, to circumstances as they arose, and that he, Jawaharlal Nehru, cannot possibly be sure of what Gandhi's view on any given subject might be at any given time since his death. Aside from certain principles, such as nonviolence, which remained obligatory throughout the Indian revolution, Gandhi's tactical variations and accommodations to change were swift, instinctive and brilliantly realistic. Gandhi did not ask Nehru to do what he (Gandhi) wished, and least of all to do what Nehru might imagine Gandhi to have wished, but to do what he himself (J.N.) thought was right. In this respect, as in so many others, Mr. Nehru differs from the devout Gandhians in or out of government.

Now, if this is so, and if it is also true that Mr. Nehru is a secular phenomenon without formal religious foundation, why is it that so many of us instinctively regard him as the torchbearer? Why is it our instinct to look upon him as "Gandhi's heir"? Not, surely, because he is Prime Minister of India. Gandhi himself never held any public office, small or great, and for long and frequent periods he absented himself, so far as it was humanly possible, from political affairs. There are few, if any, resemblances between these two men, and the mere fact that Gandhi called Nehru his "political" heir does not establish a kinship: it might only mean that for the business of government no better man could be discerned at the time. Yet we do feel, and I have felt it more strongly as the decade of India's independence was completed, that time and destiny have made Mr. Nehru into an evolutionary extension of Gandhi's genius. That is, he has himself evolved, and circumstances have evolved with him, so that his "mission" (to use a word he dislikes) is not at all a continuation of Gandhi's but a transposition of it into a more spacious field. Many men in India speak for Gandhi but Nehru speaks for himself. In doing so he has come ever closer to the essential and continuing spirit of Gandhi. This may be a paradox, and I think it is, but Nehru in being himself is closer to Gandhi today than many a saint who roams the countryside in Gandhian garments, closer than the untouchables or the lepers or the children for whom Gandhi spent a lifetime of effort. Strange to relate, this resplendent world-figure, this Brahmin of the highest degree, this man who had everything from birth—health, wealth, looks, imagination and intellect—turns out to be deeply akin to the humble spinner of Sevagram. We shall have time to show how and why, to examine and to reëxamine the evidences, but here it is enough to say that many (not only I but countless others) feel this to be true. It seems that Gandhi's instinct, which so often cut through appearance to reality, was right again: Nehru is the legitimate son of his soul.

We feel it at dawn in the garden more, probably, than at any other time on the Day of Martyrs. At least I do. This white shadow that so swiftly comes and goes, arrow-straight, seeing in the dark, gives the thrust of truth to our presence. This is the place and this is the man and we do not doubt, or if we ever have doubted, we doubt no more.

2

Jawaharlal Nehru was born in Allahabad on November 14, 1889, of a distinguished and well-to-do family. He was educated at Harrow and Cambridge, returning to India with an uncommon Englishness which has never altogether left him; his own native language, Hindustani-Urdu, was strange to him and he had to grow into it again. His father, Motilal Nehru, was an eminently successful lawyer who became, under Gandhi's influence, one of the great leaders of the Indian national movement in its earlier stages. It was easy and natural for Jawaharlal to acquire or accept leadership, since it was his both by his own gifts and by inheritance.

So much is very generally known even outside of India. It is still remembered how rich the Nehru family were, although after they turned to Gandhi they gave up most of their wealth and privileges. Mr. Nehru himself remembers that renunciation —"sixteen horses in the stables one day and none the next"— although he considers that the extent of it has been exaggerated and embroidered by legend. The Nehrus, father and son, were willing to give up anything for the national cause, but it is worth recording once more that neither of them accepted the whole body of Gandhi's teaching.

The Nehru family is of Kashmiri origin and high Brahmin in caste. It was the custom of Kashmir for centuries to call every male Brahmin "Pundit," and in fact the Brahmin caste as a whole was referred to in Kashmir as "the pundits," as one might say the priests, the lawyers or the doctors. In a state which was predominantly Muslim and (until modern times) governed by a Muslim dynasty, these pundits had a very special place and were often in high favor at the Islamic court. To this day they are a good deal more lenient toward Muslims or other non-Hindus than other Brahmins, and their traditionary rules are much less hidebound. The title given Pundit Nehru is simply hereditary, corresponding to no special training, examination or aptitudes: although the custom is rapidly dying out, it was only yesterday applied to every Brahmin from Kashmir.

And not only *from* Kashmir. One characteristic of the Kashmiri Brahmins has been their enduring clannishness even when they had migrated far and wide into India itself. They had intermarried constantly; I have heard on excellent authority that there are eleven such families, among them the Nehrus, who are all more or less related because of frequent alliances in the past two centuries. They are none of them really from Kashmir but they are Kashmiri Brahmins, pundits, living mostly in north India, and valuing the Kashmiri heritage although they may never have seen the enchanted valley. Even in India they keep up their own customs, which allow them a great deal more freedom than orthodox Hindu Brahminism permits. This, to be sure, is not much—a Brahmin of any category or origin, if he wishes to obey all the rules, must be thinking of them from morning to night in practically every act of life. Such orthodoxy vanished long ago in the Nehru family and others allied to it. Pundit Motilal Nehru, the famous father of the present Prime Minister, was a man of the world, an epicure, a traveler, and there was no room in his life for those countless tiny rules which set the Brahmin aside from the rest of Hindu society. His children were brought up according to his own ideas, and the sense of contamination which other Brahmins feel with foreigners or members of lower castes never seems to have existed for them. Many of the Brahmin rules are of an exceedingly private nature, and it would be rash to guess whether they are carried out by anybody nowadays except by orthodox fanatics. What can be said confidently is that no member of the Nehru family shows any sign of traditionalism in these respects.

The caste system is complex and powerful, with an influence upon habit which often outlasts its influence upon the mind. That is why no foreigner, however familiar with India, can be sure about its power in any one of its multitudinous aspects. Once, on a journey to Kashmir, I was delayed by bad weather over the passes and spent the night at Jammu, where I fell into talk with a fellow traveler, a Brahmin and government official. This gentleman made a thoroughgoing attack upon the caste system while we were having dinner—as a Brahmin he should not have been dining with a foreigner, an out-caste, and I made some half-joking reference to the fact. He said caste was the curse of India and must be torn out by the roots, leaving not a trace. I made some half-hearted attempts to defend the system as an element of stability and continuity, one of the forces which had kept India from being washed away in the flood of historic conquests. Well . . . We were assigned to the same room in the rest house that night, since rooms were scarce, and when he undressed I could not avoid seeing that he wore the Sacred Thread of the Brahmin across his chest.

My friend the official was probably characteristic of a huge but uncertain number of educated Indians. He could attack the caste system with vehemence and sincerity but he could not abandon the Sacred Thread. This thread, with which every boy of the high castes is solemnly invested in childhood (generally when he is about ten), plays an important part in reminding its wearer of the caste rules about eating, drinking, sleeping, praying, and even the functions of the bathroom; its ritualistic position changes with the acts of life and thus compels adherence to the rules. I have often wondered how many of the modern, cultivated and open-minded Indians of my acquaintance, avowed enemies of caste and particularly of untouchability, wear the Sacred Thread next to their skins. Many, I know, wear it from habit without obeying all the rules it is supposed to suggest; others discard it, with a considerable wrench of feeling because it represents the past; but there must be many others who, although they have abandoned every external evidence of caste-consciousness, cannot quite bring themselves to give up this symbol of their past, present and future. And as for the orthodox—well, it is enough to watch them bathing in the Ganges to see how many gyrations can be performed by the mystic strand of thread hanging from the shoulder.

Caste may be opposed, of course, far more easily from above than from below. Some of the most effective enemies of the caste system have been Brahmins; since they are its chief beneficiaries, their opposition counts for more than that of others. The opposition of holy men, great souls, saints and prophets, who with scarcely an exception have spoken bravely on the subject for thousands of years, seems to have had curiously little effect on Hinduism. For one reason, "holy men" in general are regarded as being outside caste, above it or beyond it, and their words of condemnation for the system are therefore discounted as not applicable to ordinary mortals. Thus it was with Gautama the Buddha, and thus it was millennia later with Mahatma Gandhi. Gandhi gave up his own caste when he went to England as a student, was officially read out of the caste, and never wanted to resume it afterward. He threw away the Sacred Thread (less exalted than a Brahmin's, but he had one) at the age of eighteen.

This may seem digression or even divagation: it is not. In India there is no single fact of greater importance to an individual or to the collectivity than caste. In the Nehru family caste was of no account to the great men, Motilal and Jawaharlal, father and son, but we may depend upon it that the mothers, grandmothers, aunts and other relatives who form the cocoon of a Hindu family never lost sight of it for one moment. Those who have any real acquaintance with India, outside of official or diplomatic circles, know how the old women run the households. This was a thing which Annie Besant, the British Theosophist leader, never seems to have understood in all her long years in India: she thought that when she dined with the family of Bhagavan Das in Benares, as she did once a year, the household did her great honor by putting all the food on silver plates. In simple fact it was the opposite: they did not dare use china or glass with a foreigner (out-caste), because according to the rules they would have had to smash any such dish afterward if she had touched it. Silver, like gold, is regarded as "pure" under caste rules, and thus resisted the contamination of being touched by Mrs. Besant. As the son of the house, Sri Prakasa, tells us in his valuable memoir of Mrs. Besant, she never knew this. She does not even seem to have realized that to most devout Hindus, no matter how much they might like to hear her speak or read what she wrote, she was no different from any ordinary untouchable in the caste sense.

Nehru grew up and through this tangle of Brahmin rules without allowing it to mold his thought, even in youth. His father's freedom may have been enough to insure his own, but we think, from what we know of his character, that he would have thrown off the incubus anyhow. He probably tended in his early years to think of the caste rules, and thus of the caste system itself, as kitchen business, the affair of the old women—an old wives' tale. I have Brahmin friends who insist today that it is no more than that. However, a serious mind like Nehru's must have seen very early in life how it encased and often deformed all energies in India. Its evil results are glaring, as in untouchability and other excrescences—including, in south India, variations such as unseeability and unapproachability. But quite aside from these evils, the social system itself, even for the most privileged persons of the highest rank, is unutterably and inconceivably tiresome. To be obliged to think of such things from morning to night—where another person's shadow falls; which person of which caste can hand the milk and which other person the water; purification ceremonies after the "contaminations" which are inevitable in any existence—would be the greatest bore imaginable for an alert mind. From what I know of Mr. Nehru I cannot believe he ever went through this rigmarole at any period: he detests boredom. And what, indeed, could be more boring than to trot down to the sacred river and bathe in the mud every time the shadow of an inferior fell across one's body? These, and other practices, are fading fast in India, but when Nehru was growing up they were still in full force and they certainly have not disappeared today. For example, the idea of drawing water from the same source as inferior castes is repugnant to millions of contemporary Indians and causes actual riots even now. A great modern city like Bombay, which is in so many respects a model of what civic administration can do (directly the opposite of Calcutta), constantly faces this problem in housing projects for workers.

Caste is everywhere, but I know foreigners who have lived in India for years without being aware of anything but its bare outlines. Everybody knows about untouchability, which, after all, is a relatively modern abuse in Hinduism; but the convolutions and involutions of the system within the ruling castes themselves, and most of all with the Brahmins, pass our understanding. It must be constantly borne in mind, just the same, that this condition has existed for thousands of years, is deeply involved with the religion of Hinduism, dominates the minds of the masses, creates and maintains the structure of Hindu society, and cannot possibly be swept away by a mere decade of legislation. There is no Indian, not even Nehru, who can be intelligibly discussed altogether apart from his caste origins.

Since this is demonstrably the truth, the relation of Nehru to the system is all the more remarkable. He seems to have been separate from it all his life—so separate from it that after his long years in England it seemed very strange to him, almost as strange as it does to us. I think one of his tendencies in earlier years was to underrate the power of the ancient incubus. He attacked it, yes, but I doubt if he understood for many years how obstinately it affects every activity in India. For example, the development of caste as an instrument in party politics was a surprise to him in very recent times. It could not have surprised him if he had fully taken in the terrible power of the system over most Hindus. It never had this power over him and he has found it difficult to realize the dynamism it contains. The Communists—led mostly by Brahmins!—based their electoral victory in the south on combinations of the untouchables and the dispossessed, with a sprinkling of higher castes to make the speeches. This sort of caste politics was utterly alien to the generation of the liberators—Gandhi himself, the two Nehrus, Rajaji, Mrs. Naidu. They would have thought it ignoble, contemptible, ethically indefensible, to exploit the misery of the untouchables for electoral purposes: they wanted to abolish the untouchables, not to use them. Communists have no squeamishness in the matter.

Since the system does exist in the very structure of the Indian mind and soul, and since prolonged efforts against it have resulted in a purely legal equality of the citizens, it must be seen as an advantage to be a Brahmin. Rightly or wrongly, it is. We have enumerated Jawaharlal Nehru's advantages of health, wealth, brains and appearance, his gifts of imagination, wit and charm, his general good fortune in that lottery which life is to begin with; among these it would be foolish not to name his caste. For here, too, there was a combination of the best: he was a high Brahmin by birth, but with the little extra advantage of Kashmiri origin, of being a pundit, of being liberated from some of the most irksome obligations and restrictions of the system. In the complexities of Hinduism it fell to his lot to get the best that was going—as luck would have it, luck for him, for India and for the world. The way of the revolutionary idealist, so often vowed to unpopular courses and uphill struggles, is hard; the way of the nation-builder in the actual grind of government is probably harder. Nehru, combining the two, might never have evolved as he has done, or attained what he has attained, if he had not been so dowered from birth.

This is not to minimize his adult qualities of character, intellect and will; what we mean is that these qualities were able to evolve to their present state without the hindrance which, unfortunately, Hindu society presents to many of its children. For many or most Hindus the personal goals of effort are precisely those things which Jawaharlal Nehru always had and always took for granted; aside, that is, from caste, which is fixed and irrevocable, the rest of his endowment is in itself something other men strive to acquire. Money, social position, distinctions of all sorts, even fame and popularity, do not count for much with Jawaharlal Nehru because he has always had them; they were, so to speak, in the family. In all the panoply of his gifts there is one which seems to me rarer than the others, which is the gift of ignoring them. He is able to pursue an idea or an ideal without those mean annoyances and distractions which beset most men; it is his nature to do so, to be sure, but his nature was set free to grow by a singularly propitious set of circumstances. He never had to be ambitious, really, in any ordinary way, and it is hardly surprising that he seems unaware of low motives in others until they are thrust upon him. Not so many years ago he was asked point-blank, in the All-India Congress, what was his salary as Prime Minister; the question was so unexpected that he was obliged to confess he did not remember. In the same way he does not consider it remarkable when crowds of two or three hundred thousand people gather from an entire countryside (traveling for days sometimes) to see him or to hear him speak. This has been his lot for many decades and he would probably be sorely puzzled if it did not occur. One could go on with such examples: it is downright astonishing how many rare or even unique bestowals of fate are thus taken in his stride. That is what I meant by the gift of ignoring his gifts: he can keep his mind on his purposes, and thus, in all the tumult of his extraordinary life, he can still think, in the truest sense, untrammeled by the circumstances.

And as for his intellect, I have never found it anything but secular, purely secular. I do not discover, in his printed work or in any talk I have had with him during the past twelve years, one vestige of the religiosity which otherwise obsesses Hindu culture. This is truly extraordinary in India. I have never met any other Indian who could sustain a closely knit conversation for two or three hours at a stretch without bringing into it something of a religious nature, some concept which originates in religion. (This is just as true of Muslims and Christians as of Hindus: all Indians are steeped in it.) It may be only a reference or a quotation; it may be oblique or obscure; but religious concepts always creep in. Not so with Mr. Nehru.

I do not mean that he is without religion: such a thing no man can possibly know about another. Religious instinct and religious experience are immensely variable, profoundly intimate. Mahatma Gandhi once told me that the work of Bernard Shaw—of Bernard Shaw!—had "a religious center." Upon reflection I was inclined to think that this was true, philosophically speaking, although it involved some revision of ordinary notions about religion. If Mahatma meant what I think he meant —that is, a sense of power and purpose beyond man's limits, with perhaps some aspiration to participate in that purpose—it could be quite true of Mr. Shaw. It may be equally true of Mr. Nehru. I afterward told Shaw about Gandhi's remark and he grew very solemn and silent for a minute or two. I realized, with considerable awe, that the Mahatma had put his finger upon a truth, as usual.

In the case of Nehru his secularity is open, avowed, and lifelong: his father before him was much the same. This signifies nothing whatever about the deep recesses of his being, into which no other has the right to penetrate. I suspect the existence of "a religious center" in his case, too, but it would require more courage than I possess to ask him about it. Such things are monstrously difficult to put into words and it is perfectly possible that he does not himself recognize the existence of such a center. And yet, I inquire—merely inquire—if it would have been possible for Mahatma Gandhi to rely so heavily upon him for so many years, and to speak of him as his "heir," if he had not felt the existence of this reality. Mahatma's religious instinct was powerful and not usually subject to error, even though he gave a wider sense to the word "religion" than is customary in dogmatic sects. He must have felt something —and so do I—and I shall leave it at that.

What is not in the least intimate, but perfectly public and spread upon many records, is the secularity of Nehru's views in all those matters which have concerned him, politics and literature, life in general. It is shown in innumerable details. In 1947, during my first talk with him, I came somewhere near this subject by asking what he admired in Sanskrit literature. (I had just been rereading his *Discovery of India*, published two or three years before.) He spoke of a number of things, poems and plays, particularly of the charming comedies of Kalidasa, and never once mentioned the vast religious literature of ancient India, the *Vedas* and *Upanishads*, the epics, or even the *Bhagavad Gita*. This must have been deliberate, I suppose, and thus even more significant. Similar omissions are notable in all his published works: perhaps because of the proliferation of religiosity in India—the curse of the country, so many think—

he has made it quite clear that he never wants to talk or write about religion. Shelley's line, "One word is too often profaned for me to profane it," may be applicable here; on the other hand it is likely that his mind was so busy with social, economic and political processes throughout his life that he had no time or patience for religious speculation. It may have seemed highly irrelevant, often enough—and we know from his autobiography that this was so. In earlier years he was put off by the superstitious excesses which flourish in India, and he shared with Gandhi a dislike for the "holy city" of Benares. He has very considerably modified his earlier hostility, once scarcely veiled, toward all these manifestations, but however tolerant or comprehending he may have become, his mind remains secular in its essence through every expression known to us.

Now, the fact would scarcely be worthy of remark in most countries of Europe or the two Americas. "*Paris vaut une messe*," said Henry of Navarre when he became a Catholic; Mr. Eisenhower joined a church when he entered the White House, and not before; in Latin countries, where anticlericalism used to be worn like a badge, a man could not be elected to high office (up to the present Christian-Democratic phase) unless he believed in a secular state separated firmly from any church. Since the French Revolution this has been the style and habit of the European political mind. In England, a warier and in most respects more consummate polity, religion is supposed to be a private matter and seldom obtrudes, practically speaking, in spite of the nationally established church (or possibly even because of it).

India is a very different case. So are the Islamic and Buddhist states of Asia, a good many of which have their religions written into their constitutions. ("Burma is a Buddhist state," for instance, and "Pakistan is an Islamic state"; this is fundamental law.) The Constitution of India proclaims it to be a secular state in which all religions, races and castes are equal, but the whole world knows that the Hindus outnumber all others by something like six to one; and Hinduism, as we are forced to remember at all times, is something far stronger and more tenacious than the religions known to the West. It is indeed not altogether a religion—it is a system of society, a way of life—

and it manages to entangle everything in a Hindu's existence into its own. It is not in any sense a "church" and it has no hierarchy, no central authority, no Sanhedrin, but except in a few great cities there are few Hindus who care to defy it. Pervasive and irresistible, it rules India in all the things (marriage, divorce, caste, property rights, inheritance and so on) which are the warp and woof of existence. For a man to rise to the highest position in a country of this character it might be supposed that religious support and some form of religious appeal were indispensable.

And so, indeed, everybody has supposed up to the present period. It is the merest truism in India that nobody can really lead the people or command them without "renouncing the world" and addressing himself directly to their religious consciousness. We find it in many learned works and we verify it through a long sweep of recorded history. Jawaharlal Nehru is the first popular leader to acquire secular power in a purely secular way and to wield it without once claiming any form of religious sanction. Gandhi was humble enough, in all conscience, but it cannot be denied that he usually felt (by means of his "inner voice" and in other subjective ways) that the will of God was working through him; the masses of the Indian people had no doubt of it. Nehru simply does not profess to know anything about the will of God. The unprecedented thing—unprecedented, that is, in India—is that the Prime Minister who has ruled the country since its independence makes no claim beyond that which could be made by any other elected head of a democratic government, and that is, that a majority of the citizens voted for him. By introducing this novel concept he certainly has not driven religion out of Indian politics (that may take centuries). Nor has he weakened its power where other men, even in his own government, are concerned. What he has done is to establish a glowing exception to all the old rules—an exception which, in the fullness of time, may acquire the persuasion of a precedent.

If we want to find out how true this is, all we have to do is to talk to some Indians who are not Hindus. The Muslims of India and even, in their sincerest moments, the Muslims of Pakistan, an "Islamic state," feel safe with Nehru. The extremist newspapers of Pakistan rail against him, of course, but in conversation with intelligent Pakistani officials I have repeatedly run into this sort of expression: "Oh, yes, I suppose it's all right so long as Nehru's there—but what about afterwards?" The gist of this thought (which I think a mistaken one) is that Nehru is the only Hindu capable of forbearance with, and comprehension of, the new Islamic state: that after his departure some wild and stupid effort to reunite India by force will occur. The argument comes oddly from people who themselves never stop talking of force, and yet I have heard it so very often that I can have no doubt of its sincerity. Similarly the Muslim population of India itself (some fifty millions) trusts him to see that justice is done them. To a really devout or old-fashioned Hindu, to a member of the great Hindu orthodox "protective" organization (the Mahasabha) or even to some of the more religious members of Nehru's own government, this same confidence would not be extended. The Muslims are right about Nehru, obviously: he detests communalism and religious strife. The only thing I question is whether they are right about his colleagues or possible successors: I do not find reversion or retrogression to be historically probable in matters of this kind —clocks are seldom turned back very far—and I doubt if the tremendous examples of Gandhi and Nehru, taken together, will be overcome by any reactionary force of the future.

What we consider, anyhow, is a secular figure. The word "secular" is used so much oftener in Indian than elsewhere that we ought to specify its overtones: it does not mean worldly and it does not mean antireligious. It means only, at the strongest, *non*religious, and that strictly in material matters of society, economics and politics. "The Free Church in the Free State"—Cavour's formula—comes as near defining it as any other. It is a very old story in the United States, where Thomas Jefferson, our own first "secular" protagonist, set forth its principles in the eighteenth century. England and France had to struggle for it through centuries, and the former still has an established national church, but secularism rules these democracies in our time. In India history itself has been primarily a religious expression; all the wars were religious wars; the "secular state," which India is by constitutional definition, is a new concept in that part of the world. And the secular man, meaning Jawaharlal Nehru, is so new that he is practically unique even now on the national scale. We all have dozens of Indian friends whose secularity, so to speak, whose emancipation from ancestral bonds, is complete; I cannot think of one who could carry an election on such a basis except Nehru himself.

Now, all the foregoing really does result in a whopping paradox, far bigger than those it contains or those which preceded. It is simply this: Nehru is surrounded with very nearly a religious veneration, carries the country with him on any large nation-wide question, commands the crowds as nobody ever has done except Ghandhi, and, practically speaking, personifies India in the eyes of most Indians, but does so without adopting, or even believing in, the traditional religious instruments of Indian leadership. How did this occur?

I shall list here, without discussing them, some of the explanations I have heard, in various parts of India and from various kinds of men. There is something to be said for each of them, however slight it may seem at first. These are: (1) Nehru does not have to be a saint because Gandhi's sainthood extends to him—Gandhi did it for him. (2) The people do not fully realize that he is not a saint, even though he constantly tells them so. (3) National and religious elements are so mixed in the Indian mind that the material sacrifices made by him and his family for the national cause amount to "renunciation of the world" and thus sanctity in Hinduism. (4) Ninety percent of the people pay no attention to politics in detail, and to them he is "Gandhi's heir" without discussion. (5) Hindus in the mass would never be able to believe that a Brahmin, a pundit, a learned man, was other than holy in his heart. (6) Jawaharlal (as they call him—either that or Punditji—not just Nehru) has suffered greatly, spent many years in jail, dared death often, for the sake of the people, and thus is a saint whether he thinks so or not.

This may seem a jumble of unrelated reasons for a national veneration, but on examination they can be seen to connect and even to overlap. What they come to is a final bestowal upon Nehru, nonreligious and secular though he is, of the same kind of half-mystical reverence which in the past has gone to the innumerable saints of the land. Very poor and illiterate people will walk many miles to catch a glimpse of him, and although they do not understand his words and often do not even hear them, they receive the beneficent impression which is called *darshan,* the vision of a saint. Nobody could reject the idea more sharply than he does, but it just happens to be the observed and confirmed fact for decades past, and never more than in the decade since Gandhi's death. The political classes, above all in the great cities, may attack him as they please, and do; it makes very little impression upon the immense mass of the Indian people. They may vote against local Congress Party candidates in their Gandhi caps, and do so increasingly, but few would vote against Nehru, and even those few would always turn out to see him and cheer him. The instinct of the people has elected him to something far more intimately significant to them than any office, even that of Prime Minister: that is, to be himself, and, willy-nilly, to wear an aura.

Who is to say that the instinct of the people is wrong? Certainly no foreigner could wisely do so, and for my part I suspect that it might well be right. What else could explain the feeling I have mentioned before, and have experienced myself through recurring years in Mr. Birla's garden at dawn? That is, the thrust of truth, the sensation of an irrefutable witness, which comes when Jawaharlal Nehru's white shadow silently comes and goes in the half-light? The feeling is strong in that place and at that hour, but certainly not because he is Prime Minister of India. That is a political office. The company here, at dawn in the garden, is made up only of those nearest Gandhi in life, and few, actually, even of them: with one or two exceptions they are not persons who would or could ever hold office or engage in political activities. They delve and spin; they work and pray. What do they have to do with prime ministers? And yet this man of the world in coming here puts the seal upon a testament, and all feel it to be true. He is a man of the world but this is a place of vows. He comes here not to take a vow and not even to renew one but to remember the end of that wise and good old man whose work he is doing. All in this garden do the work to which Gandhi set them, each in his own way, this one in the villages and the next one with the dispossessed, but this man of the world must work in the world, which is also Gandhi's work, and none but he can do it in the time and place. Something of the kind is what everybody there does feel in his silent presence and swift departure. They are all the Mahatma's children, but he is the eldest son, the legitimate heir, whatever the rewards or the burdens may be, because what he has to do is the largest part of the task.

3

We may define the task, and shall try; we may indicate how much of it we think has been carried out; we are free to infer intentions, directions, probabilities; but the one thing we cannot do is see it to the end. The same is true of any effort to write about contemporary men and forces, but it is especially the case with India and Nehru because in them a sense of gathering climax, of approaching culmination, seems to be in the air. We are not merely telling a story of which the end is still unknown: we are headed straight into a climax we cannot foresee. Mr. Nehru's effort to obtain a brief respite from his responsibilities in the spring of 1958—to which we shall revert later—is one of many signs of what I say. This attempt, which would have been a sort of trial retirement or resignation, an experiment or rehearsal for government without him, was greeted with such consternation in India that it had to be abandoned: as in other such cases, when the will of the people spoke clearly enough, Nehru yielded to it.

Even so, it was a warning signal. This is not a man who easily abandons an idea or qualifies a judgment. If he felt it necessary to give his own government the experience of ruling in his absence—and if he felt in himself the necessity for solitude and thought—those necessities were not obviated by postponement. It is clear to everybody that India someday must do without him, and yet the government, party and people are still unprepared to do so. This is a dilemma more crucial in a young democracy than in an old one. It might threaten the institutions which were established with such struggles little more than a decade ago. It might affect, in its unforeseeable consequences, the whole life of the world.

Nehru himself, whose mind has never been stronger or more flexible than it is now, sees the dilemma in all its harsh reality day by day. A tendency to put upon him all decisions and all responsibilities, even (we dare to say) to substitute faith in Nehru for faith in India, has grown to an alarming extent in the decade of power and independence. His incredible capacity for work has not discouraged such tendencies, and all the circumstances have conspired to create a kind of personal centralization of authority which has few parallels in democratic societies. We think of Roosevelt and Churchill in wartime, ruling like dictators of the Roman Republic under emergency powers, but the cases are not really parallel because in India no emergency powers have become necessary. (The emergency powers granted by the detention laws are powers of the separate states, not of the central government.) What we see in Delhi is an intense concentration of personal authority in the Prime Minister, not by virtue of special legislation, but under the normal operating procedure of the government. In other words, it is personal, extraconstitutional, and depends most of all upon Nehru's unique position as a man rather than as an official. Another Prime Minister, when and if he eventuates, would have far less authority over the government if he had less over the nation as a whole.

Nobody could be more deferential to the elected parliament or to its methods of action than is Nehru. To hear him in debate in the lower House, the Lok Sabha, is a lesson in democratic manners. And yet we all know—everybody in that assembly knows—that when it comes to the vote he will have his way. His views prevail because he controls a large parliamentary majority. Within that majority—and within his own government—his views prevail because his party and his colleagues feel the weight of the whole people behind him. Thus his power, although democratically exercised, is in reality independent of democratic forms because it comes on what we might call a national wave length, arises from the people in a highly nonpolitical form, more ancient and far more familiar than political democracy to the masses.

"So far as the people are concerned," a leader of importance said to me, "there is not one of us who can stand against the Prime Minister."

This, after all, is an objective statement—it refers simply to a fact verified by experience. Similar facts have been experientially verified in other democracies from time to time. But there is another attitude prevalent in India which seems rather an assumption than a fact: "Punditji knows best," is the most succinct expression of it that I have heard.

It may or may not be true that Punditji knows best. It is not susceptible of proof, and a citizen who concludes an argument with that statement has thereby abdicated his democratic right to his own opinion. Furthermore, such an abdication leads to the most dangerous extreme inherent in this situation—that which I mentioned before as being faith in Nehru rather than faith in India.

The man who made that statement was an intellectual of considerable attainment who disagreed with some of Nehru's ideas in foreign policy. After stating his disagreements and amplifying his own opinions, this mature, enlightened man was capable of concluding literally in these words: "Well, after all, that's only what I think—but Punditji knows best."

Mr. Nehru has been at great pains for the twelve years of his trusteeship to make no such claim for himself; he is ever conscious of the possibility of error; he says what he thinks, it is true, but he does not pretend to final wisdom on any subject; he expects others to say what they think and to convince him if they can. Yet after this decade and more of democratic self-government it is apparent that India tends, more than ever before, to entrust its fate to one man, and thus incurs risks as grave as they are obvious.

The political and intellectual classes, which are roughly equivalent to the English-speaking, see this plainly enough and talk of it a good deal. Lawyers and journalists, teachers and preachers, engineers and technicians, must use the English language as the instrument of their work: no other national language has taken the place of this alien tongue which rules the law courts, universities, legislatures and press. There are thought to be about four million citizens of the Indian Union, in a population now approaching four hundred million, who can more or less use English, and these are the vocally political. They have a little pet question which, with sloganlike concision, recurs constantly in print and in talk. This is: "After Nehru—what?" We see this blunt simplicity staring at us in the newspapers almost every day in one shape or another. Journalists even ask foreign visitors their opinions on the subject, which is going pretty far, and it seems a favorite theme for any writer of editorial leading-articles who has a space to fill. It reflects an anxiety as well as a mere speculation. The anxiety is patriotic, whereas the speculation is a political game. In more experienced democracies they are seldom united: we all wonder who the next President of the United States may be but it never crosses our minds that our lives may depend on it. In India many persons known to me are filled with forebodings which concern that normal, natural and inevitable event, the succession to the Prime Minister's office.

There is no use denying a good deal of cogency to the thoughts which make them anxious. There are many sharply divisive tendencies in the Indian Union which are sometimes concealed, sometimes overcome, by the vast popularity of Jawaharlal Nehru. Union and independence are so new that they do not seem permanent, solid, indefeasible; they have by no means reached the stage wherein adult and sensitive minds can take them for granted. The first decades of the American Republic exhibited the same uncertainties, but the American states were neither rich nor powerful enough to attract enemies. They were, moreover, geographically remote from the contending powers of the eighteenth and early nineteenth centuries, so that they had the possibility of undisturbed growth. India stands, so to speak, in the very middle of a world in conflict, and the tumults of the world outside affect her deeply. Many and perhaps most Indians feel sure that only Jawaharlal Nehru's instinct and intellect have steered a safe course through the external dangers of the past decade. They see no other such national idol as a power for internal unity, and they fear that there is no helmsman of equal skill for the perils outside. Within and without, the prospect of trouble beclouds the future for many in this frame of mind.

No foreigner known to me has quite this kind or degree of anxiety, perhaps because most of us have more faith in institutions than has yet become common in India. Even so, it is worth recording that the dismay among foreigners was notable at the mere suggestion of Nehru's retirement last spring, and even the heads of great states did not hesitate to say so. This appears to be one of the few matters on which the American and Russian governments hold similar views.

The climax, then, however inevitable it may be in time, involves future uncertainties which go a good deal beyond the borders of India itself. "After Nehru—what?" is the headline writer's way of expressing an uncertainty which, however much we may deplore it, is certainly spread throughout the world. We may feel, as I do, that the Indian Republic deserves more confidence in itself—that it is well enough founded and built to survive many shocks. We also may know (as I think I do) that there are a number of men well able to continue Nehru's work in specified fields, although there is certainly no single one who at the present moment could command the same following in so many fields. The fact remains that the world in general, and India in particular, are uneasy at the prospect of a government in New Delhi without Nehru.

Under these circumstances one might well rise to inquire, point-blank, why there is any necessity to consider the question at all. Nehru is at the very height of his powers; he has gained confidence, poise and a new serenity in this past decade; his knowledge of the world "at the summit" has been deepened and enlarged by an experience which must be unique among men; his health is unimpaired, his courage indomitable, his energy equal to an amount of work which stuns the beholder. *Time*, says the poet,

part steals,
Lets part abide.

Nobody can quite expect the head of a government, in a country the size of India, to go freely among the people or even to be constantly "accessible" to all elements. The complaint of Nehru's "inaccessibility," so often heard in India, does not seem reasonable to me. In compensation for a certain remoteness which is inherent in his position, India has in him a brain, will and intuition of the highest category, and I do not see any objective reason why they should not be at the service of the nation for a long time to come. Nehru was seventy on November 14, 1959, and the annals of statecraft are studded with examples of men who performed their greatest services after that age. His is not, really, a trade for young men: they may make energetic campaigners, inspiring orators or capable politicians, but statecraft of the highest order is most often attained after long experience. There are dozens of examples on both sides of the question—the young Pitt, the old Churchill, for instance—so that each must be considered individually. To my own way of thinking some remarks made by Nehru's doctor, in the course of conversation one day in Delhi, are highly pertinent. The Prime Minister, said he, has the body of a young man, the reflexes of somebody decades his junior, the physical security of the prime of life. This being so, what is this pervasive anxiety about "after Nehru—what?"

Of course there is a sense, among politically-minded persons, that the inevitable should be faced now, no matter how far off it may be, and that so far nothing has been done to provide for it. So far, so good—we might all agree, and I think that Mr. Nehru's trial resignation last spring would have been a real attempt to prepare the nation to do without him: I think it was so intended, although he put it on other grounds. Indians and foreigners alike consider that some untoward accident, of which life affords so many, might very well remove what has been, throughout the decade of unity and independence, the central governing phenomenon. There is something fateful about Nehru's flashing passage through the history of our time. To the imaginative it is in itself dramatic and therefore, quite irrationally, suggests a dramatic termination. In sober fact, so far as I can see in the array of probabilities, there is only one valid reason why he might not continue to govern India for years. That reason is that he may not wish to do so.

It is enough, of course. If he determines to retire, he will. It is well known in India that he used to fix seventy as the age for his own retirement from public life. (Men of forty or fifty often have such ideas.) The inroads which experience may have made upon this intention are another thing. None of us who have watched the evolution of the Indian Union from the time of independence can possibly imagine a state of affairs in which Nehru would be without great influence upon government, even if he held no office: that is another consideration. India is used to counselors who are not officeholders: that was precisely the magic of Gandhi from beginning to end. There is the clear possibility that Mr. Nehru may someday want to lay down his burden without altogether depriving the nation of his services in other ways. If I were compelled to make a guess, a rash and temerarious proceeding in this matter, it would be that some such course is the most likely outcome. But it is certainly my hope, based on the total observation and reflection of the past twelve years, that the outcome will be long delayed.

For here, in essence, is the positive side of the question, the side that is uppermost in one's consciousness at dawn in the garden: there is hope in this man. Too often there are nothing but negatives brought forward in discussions on the subject—negatives which, no matter how profusely accumulated, never work out to a positive. We are told that Nehru is not young, that he cannot remain in place forever; and we are similarly told that Mr. X or Mr. Y or Mr. Z, among the possible successors, are "not Nehru" and never will be. It is my own considered opinion that Mr. Nehru is a wiser man today by a great deal than when he took office, and that the accretions of poise, calm and wisdom have come without sacrifice of vital energy. To me he looks and seems younger than he did something like twelve years ago when I first saw him. I made this remark to the Prime Minister's present physician, an eminent man in his profession, and he replied that he found it quite easy to believe. The ardent, impetuous revolutionary whom we find in his autobiography and in other works of the 1930's has turned into a mature, thoughtful man of state, a ruler with the unmistakable gift for it, and, what is more—what makes him unique in this world—to his highest purposes forever loyal. If I may state my own conviction bluntly, it is that his mission is not complete. It is, further, that he never has been more fit in every sense to complete it than he is today.

That mission is, of course, twofold: what he set out to do was to put the union and independence of India on a firm basis and at the same time to serve the cause of peace in the world. They are intertwined, of course—great war, general war, might well be fatal to India—and thus the national and international aspects of his effort can never really be separated, but they correspond roughly to what we call, for convenience, domestic and foreign policies. These two aspects of his work are cut across by a very special problem, that of relations with Pakistan and the situation in Kashmir, which may be called both domestic and foreign policy at the same time: but for these grave preoccupations, involving military expenditure which could otherwise have been kept down, India might have done a good deal better in the past decade. Nehru himself has said publicly, in a speech last spring in Kerala, "I think we have done pretty well." By my own view this was a masterly understatement.

Anybody who was in India in the first period after its liberation will recall the dire prophecies that filled the air—prophecies which had been given currency first by the opponents of freedom—and the even direr events which accompanied partition and the birth of two new nations. There were times in 1947 and 1948 when it required a good deal of optimism to have faith in the future. Nehru himself says that the terrible experience of that initial period, when massacres disfigured the land both for Hindu and Muslim, was an ordeal with a result: since "the worst had already happened, right at the beginning," he was able to keep to his course with the grim certainty that nothing worse could come. It was a hard-bought confidence, but it has helped to make possible the achievements of the decade.

These achievements have been very considerable, but the point I make now is that Nehru today, the very same Nehru who was seventy on November 14, 1959, is a man of hope. The resilience of his physical presence, as, for instance, in the garden as he comes and goes before the first light, evokes it, and it is not an illusion. It is hope based on reason, tempered by wisdom, nurtured by experience, but it is a real thing of the deepest value, and I believe it is renewed by resolution on such occasions as this—resolution that the great dead shall not have died in vain. This, then, is what arises from those brief moments in the garden before dawn: a perception that such a man as this is not one to turn back from an undertaking, however vast, until he has given it all he has to give. He might give it in some other form; that remains to be seen; that is our unknown climax; but give he will, to the end, and greatly.

II *The Potter and the Welder*

THE EMPIRES that have come and gone on this earth are without number. Some strut their hour for a century and some for a thousand years. When and where they have left remains, the predominant characteristic of these remains is the boastful and vainglorious assertion of success. Poets and philosophers have taken due note: "My name is Ozymandias, King of Kings," is a line known to all in English.

India is richer in vanished empires than most other areas of the earth, owing to its size and antiquity. Not even the so-called "Middle East," the blighted and deforested land of Asia Minor, has so many. These Indian empires are distinguished from others by being even more unknown to us, heirs of Europe, and also to Indians themselves. The archaeology and chronology of Indian history are still too imperfectly studied, as the ancient languages of India are still too obscure, for any kind of full knowledge; and, besides, the existing remains are nowhere near so plentiful as in the Mediterranean and other regions. What we do know is that many dynasties ruled mightily in this country for many centuries, and their achievements, often great, are sketchily known to their own descendants. We may say, with considerable confidence, that foreign scholars have shown the way here, and even today a moderately well educated foreigner usually knows more about the echoing past of secular Indian history than do most Indians. That is, he knows more when he goes to see the monuments of that past: he has the habit, ingrained in all of us, of "looking things up," of verifying his data. The Englishman or the American or the Frenchman (and chief of all, naturally, the German) generally has a fairly exact notion of what he is beholding when he goes as far as Ajanta or Ellora, Mahaballipuram or Elephanta, to gaze upon a relic of some imperial splendor lost down the ages.

Still, even so, the familiarity is transitory. I know from my own experience that one may become highly learned for a day or so in the affairs of the Gupta or the Chola empires, only to forget it all a week later. These tumultuous and triumphant satrapies, these gorgeous sovereign creations, mean very little to us in reality. They do not connect, as do Alexander and Caesar, with our own continuing experience. This is mainly because Hinduism itself (not the race but the essence of the thing, which is primarily religious) is strange, and seems to have been directed through aeons toward an end which we do not recognize as a social end at all: that is, toward the elevation of the soul and not of the society.

We may cheer up a little when we discover that to most modern Indians, no matter how extravagantly educated, these ancient monuments mean still less. I have often wondered how it is possible for my cultivated contemporaries in India to be so unaware of their past: there is hardly one friend of mine who has been to look upon the ruins at Mahaballipuram, the frescoes and carvings at Ajanta, the rock-temples of Ellora, the lesser glories scattered north and south. Artists, archaeologists and connoisseurs in general are to be excepted, of course (they are few in any country). You may find a man who can quote Shakespeare by the yard, knows English poetry, Italian painting and German philosophy, can recite the whole second chapter of the *Gita* in Sanskrit and tell you the precise dimensions of the Empire State Building, and yet this man has never been to Mahaballipuram. Or you may find, equally well, an extremely erudite person familiar with the ancient tongues (I know one such, a professor of Buddhist literature and philosophy, although himself a Hindu), who knows every single detail about all of these monuments and has never taken the trouble to go and look at them.

Well, *tout dit,* you can find the same thing everywhere, but it is more astonishing in India because nationalism has had such a memorable outburst here. You would think (or anyhow I should always think) that part of nationalism consisted in pride for the past, esteem and self-esteem in the achievement of the ancestors. This hardly seems to count in India. The most extreme nationalists are those who most brutally condemn the past. I have heard rabid ultranationalists declare that they would destroy all monuments of the past. This comes weirdly indeed from a people in whose basic law there is enshrined the principle of sacrifice of "the whole cake" to the ancestors in three agnate (i.e., wholly male) generations and of "crumbs of the cake" for the next three agnate generations. Revolt against the past may be accompanied, as I suspect it is, by dutiful ritualistic sacrifices to it, and by the wearing of the Sacred Thread.

Never mind. The ruins of Mahaballipuram stand against the sea and the sky in beauty. It is very difficult to compare these temples, shrines and pillared halls with any other. It is a ruin of the Pallava Empire in the seventh and eighth centuries A.D.—that is, just before Charlemagne in Europe, from whom, so far as I know, nothing is left comparable to this. Mahaballipuram is some twenty miles north of Madras, on the east coast of India, and by its accessibility has become one of the indispensable points of attention for any visitor. It has rock carvings of the rarest quality, such as the one of Vishnu reclining, and of Krishna holding up the mountain; its "Temple on the Shore" is an evocation to be compared with the Temple of Neptune at Paestum; the area of the ruin is great. Since independence the Archaeological Service has had greater authority and (I suppose) greater resources; much has been done to clean up the area and give it order. Silent and august by the ocean, it gives its own testimony, and there is not much in India or anywhere else to challenge the awe we feel here.

Now, what was the Pallava Empire? It was at its height in the seventh century A.D. The Pallavas came from the north but united the south. They were succeeded, or overwhelmed, by the Cholas, one of the ancient Tamil (south Indian, Dravidian) dynasties, who united all South India and Ceylon in the tenth and eleventh centuries, succumbing in their turn to the Pandyas for that brief final gasp before the Mohammedan conquest of 1310.

Who cares, alas, who cares? The Rashtrakutas (eighth century, contemporary with Charlemagne) have to their eternal glory the rock carvings at Ellora, in what is now Bombay State, and in particular the great Kailash Temple, but they, too, are forgotten of their own. The fact is that all these empires of India are too confused, dynastic and similar to have much meaning for their own descendants: they do not continue and connect, as history should. Perhaps the fatality that fell upon them was mainly the Mohammedan conquest, obliterating much of their history, cutting them off from what preceded and what followed. Anyhow, what we have left is a series of majestic memorials from Buddhist India (roughly 200 B.C. to 700 A.D.) and Hindu India (overlapping, but vaguely 500 A.D. to 1500 A.D.) and Mohammedan India (best in its later eras, the sixteenth and seventeenth centuries). It has been India's characteristic effort, in many periods, to combine elements from various sources—that is, to "syncretize" in the religious sense, or adapt parts of one religion into another—so that we find Hinduism slowly but surely creeping back into Buddhism, and the Mohammedan conquerors becoming gradually Hinduized in a greater or lesser degree. This is visible in architecture and painting as well as in the doctrines that slowly evolved through all these centuries of struggle, conquest and revolt. The visitor today, unless he is a specialist, is quite likely to fuse the forms in his mind and go away with a rather hazy general impression, as of a world unimaginably ancient and complicated but blended into one continuity which produced, in the end, the Indian Republic, a state and society of today. I do not mean that the Pallava Empire produced Jawaharlal Nehru, or that the Taj Mahal has anything much to do with the new steel mills: such jumps are hard to take. What I do mean is that I feel, and believe most visitors feel, greater continuity of essence than used to be generally conceded. The days when you could dismiss the whole Indian past as a chaotic jumble of small states warring through history with each other—without continuity or development—departed with the nineteenth century.

So we go to Mahaballipuram, as we go to the other great monuments, to refresh our awe, so to speak, to keep that past alive in mind. This last spring when I went there it was for the third time in about eight years—that is, whenever I have been in Madras. (All tourists do the same.) It is different every time in some way, if ancient ruins may be said to change. A different light, perhaps (and a different you), combining with some distinct improvements in maintenance and surroundings, give another impression from the time before. And this year my visit to the Pallava ruins took place just the day before I went out to the Integral Coach Factory at Perambur to one of the most spick-and-span modern factories I have ever seen anywhere. And on both of those evenings I discussed the things that arose in my mind with Rajaji.

Rajaji, as all India calls him, is Chakravarti Rajagopalachari, a name which was mercifully shortened many decades ago into "C.R." or usually just Rajaji. He is a sort of local monument in Madras; he says everybody makes the same rounds—they go to the temple ruins and then call on him. He was an old friend and associate of Gandhi's in the national struggle, became the first Governor-General of free India after Mountbatten's departure, and at various times over a long period was responsible for the government of his native city and state of Madras. A gentle, benevolent and scholarly elder statesman, yes; but also a sharp mind and tongue upon occasion. Occasionally he emerges from his retirement to speak his mind on some subject, and when he does, he commands wide attention. The people in general tend to think of him as a member of Gandhi's generation, the liberators, because he was involved in the movement from the very start; it was in his house in Madras that Gandhi had the curious experience, half asleep and half awake, in which he hit upon the idea of *hartal* (a day of staying at home to fast and pray) in protest against the British rule. *Hartal,* suspension of activity, worked out more or less like a general strike and became a powerful weapon in the freedom movement from 1921 onward (and very often without the religious overtones Gandhi gave it in his own mind). Rajaji actually was younger than Gandhi and older than Nehru; a decade separated him from them on both sides: during most of the twenty-five years of struggle for freedom they were so closely associated that such differences disappeared. (They count most at the beginning and at the end, anyhow.)

So, you are the typical tourist in Madras, as Rajaji says, and you go to the city of ruined empire and then to the Integral Coach Factory, jumping about twelve centuries in time and aeons in thought; and then you go to see Rajaji about it, and what is the result? I shall try to tell about it without exaggerating the significance it has for me.

On the drive back to Madras from Mahaballipuram I was bemused by what I had seen and not really taking much account of the landscape or the villages through which we passed. It is a two-hour drive and I had taken full account of the hot, still, flat land on the way up to the ruins. My companion, a government official, had run out of conversation, the sun was high, and we may have slept. Suddenly in one of those villages the driver of the car stopped abruptly, turned around and said something in Tamil. My friend the official translated: "The driver thinks you might want to see a pot coming off the wheel. Just there, on the right. The potter has practically finished it."

And there it was, a medium-sized tallish pot twirling, twirling on the wheel, obeying the potter's hands and feet, glistening and twirling in the deep shade of the grass roof, just such a thing as might have been seen in this same place four or five thousand years ago. As we watched the last revolutions the potter judged the moment had come and separated the pot from the wheel with a deft, decisive movement of a thread held high. It was over in a moment, the pot was finished and set on one side, and the potter stopped for a moment to stare at us. He was a man of middle age or beyond it and had probably done nothing in his life except make pots of this kind, the earthenware which is the commonest object in every Indian household. His skill was great, his time was his own, his earnings small, and—since the potter is a caste as well as a trade—his ancestors before him had done exactly the same for generations without number.

We went on in to Madras, of course, but my mind would not or could not get the potter out of it for another day or so. Old village industry, caste system, education—all those things which are the main strands of life in India—seemed to center upon this potter and his life, what was to become of his son, how the great changes of the present decade are affecting him. After my first talk with Rajaji that evening, his slow and wise old voice with its curious reminiscence here and there of Gandhi, his general tone of being (at last) above the battle, combined perhaps with the influences of the surroundings—an old house in a sleepy, shady suburb—to make me feel that perhaps I was unduly thoughtful in matters beyond my ken, and that the potter and his India would greatly survive all the possible changes of the present time.

The subject recurred the next day, just the same, and in a form which gave me even less chance of getting it out of my mind.

The Integral Coach Factory at Perambur is as modern as the year after next, with equipment of power and precision from more or less everywhere in Europe and America, with a staff of highly trained engineers and a skilled labor force recruited in India but trained (mostly) in Switzerland. What it makes is an all-steel third-class coach for the Indian railways, lighter and stronger than any known before, all in one piece—"integral" —and its production in three years has gone beyond the targets set for it in the Five Year Plan. I saw it in considerable detail, both the parts and the whole, in the company of an engineer trained in America, but it would be absurd to pretend that I absorbed, or have retained, much technical detail from the experience. What I have kept in mind ever since, and even after seeing some other technological marvels of a high order, is that first impression of cleanliness, efficiency, the quality everything had of being spick-and-span and in apple-pie order as the integral coaches became more integral every moment, moving through the assembly lines and on out to the rails of India. There were workmen of great skill, naturally, but what struck me more than the skills involved was the degree and intensity of the *attention* which must be necessary at every moment. A welder working with a flame at fifteen hundred degrees of temperature cannot let his mind wander a moment (whereas the potter can). We had some talk with a few such skilled workers, one welder in particular who had been trained in Switzerland.

He was from a village in the Madras neighborhood and had been chosen for training from his school, after passing certain examinations. After we had gone along for some further distance I asked my engineer guide suddenly, "Was that man's father a potter?" My friend laughed and said he didn't know, but that it was perfectly possible.

"Do you want me to go back and ask him?" he inquired.

"No matter. I see that it's quite possible, and whether that particular one is the son of a potter or not doesn't matter."

"It depends partly on how well he did in school," said the engineer. "It's also his own character and aptitudes. But we get them from every kind of origin in the villages. You'll see our training school later and can get an idea."

I did see the school, with its hundreds of young men learning how to make tools, or read blueprints, or any of the other elements of their craft, and talked to some of them, too. There were Christians and Muslims among them, too, although in that area the Hindus would naturally be in a big majority; and these Hindus were of all castes. They lived in modern dormitory quarters which, like everything else there, looked spanking new. But what struck me in the school and was to strike me repeatedly in others was the extraordinary neatness of the arrangements with tools, books, etc.—everything in its place, each boy responsible for keeping his own materials in order. The entire establishment seemed far removed in time and space from the nearby villages out of which, after all, its labor force chiefly came.

After the whole tour had ended my engineer friend asked me to come up to the director's room for tea. This was in the main building, a gleaming structure with a garden ablaze with flowers at its entrance. There I met six or eight executives and engineers who drifted into the big room, with its big mahogany table, its air-conditioning and leather chairs and silver cups won in factory athletics, for all the world like the same room in the most modern of American factories. (It was probably German or Swiss more than American, but such things usually do seem American to us because we saw them first at home.) All the engineers I met at Perambur were Indians, by the way, although there still were five or six of the Swiss technicians left in the works. We fell into talk about the coach factory and its brief history, its rapid rise in production, its future. Somehow or other, because he was still in my mind, I spoke of the potter I had seen finishing a wheel the day before.

"He might be a little bewildered here," I suggested.

"You will see such contrasts everywhere in India," the director said. "It is our stage of development."

"The potter doesn't work as hard as our people do," one of the engineers said. "He can think, you know, while he's working. He can sing a song. Perhaps he is a little freer."

"He makes a good deal less money than his son, providing his son is that welder you saw downstairs," said my engineer friend, the one who had accompanied me through the works. He laughed and added, "Isn't that the main consideration?"

"I wonder if it is?" said another executive. "He might be better and happier than his son—we can't really be sure of that. The little he makes may go further. He spends less. He isn't attracted to the city and the bright lights as his son is."

And so it went; the young engineers—several of whom had studied in America, two of whom had worked in the Baldwin Locomotive Factory—took hold of the notion and threw it about in the air, assuming easily (as I did) that the welder I had seen downstairs might be the son of the potter I had watched in the village, and thus a social phenomenon. They were not at all anxious to transform the whole of India into a factory, and one or two of them very seriously pointed out that the best way to avoid the evils of the factory system was by careful planning, such as had taken place here. They were imbued, most of them, with Gandhi's familiar idea that industrialization could be accomplished without exploitation, without slums or overcrowding or inroads on the health of the workers—and of course, in these surroundings, they proved their point by everything I had seen that day. I left them with the feeling that if they represented the future, or even part of it, the future was in good hands; and still I could not get the potter out of my head.

We drove back to Madras with all possible speed in the evening heat and I was a few minutes late for my appointment with Rajaji in his quiet suburb. (The name of that suburb is Thyaga Raja Nagar.) As on the preceding evening, we were left alone for a long talk. My distinguished friend, if I may so call him, was in the same elegiac mood, to start with, as on the evening before when we had talked about Gandhi and the vanity of human wishes. He had told me the contemporary India, that of this moment, did not represent what he and Gandhi and all the countless others had borne in mind for all the years of their struggle; power and place and position, he seemed to feel, had corrupted the patriots; the reality was far from the ideal. This vein of talk (which had caused me to write in my notebook the night before, "It all makes me feel sad") was soon abandoned when I put before him my various questions and suppositions about the potter and welder. He caught fire and began to talk with animation as he got into the subject, years or even decades dropping off him as he developed his theme. I took no notes but offer this as a fair paraphrase of what he had to say:

"Industrialization has become a slogan and a fetish, a kind of obsession, regarded as a good thing in itself no matter what dislocation it may bring to the country at large. The life of India is still in the villages, and you may see the broad, general standard of living, which is very low, in the villages only. The potter's son, after going to school and being fired with ambition, wants to leave the village; he wants to get into an industrial school, to be a welder and earn a great deal more money than his father did. Supposing he is the only son. In many cases he may even fail as a welder, have no aptitude for it, but he will not then return to the village, which is therefore, for the first time in centuries, without a potter. If in this dislocation you were able to bring up the whole level of standards, so that it doesn't matter whether the villagers have pots or not, it would be different; but the fact is that the villagers can't afford modern industrial products and even the pot itself is going up in price all the time. If having more welders means having fewer potters, it is not progress but dislocation. I would never push the rate of industrialization, or even encourage the villager to go to the city or factory, in this stage of India's evolution. There is too much suddenness in it all, not enough preparation."

This is not only a paraphrase but a summary, since the talk was quite a long one. I gathered that Rajaji's dislike of industrialization was at least partly temperamental—a natural dislike

—and as such was akin to Gandhi's. However, Gandhi had intimately seen and strongly deplored the factory slums of Europe, whereas Rajaji had never been outside of India and could not possibly maintain, on the limited experience of industrialization India has known up to the present, that the slum, poverty and disease were its inevitable result. Indeed the greatest Indian industrial plant of pre-independence days, the Tata steel mills and connected works at Jamshedpur, was an early model of enlightened paternalism and could have given lessons in many respects to the "advanced" industrial countries. Rajaji's argument, so far as I could follow it, concerned certain social and economic dislocations between village and city, between old-established caste guilds and the factory system, which could, as he said, upset or diminish the old virtues without adequately substituting new ones. This assumed that industrialization was going to be undertaken on a vast scale, which, under present conditions, seemed to me doubtful. I had no question in my own mind that the workers I had seen in Perambur, with their fixed cash wages and bonuses, with their model houses and schools, were better off than their relatives in the villages where they originated. The only question was whether they were happier, and whether old and new could exist together without multiplying the discontents. Rajaji's answer was clear: the village is still India, the Five Year Plan and all other schemes for industry are rash and precipitate, and grave social discontent and disorder are inevitable.

I had not gone there to argue with an eminent patriot whom I so greatly respected. Therefore I was glad to get his views without opposing them, although in truth I have never been able to see how a vast agricultural country much afflicted by climate and topography could combat poverty without industrialization. In Rajaji's view when the potter's son becomes a welder the village then has no pots, and since it cannot afford tin and aluminum vessels, and since the price of earthenware pots must then go up, the net result in the village is more poverty rather than less.

He fixed the price of a pot in the village, such a common pot as I had seen, at four annas (a quarter of a rupee), which comes to about five cents, and no doubt that was its price the last time he inquired. I learned afterward that the price paid to the potter at the present moment is generally twice as much—eight annas instead of four—which would seem to support his thesis that the present programs are driving prices up for the very poor.

In all such talk in India I had to make an effort not to compare prices or wages with those prevailing in my own country because such comparisons are worthless. The truth of the matter is that I was appalled at Perambur by one thing, the low wage scales (by my own standards) of skilled workers. I had to make a serious effort, then and afterward, to realize the conditions which make this wage scale fair and even good. A welder makes, with cash wages fixed on a uniform basis, and counting in his bonuses, some hundred and twenty rupees a month (thirty dollars). He can have a company house at a very low rent if he wishes, ten rupees a month or less in most places, and his transportation to and from the factory is free; he has free medical attention, schools, recreation centers and other benefits which certainly bring his real earnings up to much more than their cash value.

But even the potter in the village, although his earnings may be tiny in the eyes of foreigners, has compensations of another kind. Under the Hindu family system, it is more than probable that he shares in some plot of land and its produce. This complicated system, old by perhaps fifteen centuries or more, rules the villages of India and makes standards of cash earnings almost inapplicable. I do not say that Hindu villagers, especially the young, do not want cash when they can get it; they certainly do; but the fact is that they can get along with far less of it than Western minds would ordinarily consider possible.

Visitors to India, especially those who make brief visits, would maintain that Indian prices were on the international scale or close to it. This is true of the big hotels and of shops dealing in imported objects or materials. At times these prices may be above the international or dollar level. But if you ever have to have a loose heel tacked on to a shoe, for example, you will find that the price for this service, which depends on a craftsman, is far below what it would be elsewhere—even in Delhi, and even allowing for bribes, commissions or exaggerations on the part of the hotel servant who takes the shoe out to be mended. The servant goes to a relative, if he happens to belong to a leather-working family (that is, Muslims, untouchables, Christians and certain others outside the caste system), and the small sum you actually pay may be either subdivided or go into a family pool; that is not for you to inquire. What you do inevitably observe is that for such work as can be done by hand without the intervention of a machine or a shop you may, indeed, pay much more than an Indian would, but it will still be minimal by world standards.

Even the most casual visitor on the briefest tour must have observed the gap between foreigners' prices, as paid chiefly in hotels, city shops and the like, and for imported goods, and Indian prices. If you are content with Indian soap—Tata makes a number of good ones—you pay a great deal less than you do for the standard, but ordinary, brands of Europe and America. In short, the foreign visitor pays the prices of the rich, which are more or less international—the rich Indians pay the same, of course—but this has little or nothing to do with the immense mass of Indians living in the villages and on the land.

I digressed so far because in this last talk with Rajaji we spoke a good deal about prices and wages, and it would be more or less incomprehensible if this cannot be understood *in Indian terms*, with regard to all the surrounding circumstances.

Rajaji's conclusions are not at all mine, but they are based on far greater experience and knowledge, of course. I think the general excitement set up by discussion, in which he obviously revels, may have caused him to overstate his case a bit, but he ended up by saying that unless or until the government can supply aluminum or tin utensils at prices the villager can pay, no potter's son should be encouraged to leave his caste, his village and his inherited task. Such a degree of industrialization as that —the substitution of factory-made utensils for earthenware— is utterly impossible for a long time to come, and Rajaji was well aware of it when he made the statement. He was merely pointing up, emphasizing, and reducing to the absurd, the conflicts he perceives in the present program.

Some of his other criticisms of Indian policy were touched upon during these two conversations, of course. He dislikes all expenditure for military purposes and would not be averse to unilateral disarmament for his own or any other country. He deplores corruption, office-seeking and dishonesty of any kind, as does everybody else in India who ever spoke to me. He does not believe the program of village improvement, known as the National Extension Service, has even scratched the surface of the village problems. He sees a good many Potëmkin villages, so to speak, in the model establishments which are shown to foreigners. When these talks took place he was genuinely disturbed over the language policy which favors a gradual introduction of Hindi as the successor to English in government services, legislatures and courts. Naturally he speaks for his own South Indian people, but although his views are not welcome in New Delhi, I have met almost countless persons who agree with him—even, actually, among native-born North Indians to whom Hindi is the mother tongue.

Rajaji is, after all, a Madrassi Brahmin, and the Madrassi Brahmins have filled the government services for a century. Their command of English, which has always been well taught and learned in Madras, has been one of their most valued accomplishments. They grow up speaking Tamil—as other southerners in other provinces speak Telugu, or Malayalam, or Kanarese—and to this mother tongue they add English as the language of instruction in school after the earlier years.

What Rajaji said, restricting himself to his own city and province, was that if Hindi is added to English, as would have to be the case for many decades, the mind of the growing boy will be so cluttered with dissimilar languages that he can learn scarcely anything else. To pass government examinations in two foreign languages would not merely double the task but make it ten times more difficult. And government service is today, more than ever before, virtually the only career open to middle-class boys in India.

Rajaji points out with acumen and humor that the southern languages are so different from the northern that they actually bear no relation: they have no common roots at all. Hindi is a language of Sanskrit origin; Tamil and Telugu have nothing in common with it. The teeming south (like the teeming province of Bengal!) has enough crosses to bear, he seems to say, without adding a new foreign language. In sum, says he, English has been immensely useful to India, it is the only language all India possesses for communication between regions, and it would be far simpler and better for India to retain English as a national language superimposed upon the existing regional structures (the Tamil, Telugu, etc., in the south, the Hindustani-Urdu and Bengali in the north). The remedy is not to impose a new national language but to increase and improve the existing knowledge of English.

On such a question no foreigner can have a really valid opinion because whatever it is, it will be intellectual only: the deep emotions aroused by regional languages are not felt by us, and therefore not understood. Language is a basic thing. As Stalin ruled, I think quite correctly, in his conclusion to the famous linguistics debate in the Soviet Union, language is at the base of human society and is not a part of its superstructure. As a basic element it involves the subconscious and the unconscious, an emotional field in which the intellect is not of much use.

My views of the language question, therefore, are not worth giving. I understand the practical arguments on both sides but their emotional content is beyond me. What I can say, however, is that many persons in India agree with Rajaji in the matter, and so long as this remains true it seems most unlikely that English will be driven out, or Hindi substituted, as the means of communication between regions. As Rajaji says, English is "a window on the world," and the difficulties involved in putting all learned works (scientific, legal, technological) into Hindi would be endless: therefore, in practice, whatever extra heat may be generated in the debate, it seems fairly sure that English will remain for a long time to come.

These are the principal elements, let us say, or a summary of them, in which Rajaji is at variance with the ruling tendencies in contemporary India. It is worth taking them into account because in every case he takes the unpopular side, voices the unpopular opinion. I have heard political arguments almost constantly since my first visit to India, and they are most common in New Delhi, but they tend to concern persons rather than policies. They also contain a great deal of the backwash of current events, involving "what really happened" in this or that recent episode; they are like political discussion in most capitals, partly sheer gossip.

With Rajaji in those two Madras evenings there was not a scrap of triviality: he gave his views without even naming persons. He was partly musing aloud (some of these things were made the substance of a public address he made weeks later in Calcutta) and partly whetting his mind on whatever stones of observation I could put before him. As Gandhi's old friend and lieutenant he has a special status, and perhaps for this reason alone can go so far in criticizing the prevailing climate of thought in India. Among the ranks of the Congress Party faithful, all of them Gandhi's followers, you may find disagreement on specific questions, but only Rajaji seems to have a fundamental dislike for, or disappointment in, the main lines of contemporary policy. In all these grave matters, industrialization, defense and disarmament, the language question, the work among the villagers, he is saddened by what he regards as error and falsehood.

Now, to tell the truth, I could not be sure of how much in this sadness or disappointment came from age and inevitable disillusionment. When he said quite plainly that it was not for this (contemporary India) that his generation had struggled so hard, I asked him if he were not, essentially, complaining of the vanity of human wishes. He acknowledged that it was partly true.

"But only partly," he went on. "It is true that we all hope too much and we are all disappointed. But in these matters there were other choices—other things could have been done."

In other words, he is reconciled to the fact that every great movement of an idealistic nature aims too high and must be disappointed in the realities which come after success. But he also thinks that in India much that has gone wrong could have been put right. Strangely enough, he was regarded for thirty years and more as one of the most practical politicians in India. "Subtle and astute," Frank Moraes calls him in his *Jawaharlal Nehru, a Biography*. And yet today Rajaji, in his yearning after a homespun and disarmed society, a sort of Gandhian abstraction, seems to have left everything practical behind him.

It is good, nevertheless, that such voices can be heard. They instigate thought and evoke questions. I could not myself easily imagine the Platonic society or state he has in mind: it would be too good for this world, as it seems to me. But that he can see it and speak for it, under the prevailing conditions, seems to me good whoever listens—and even if nobody seems to listen there must be somewhere an echo.

2

As I went on with my journey among potters and welders, all over the vast country, trying to piece together an intelligible concept of India today, there were not many occasions when fundamental dissent could be heard. Enthusiasm in all the new plants and projects, the great new dams and steel mills, the establishments for scientific research, is very high. I found it frankest and most inspiriting among the young technicians, engineers and the like, but it reaches into the directorship, too—men in their fifties who are seeing achieved, in actual fact, a transformation they could not have expected in their own lifetimes. Most of these people, young or middle-aged, are far too busy to indulge in abstract argument anyhow. An eminent research chemist, thoughtful and deliberate in speech, said to me at the end of a long talk: "We are taking the only way there is to take. No other course is possible for India." This seemed to be the view of mature, highly trained specialists all over the country who were involved in the Five Year Plan or associated schemes of development. It is worth mentioning that I believe I never found a Communist among them, although, in the nature of things, there must be a few.

What is this "only possible course for India?" It is planned development under state ownership and control, but without the sacrifice of either freedom or democracy.

Up until a very recent period the thing itself has been regarded as impossible. Economic theory may have allowed for it, but economic practice certainly never yet has confirmed it. We had on the one side those who believed industrialization, modernization, development in general, depended upon the free flow of private capital and enterprise. We had on the other the theory of the omnipotent state, which alone could plan and execute such vast schemes by total control of all persons and all property. What India is trying to do and is in fact already doing is wholly new and so far unique in the world, a combination of the two.

Jawaharlal Nehru is the chief originator of the great experiment, although he had the assistance of the best specialists in the country. He started with the premise that the new government of united, independent India must make an attack upon the central problem, which was poverty. Not to do so would have been a betrayal of the many millions who struggled so long to set India free. To attack poverty on such a scale demanded a coherent plan and a capital investment which, in such a country, only the central and state governments could possibly provide.

The new government, Nehru most of all, were firmly vowed to freedom and democracy. In their thirty years' war against British imperialism they had talked far more about freedom than about poverty, far more about democracy than about economic planning. The British themselves had sponsored a good deal of economic planning in the last part of their tenure in India, and it is always well to remember that some important elements in the two Five Year Plans were started by them. It was necessary for the new India to move decisively into large-scale development, but it was equally necessary to do so without upsetting the rule of law, the democratic structure of legislatures, the freedom of the citizen. The Republic of India came into being in response to a demand for more freedom, not less.

Thus the two main lines of development in the first decade were imposed by the historic conditions. There had to be a determined attack on poverty by means of economic planning, which could only come from the state structure (central and provincial); and it had to be done in freedom, with all the flexibility and caution and persuasion which that involves. Any abrupt exaggeration of state powers would have been dangerous to stability; any relaxation in pursuit of the aim would have impaired the faith of the masses.

That is why the planned economy in a free society is "the only possible course for India." The historic conditions made it so. But once this necessity is acknowledged there opens up a field of activity in which the possibilities of experiment, improvisation and even sheer invention are large. In a tactical sense, you make it up as you go along; you learn by doing; if you cannot get over a difficulty you must go around it. In this effort in both the Five Year Plans, and especially in the second of them, the fertile brain and indomitable spirit of Jawaharlal Nehru have been of the utmost value to the scientists, engineers and other specialists who do the field work. They have needed constant support from New Delhi, not only in funds and authority, but also in the incessant day-by-day grind of administrative decisions. This support they have received in full. Many times I heard the same words from plant managers or the directors of scientific institutes: their best friend, the best friend of the whole Five Year Plan in its struggle for life, has been the Prime Minister.

It should therefore be plain that the views of Rajaji are not at all those of Mr. Nehru. They are the views of one eminent citizen, but I could not find them echoed on any scale through the country, unless it be on the language issue. So far as industrialization is concerned, India seems to want more of it rather than less, and on the question of military defense there is not much difference of opinion. The most vocal opposition to Nehru's government comes, of course, from the Communists, whose principal complaints have to do with big business, the "vested interests," and various accusations of moneymaking in government. They do not oppose industrialization, but they want a more thoroughgoing scheme of state ownership and control. When I have listened to them in parliament, or have read their press, it has seemed to me that they attacked persons, or episodes, or incidents, rather than principles. In their present phase, while they were trying to make a go of local state government in one of the new provinces—Kerala—the Communists did not show their hand plainly. They oppose for the sake of opposing, but they seldom declare or even acknowledge their fundamental aims. We know that they must fundamentally want nothing else than absolute power in all India, with the creation of a Soviet state as its instrument, but this is not what they say. When they speak, it is of lesser things—and most of all they are in the central parliament to obstruct at every turn, to make up in noise what they lack in numbers.

So we may justifiably say that there is no real opposition in India on the great questions of policy. The Socialist Party, divided into two parts, has grown weaker rather than stronger during the years of independence. Up until the 1957 elections, which put a Communist state government in power on the Malabar Coast (the new state of Kerala), the Congress Party's majorities everywhere were so great that, as Mr. Nehru himself has said, "We were becoming almost monolithic." There are signs that this state of affairs may not endure, but so far the central government is securely in Congress Party hands. It is not likely to be otherwise so long as Mr. Nehru commands the immense popular support which is always his for the asking.

3

My journeys into the Five Year Plan touched upon numerous establishments of older date, such as the silk manufactories of the state of Mysore or the cotton mills of Tata in Bombay. Private industry did exist in India under British rule and continues today, although its efforts are now counted into the total of the Plan. There are scientific institutions of earlier date, too, and some of them admirable, such as the Indian Institute founded by Tata at Bangalore. Even in the great water-control systems, whereby the rivers are harnessed for irrigation and power and floods are reduced, there were conspicuous beginnings under the British: the wonderful dam at Hirakud (state of Orissa) was fully planned before independence.

It is only natural, however, that the new projects, plants and dams should arouse the keenest interest in most visitors because they are the fruits of freedom. In themselves they are often so tremendous that they inspire something of the awe one feels before the monuments of the ancient empires. Such a one is the vast Bhakra-Nangal dam in the Punjab, a towering structure yet unfinished, or some of the river diversions which are undertaken in the south. It might be useful to make a list of the principal enterprises which I was able to visit in some detail last spring. The mere list itself, although it may be geographically unfamiliar, indicates the variety and extent of the effort being made under the second Five Year Plan. To wit:

Integral Coach Factory at Perambur, near Madras—an impressive achievement already discussed.

Gandhigram outside of Madura: a training school for workers in village industries, social education, home economics, care of children, etc., etc.—a big, lively and inspiriting institute for boys and girls who will go into the villages.

Cochin Harbor (state of Kerala): the channel to the open sea is four miles long in a straight line from the land-locked harbor, an excellent one which must be more or less unique in form. It requires constant dredging, of course, and a great deal of work is in progress.

Cochin Naval Station: to my untutored eye it seemed as modern as anything I've seen, especially in electronics.

Bangalore (state of Mysore) is a thriving industrial city where there are many factories, old and new. I visited the Bharat Electronics Factory, which was brought into being under French technical advisors; the Hindustan Aircraft Factory (originally American), which makes trainers and fighters and repairs bombers; Hindustan Telephone Factory, the Machine Tool Factory (German technicians), the Indian Institute of Science (Tata), and other establishments with their attached social services and housing. According to my diary what constantly impressed me in all of these plants was the apprentices—those learner-candidates whom I had first seen at Perambur, so serious and so unbelievably careful of their equipment. The plants in Bangalore are of different origins and dates; the newest are the electronics, telephone and machine tool factories (all Five Year Plan); and of all the new works it may be seen by the cornerstone that Jawaharlal Nehru was there. He must have laid more cornerstones than anybody of this age.

Krishnaraja Sagar is a wonderful big dam with an illuminated garden at its base and an excellent hotel alongside: it is one of the early dams of India (completed 1913) and thus has nothing to do with the Five Year Plan except to be, of course, integrated into it. It was built by the old Maharajah of Mysore, grandfather of the present prince, renowned like most of his family for public beneficence.

Central Food Technological Research Institute (Mysore city), where an amazing work goes on for the development of new sources of food, prevention of contamination or waste of food, or new combinations of food values; a number of the specialists had been trained in America; and I tasted a new "synthetic rice," so-called, a food on a wheat basis which tastes something like rice when prepared.

Himayar Sagar (near Hyderabad city), a training center for block development workers, those who go into the villages to teach and serve; it was a good one, one of the four in India, and I was delighted to see that the library contained a fair number of books which had been presented by the United States Information Service (works of popular education in paperbacks).

Aarey Milk Colony (near Bombay—opened 1949) which has thirty units of roughly five hundred cattle each, now supplying half of Bombay's milk needs: ultramodern, sanitary, scientific. The problem of the cattle and the milk seems to be on a fair way to solution in Bombay city.

Bombay city itself contains a considerable number of plants and factories, old and new, which together make up its contribution to the Five Year Plans. These include the Stanvac Oil Refinery (1954) and the Atomic Reactor, a one-megaton job almost entirely produced on the spot—and these two are modernity itself—along with the older Tata mills and many others; the Cancer Research Institute (in conjunction with the Tata hospital) fascinated me above all by some investigations of heredity in the caste system; the celebrated Haffkine Institute, for immunology, produces serums and vaccines of all sorts, including the best one known for snake bite. Mordecai Haffkine, a Russian Jew who was a pupil of Pasteur, came to Bombay in the great plague of 1896 and has undoubtedly left an enduring monument. At present the plague is virtually unknown in Bombay and cholera is very rare—which cannot be said of the other great port, Calcutta.

Poona has the National Defense Academy, in which Army, Navy and Air Force cadets are trained together, and two great scientific institutions in its immediate neighborhood—the Central Water and Power Research Station and the Chemical Research Institute. In the Water and Power Station, models to scale are made of every problem brought to them—the Bombay Harbor, for example, which needs dredging and enlargement, or the river systems around Calcutta. Upon these models, which are accurate in every detail including tides, currents and silting, can be seen the actual behavior of rivers, ports and harbors, so that the engineers charged with their improvement can draw plans. The huge Chemical Research Institute, where chemistry is put to work to aid in production, was no less marvelous to me, although somewhat harder to understand.

The Damodar Valley Corporation and the works undertaken in the same neighborhood are obviously dear to the planners in general and represent a heavy investment. There are big dams at Konar, Tilaiya and Maithon on the Barada River, the huge Maithon dam (1957) being the latest; there is a big Thermal Power Plant at Bokaro; there are model factory towns at Sindri and Chittaranjan in this general region. Dust and a touch of fever made it difficult for me, but I retain vivid impressions of the fertilizer factory at Sindri (ammonium sulphate from local coke and Rajasthan gypsum) and the locomotive works at Chittaranjan.

The new steel mills at Durgapur (English under contract), Rourkela (German under contract) and Bhilai (Russian under contract) will soon be in production and constitute a separate element in the Five Year Plan. They are really quite extraordinary, whole cities evoked from the dusty plain. The plants are designed and partly manufactured in the countries of origin, and the contractors bring ready-made pieces to India to be fitted together by (chiefly) Indian workers. The German-built plant is perhaps furthest along, although the Russian one at Bhilai is well advanced, too. Durgapur, the English one, is the newest and therefore least advanced. It was obvious that all the engineers and technicians employed in these projects had brought their tastes with them; the food at the hostel in Bhilai, where two hundred Russians are employed, was strongly Russified, although all the cooks and boys were Indians. The product of these three plants will reach six million metric tons in a relatively short space of time, it is said, and each is to some degree specialized so that their efforts will complement one another.

If we add the great dam at Hirakud (the oldest in this northeastern area, and the longest in the world) and the other at Bhakra-Nangal in the northwest, the highest in the world, we have something like a prospectus of the Five Year Plan as it has so far gone. You will see that old and new are combined in the general view, as they are combined in the calculations of the Planning Commission. Each has its fixed dates for completion, targets for production and special contribution to make. No doubt it is true that the economy of India remains based upon the village, the small agricultural village, and must be so for a long time to come, but it is also true that remarkable advances have been made in industrial construction, flood control, irrigation and power. In this list, which includes only the principal establishments I was able to visit, there is no mention of numerous other projects (such as river diversions of considerable magnitude in the southern mountains) which I saw only in the form of models. Such as it is, and in most summary form, the list may give an idea of the extent of the effort now being made toward development. We can have no difficulty imagining the fructifying influences of irrigation, for instance, in those half-desert regions of Rajasthan and other dusty wastes where the need has always been for water—water which is withheld from India, by nature itself, for all but a few weeks of the year during the monsoon.

4

For here we come back to the principal consideration, which is that nature itself has been harsh to India. That implacable geographer, Sir Halford Mackinder, used to say that India was "governed by the monsoon," and this must remain true for a long time. The rain that forms in the summer clouds may be copious or stingy; it may be too much for the crops; it may not be enough. The hundreds of millions who live by agriculture have always been dependent upon it, and with them the food supply of the country. For the rest of the year there is no rain. The dust invades, takes over; the desert areas grow larger; land passes out of cultivation.

Again and again, as you drive through the flat dust-haze of the limitless plains, perhaps with a big handkerchief tied across your nose, you are forced back into the same reflection. Nature has been a cruel stepmother to this country. ("*O vraiment marâtre nature!*" said Ronsard.) Deforestation, ages ago, may not have been nature's work entirely, but since then there has seemed very little man could do to overcome the relentless harshness of the seasons. The temperatures recorded in my diary for last March and April look difficult to credit in another climate; day after day the Fahrenheit recordings were 104, 108 or 110. This is in an industrial area where a stern effort is being made—in the Damodar Valley, for instance—and where work must go on whatever happens. In such a climate disease is far more of a problem than in more moderate regions, and here, too, a great struggle is taking place. One of the most encouraging results has been obtained with malaria, which was the scourge of many areas until very recently. By drainage and the destruction of swamps, by chemicals and by the treatment of disease once it has declared itself, much has been done in these past ten years to make life more bearable.

It is still true that nature is harsh. It costs more in human energy to go out into these plains and evoke new cities, new sources of wealth, than it would cost in most other countries. More and more irrigation, more tree planting, more vegetation, will in time make a difference, but the time is not yet. In a model town like Chittaranjan, the locomotive center, trees have been planted everywhere; it will be another decade before they begin to deflect or modify the blaze of the sun.

And as for water itself, of course the amounts available for irrigation and power do not compare with those in temperate zones. An engineer at Hirakud, who had traveled in Europe and America, talked to me rather sadly one night after dinner about this very thing. He had been to Niagara and the region of the Great Lakes, where the amount of water at the disposal of his fellow engineers in one year is vastly greater than it can ever be in India. He was not at all despondent—indeed he had great faith in the new projects and what they would do for the country—but he pointed out that the disparity in natural endowment made every achievement in India more precarious and hard-bought than in my own country.

So it is with coal and iron—both are of low grade even in those districts where they are relatively abundant; petroleum has not yet shown itself; aside from the radioactive sands of Malabar, nothing new has been discovered in recent years to add to the sparse resources of the country. The whole effort to seek new sources of wealth in industry, however necessary it may be, is a dire struggle, uphill all the way. So much of what is fundamentally necessary must be purchased in foreign countries that the demand for foreign currency incessantly grows with the very development it feeds. The amount required to complete work already started under the Five Year Plan (up to 1960) was being estimated at an extra billion dollars when I left India and the sum has since risen. This is exclusive of the amounts already made available in dollars and other foreign currencies before the past summer.

These are some of the obstacles. Without being an economist or technologist of any kind, a visitor who sees as much as I did of the work undertaken must be simultaneously encouraged and anxious. Encouraged because the human contribution is so great and has already done so much—anxious because the difficulties ahead seem so serious. The essential supply of foreign currency may be found, and at present it seems that it will be, but the enmity of nature is something nobody can correctly estimate or foresee.

Mr. Nehru once said to me, "One bad harvest is bad luck and two are far worse. Three bad harvests in a row are beyond any normal computation of bad luck, and yet it happened."

This, of course, is the basic misfortune: food supply for the population is always precarious. Reserves are extremely limited —two or three months away from famine in many areas— and too much water, or not enough, can ruin any harvest. Flood is an ever-present peril in one season and drought in another. The great dams which one day may control the floods and distribute the water do not yet reach a large enough part of the whole country to save the land mass from these disastrous natural fluctuations. It is true that food production in a normal year is higher now than ever before, but the population also has grown rapidly—an increment of some four million a year. Birth control, officially approved now by the central government, seems to have made little progress outside those well-to-do classes (mostly city dwellers) who take to it in all societies.

All these things put together make the problem of progress and poverty far more acute in India than in other great countries. The natural resources of the Soviet Union and of the United States are both incomparably greater; China alone, of the largest countries, may be a comparable case, but under its present regime we are not allowed to know much about it, so the comparison cannot be carried out in any detail. What is obvious is that India's way, the planned development inside a free society, is very much a test case, very much under the observation of all Asia. Since India is a free country and anybody who wishes to do so may see what he likes there, our information on its successes and occasional failures is profuse. Of China in recent years we know little; even those who go there, judging by their reports, see almost nothing. It is only by the results, somewhere in the unknown future, that any valid comparison could be made.

These dark realities have to be kept in mind; they account for a great deal. They cannot obliterate the impression made by other realities, such as the towering dam of Bhakra-Nangal or the new, clean, thriving industrial communities which have been created from nothing in the bare plain. The youth of India, whenever it has received training and opportunity, responds almost magically to the challenge of the hour. I can remember scores of them whose names I never heard or have forgotten—a chemical research worker here, an engineer there—whose keenness in the work and belief in its purpose would gladden any heart. They have a quality which often made me think of the American West—not only because their surroundings are sometimes rather reminiscent of Arizona or New Mexico, but because they have that same alert, eager confidence which belongs to pioneers. They do not go so far as to think that men can do anything or everything, but they are not afraid of nature—that shrewish nature which is India's stepmother.

The inspiriting effect of this human contribution to progress is not confined to engineers, scientists and technologists. I confess I found them to be of the highest character and interest, especially when they completely forgot my existence, as they so often did, in the eagerness of their exposition. It would be equally impossible to forget the village social workers, the teachers, the veterinarians and country doctors, all those who are involved in the National Extension Service. This program has not yet reached into every village but it has covered a large part of the country and hopes, when there are trained workers enough, to touch upon it all. The results vary from place to place, and it is quite true that there has not yet been enough time to estimate their effect. At this moment we may disregard the future results only to say that in this category of workers I met many memorable men and women, almost all of them very young, who seemed to have the same kind of indefatigable zeal as the engineers and technicians in a totally different way.

Engineers, scientists and technologists, although they may work in an extremely adverse climate, have numerous advantages: their housing, their recreation, most often their actual cash earnings, are in a special category. They are not strangers to air-conditioning, good food and a well-stocked general store or canteen. The same could not be said for village workers in the block development services. I remember a veterinarian in the province of Madras whose "block" was 112 villages scattered over 141 square miles. This was at Tarukalukundam (a neat name), not far from Chingleput. The young man gave me a complete lesson in artificial insemination but also told me his gravest difficulty was in persuading the country folk to feed and care for the cattle obtained by this method. The upgrading of the breed of cattle which might result in some countries in four generations (twelve years) takes much longer in India, and among all the hardships of that young veterinarian's life, which were obviously numerous, he counted this the worst.

Furthermore, there were many men and women who seemed to me to be doing their energetic best for the Five Year Plan in quite different walks of life—not specialists of any kind, but even, if I may say so, among the most maligned of all, the politicians, the journalists, the civil servants. These are the groups or classes which are often said to live only for salaries and promotions, for corrupt and illicit gains, or for self-aggrandizement. It was my luck to find many who could not possibly have deserved such accusations, and many more who were filled with unmistakable enthusiasm for their own particular work and for the whole national movement—as it ought to be called—which the Five Year Plan has, in my opinion, brought into existence.

On the whole it is the eagerness, the enthusiasm, which distinguishes all these boys of the Five Year Plan. Among them there is not a trace of that hopelessness or despair which many visitors used to see, or said they saw, in India in the past. Hopelessness and despair there must be, on a great scale, in villages swept by flood or famine, but those who are now giving their lives to combat these conditions are filled with a new energy based either on hope or confidence or a combination of the two. There were actually ministers in various states—full cabinet ministers, and even chief ministers—who were touched by the same quality. We are constantly hearing in India that all the governments, state or central, are filled with "old men," but I ran into a considerable number of young ones who had nevertheless managed to get into high places. And it is probably not necessary to say that the Army, Navy and Air Force have their full share of this lively, energetic and forward-looking youth: such services get it in all countries, and India is not at all an exception but rather a prime example of the rule.

Thus we have human beings pitched against inimical nature in a grand effort. I have called it a national movement and that is what it is, because it is not all directly connected with the Five Year Plan. The Plan has, not on paper but in operation (especially in the second installment), sent a thrill of life along India's keel. It arouses, evokes and partially creates the vision of a better future, to which each citizen as he matures has something to give. In this respect, which is psychological, and in the practical consequence of work done, there is something to set against the harshness of natural conditions. Nobody wants to exaggerate the changes which have set in—and, remembering Rajaji, we must repeat that the countless villages are still the basic India—but we should be deaf and blind, as well as a little stupid, not to perceive that change is afoot.

Here, too, we encounter the fact that Nehru has been the prime mover. I have already quoted the field workers who called him their "best friend," and who have relied so heavily on his support for the past six or eight years at least. That is his practical task; that is what he *does*. There is also to be considered the immense effect of what he *is:* he has done more by mere being—and by being in so many places in rapid succession—than anybody else. The keenness of the young, the national movement of hope, although it has diverse origins, is sustained by his presence. And what a presence! I have traveled far more in India than most people ever do, Indian or foreign, and I have yet to see any work, plant, enterprise, school, hospital or laboratory which he has not visited. The workers in these places always told me about his visits, what he said, how he looked, incidents of his passing. He has an eagerness about the new projects which equals that of the youngest engineer returned from America or Germany or England; he wants to see everything, and does. His own vivid curiosity appeals to the pioneers more than his public acts or speeches. They all take photographs of him and tell stories about what he said in this, that or the other place, crawling around on scaffoldings and into half-built shafts. Often he tells his technician guides that he is not equipped to appreciate all their work, but his eagerness to see it never wavers. He is evidently able to tap extra reserves of energy for these detailed visits, which often left me exhausted. In almost every important structure during the past decade, as I remarked before, the cornerstone bears an inscription saying that he laid it. This is to be found north and south, east and west, in every corner of India from Comorin to Kashmir, and applies to schools, museums and hospitals as well as to developments under the Five Year Plan.

This omnipresence, made possible by the airplane, is an element of unity for India, as has often been remarked before now. No matter what he says or does, it is his being there that counts, and helps in great measure—nobody can say how much

—to overcome those divisive forces of region and language which afflict the country.

How much more, then, must be the effect of his presence upon the eager youths in the steel mills, power projects and new factories! With all their enthusiasm they must tend sometimes to think their work hard and its importance unappreciated. Climate is almost always against them and the diversions of the cities are far away. They have come, let us say, from the Massachusetts Institute of Technology, back to India for this very purpose, and they do not regret it, but living for a year or two or three on the dusty plain while some huge project makes its way from blueprint to actuality, wondering sometimes if the rest of the country really knows what they are doing, they value these visits from the Prime Minister beyond rubies. Every boy I saw on those projects was able to say with perfect precision what was the date of the Prime Minister's last visit, what he saw and what he said and did; above all, those little remarks he so often throws off, more or less unconsciously, which are treasured by his listeners thereafter.

It is also noticeable that the new generation of engineers and specialists tends to refer to Mr. Nehru as "our Prime Minister." This form of reference to him is almost universal among the young. The graduation of terms is fairly interesting: these young men have known him only as Prime Minister and they have never known any other. Their immediate elders were likely to call him "Punditji," which is more or less "Mr. Pundit," a form of reference still common in New Delhi. And a still older generation had the habit of calling him "Jawaharlal" whether they actually knew him or not, in accordance with a very old Indian custom. The boys of the Five Year Plan have certainly not thought out the implications of their reference, which comes naturally from their consciousness, but again and again it struck me that in using these words, "our Prime Minister," they seemed to be making a symbol in which India and Jawaharlal Nehru were one.

At a later point—in the chapter on Nehru in politics—I shall have occasion to show what an element of strength to him, too, is this simple, unthinking and unquestioning faith, which he encounters most of all among the youth and in the broad masses, far removed from parliamentary debate. It seems to give him a special restorative which (luckily) he enjoys as much as they do. The miracle works both ways.

If I have clearly stated both terms of the conflict between nature and man in this land, it will be seen that India's greatest resource is its people—the one and the many. I do not find them to be so very separate or different.

5

The question often arises in discussion, not with skeptics or critics in particular but even with the friendliest observers, how much or little the development schemes have affected the life of the Indian masses. The masses are agricultural: what good does it do them to have good steel coaches produced for the Indian railways? What do they get out of an increased steel production or an electronics factory? How is the life of the village responding to these innovations, or to the Five Year Plan in general?

Those who ask such questions are often familiar enough with the development schemes on paper; most Indian intellectuals of the cities know the plans well enough. Not many, however, have seen the concrete evidence except here and there. Even the workers in the Five Year Plan know chiefly their own part of it; they are not likely to have time for other observations in such a large country. They see wages, prices and taxes all gradually but steadily rising, and it sometimes appears to them that this is the only tangible result of the effort at development for the country at large. The Communists, of course, exaggerate every such question into a vast interrogation which, essentially, puts the whole value of the Plan in doubt. There is a clear tactical reason for them to question the Plan, and all plans made under the present regime, for their hope is to see such a catastrophic failure as would give them their chance at power.

It is not for them, however, but for the men of good will, that answers should be found. I am not thinking here of the young but of the middle-aged and older generations, particularly those in the cities. Outside of India such questions arise even more often. The foreigner is most likely to put it in the bluntest form, as I have heard from some Americans: "What difference has the Five Year Plan made?" Indians are more likely to inquire, of themselves and of others, what changes it has introduced into the life of the broadest mass.

We can immediately stipulate one thing, which is that hundreds of thousands of villages have so far been untouched by the immediate results of economic planning. They have been reached, either thoroughly or (as in most cases) rather sketchily, by the National Extension Service, but industrialization, with the water power and irrigation schemes—all the newest part of the planning—has so far affected only contiguous areas, not India as a whole. This is natural enough when you consider that the first plan was somewhat modest and the second, which goes more to the root of the matter, is only three years old. Time does not permit the kind of wholesale transformation which such questions imply. Even in Russia, with colossal natural resources and a wholly subject population which can be moved about at the will of the rulers, it took about thirty years to get a result commensurate with its possibilities. (And at what a cost!) We shall do better not to expect fantastic results in the case of India in these very few years.

What can be seen with the naked eye is that areas contiguous to the development schemes, where those are already in operation, have profited by them. Some of the biggest schemes for power and irrigation are still unfinished and we must use our imaginations to see what the life-giving water will do for the land in only a year or two more. But in what has already been completed the results are visible. They are equally visible in areas where cheap electricity has resulted from the water power schemes. Land reform, where it is fully operative and not just a legal project, has played a part in this obvious improvement of certain areas. Even some very primitive voluntary efforts, such as the deepening of the village "tanks" (pools or ponds for storing monsoon water), have had some result. When we see what water control has already done, no matter how vast and parched this land may be, we must feel convinced that it will do much more for the standard of life.

And aside from what we can see by looking—if we look in the right places—there are many other indications that something quite new has arisen in the life of the villages. One is the insistent demand, which by the nature of things becomes political, for more water, more electrification. Some of the politicians in local governments are harassed by this more than by most of the other problems they face at the time of the annual budget. The villagers have had enough acquaintance with rural electrification to want more of it at almost any cost, and to vote in accordance with their wishes. The ministers who plan and present a budget according to their estimates of revenue find themselves under severe criticism because they are not instantly damming up *all* the rivers and dotting the countryside with power stations. Last spring I was in a number of state capitals just at the time of their budget debates and was struck by the recurrence of this demand. Next to the questions involving food prices and food control (government "fair price" shops and the like), the demand for electricity probably ranks second in the minds of rural representatives. In a case like that of the state of Mysore, which is in the happy and rare situation of having enough rice, electricity takes first importance.

Mr. Nijalingappa, who was then Chief Minister of that state, said to me on the second day of his budget debate, "Nobody wants to haul water out of a well any more. In every village they want an electric pump!"

Neither he nor I could blame them, of course, but the capital investment required to satisfy such a demand cannot be provided—even with help from Delhi—overnight.

The indirect benefits to the village from far-off industrial schemes are difficult to observe or measure, but they must exist: if India can produce its own railway coaches or telephone switchboards or chemical fertilizers, the general level must go up, however slightly. And in fact, if I am not suffering from delusions, it actually has. No foreigner can feel safe from error in such a matter, but I certainly thought I perceived some improvement in clothing and in commodities offered for sale even in remote villages. This is, of course, improvement over ten years ago; the standard is still very low but it seemed to me higher than before. I also thought I could see some result from the agricultural lectures which are periodically given in so many villages. Certainly there has been a great deal of volunteer work done in the past four or five years on irrigation ditches and tanks, with an increased use of chemicals.

These are matters in which an increase of supply produces an increase of demand. It is so in most places where the human race has dwellings. In the overwhelming prosperity of the United States there are many millions today who could hardly face life without television, although they were unaware of its existence a short time ago. In the Indian cities, which are fed by the villages, supply and demand have the same perverse way of increasing each other, so that progress can scarcely keep in step. The lovely lady Mayor of Madras, Mrs. Cherian, smiling over the teacups, with a rose behind her ear, said to me, "I wish you could find some way of persuading our city dwellers that *even in advanced countries* people have to live rather spread out, and use public transport to get to their work."

She had been discoursing about overcrowding, along with sewage, electrification and kindred matters. She made me see that even in Madras, a city which has had somewhat better conditions than others in India for decades, one result of progress is the demand for more progress.

Now, of course, we have plenty of statistical evidence that the Five Year Plans, both of them, have been producing a steady increase in the national income as a whole. I have tried to avoid statistics, which are in any case readily available in all public libraries, but the two plans have aimed at a five percent annual increase in national income, measured in real values. That is, if prices keep pace with rising income there is no increase in real values; if they can be held in whole or in part, or the income rises faster than the prices, the "real values" can be seen to grow. In this sense the plans have gradually, year after year, brought the total national income up until it is now rising somewhat faster than the five percent originally desired. The average income of an Indian citizen is at present about $60 a year, a little more perhaps, and at the beginning of the planning it was reckoned at $53 a year. In twenty years, at most, it will go beyond $100 a year—all this in "real values," regardless of what accidents may occur in the meantime (flood, famine, even inflation). It is not much, and it may cause many of us to ponder over the state of affairs which obliges the central government to pay a million dollars a year to the Nizam of Hyderabad for his privy purse, in addition to $500,000 a year for the upkeep of his palaces and $500,000 a year in compensation for the loss of revenue from his former crown lands. India inherited not only a grueling poverty but an assortment of other liabilities from the past, and one of these liabilities was certainly the feudal princes. And yet, without using forcible and confiscatory methods, which are alien to the temper as well as to the Constitution of India, the past must be pensioned off while the future is being so hard-bought.

Statistics, however, to which one may make a bow without undue reverence, are not particularly germane to this account of things seen, felt and heard in India. The telephone that you see introduced for the first time in a southern village, the electric lights that twinkle at you all along the Malabar Coast, the new school in one village or the new deep well dug in another, convey a great deal more to my own receptivities than all the tables of statistics in the world. And I think that most persons are alike in this. Statistics belong to statisticians.

The accomplishment is plain—as plain as its limitations. It is designed as a beginning, a realistic beginning for a larger program. In speaking to the nation over All-India Radio at the time the first plan was published (1951), Nehru said:

"Our economy and social structure have outlived their day, and it has become a matter of urgent necessity for us to refashion them so that they may promote the happiness of all our people in things material and spiritual. We have to aim deliberately at a social philosophy which seeks a fundamental transformation of this structure, at a society which is not dominated by the urge for private profit and by individual greed and in which there is a fair distribution of political and economic power. We must aim at a classless society, based on coöperative effort, with opportunities for all. To realize this we have to pursue peaceful methods in a democratic way.

"Democratic planning means the utilization of all our available resources and, in particular, the maximum quantity of labor willingly given and rightly directed so as to promote the good of the community and the individual."

A year later he said:

"Our ideals are high and our objectives great. Compared with them, the Five Year Plan appears to be a modest beginning. But let us remember that this is the first great effort of its kind and that it is based on the realities of today and not on our wishes. It must, therefore, be related to our present resources or else it will remain unreal. It is designed to be the foundation of a bigger and better plan of progress in the future. Let us lay the foundations well and the rest will inevitably follow."

In speaking to me of these matters Mr. Nehru said that the first Five Year Plan had met or sometimes surpassed its aims, harvests had been good, and the second plan was made, therefore, in an atmosphere approaching (his word) "complacency." If it was too ambitious, which has not yet been proved, this may be the reason. Three bad harvests in a row, which have been one of the chief misfortunes of the second plan, could not have been foreseen. Even these bad harvests and the diversion of currency they entailed may be overcome by the action which has already been taken by the United States (in chief) and the United Kingdom and Germany to supply the needed foreign exchange and/or capital goods. Already at this moment, in spite of the mountainous difficulties in the way, the success of the second Five Year Plan can be counted on with some confidence for the year 1960.

The potter's son, therefore, if he can pass his examinations, has a good chance of becoming a welder, leaving behind him the caste system, the village, the untold and untellable past of centuries without number.

With all respect and even reverence for Rajaji, it appears to me that his view of these matters, although closely molded upon various of Gandhi's views in the 1920's and 1930's, no longer applies to the existing situation. Forces which Rajaji dismisses as chimerical are in fact *already* operating upon the body of India. Results which he thinks unimportant or unobtainable have *already* been obtained. It is not lightly that any nation or society can embark upon a transformation of its structure, but once this has begun there is no turning back. With all my own reverence and affection for Rajaji, I cannot refrain from quoting the words Gandhi used to the Congress Working Committee in session at Wardha, near his village, in 1943:

"Somebody has suggested that Jawaharlal and I are estranged. It will require much more than differences of opinion to estrange us. We have had differences from the moment we became co-workers, and yet I have said for some years and say now that not Rajaji but Jawaharlal will be my successor. He says that he does not understand my language, and that he speaks a language foreign to me. This may or may not be true. But language is no bar to a union of hearts. And I know this, that when I am gone he will speak my language."

Gandhiji was specifically referring, at that time, to differences of opinion between himself and Nehru about the position of India in the Second World War. Nehru was internationalist, anti-Fascist, fiercely devoted to liberty, anxious to do nothing which might cause the victory of forces he detested, Hitler's Germany and Japanese militarism. Gandhi held similar views and was certainly as pro-British as Nehru by temperament—strange how long it took the British to discover that both these enemies were their friends! They disagreed upon courses of action because Gandhi objected to India's being involved in war without its own consent.

Those who ask the questions about concrete results of the Five Year Plan, who are free to condemn without regard to truth or justice, are not so much its enemies, but rather the placid and thoughtful citizens who often look at every innovation and say, "I wonder." The most famous American development plan, that of the Tennessee Valley Authority—which was the model for the Damodar Valley Corporation in India—had the same experience for a good few years. But I should never say that those who wonder and speculate are more numerous than those who whole-heartedly go along with these schemes. Above all, those who are involved in the development plans, and I have already said how youthful they are for the most part, are a source of faith and hope.

6

Nehru has presided over the Planning Commission since it was appointed in 1950. It was in his nature for years past to look toward this kind of comprehensive scheme as the only solution for a country which had fallen so far behind the other great units of mankind. As soon as it was possible to do so after independence was achieved—and in spite of the horrible turmoil produced by partition, with a form of civil war, vast population movements, a refugee problem without precedent—he set up a committee to study how to make the plan. It was, as he told me, partly for these experts to show the way, and partly to give earnest of his intention to proceed to planning as soon as possible. The Planning Commission came into being in 1950 and the first Five Year Plan was published for public discussion and study in 1951. Its target date was April 1, 1956, but before that had been reached the second Plan, a far more comprehensive scheme, had been drafted and issued to the public (spring, 1955). It is this, the second plan, which goes wider and deeper into the matter, that critics have said was "too ambitious." We shall not see the result until 1960, but on the present showing it is most likely that the plan will be successfully completed and that the foreign currency, which has been one of its aching needs, will be found in time and in sufficient quantity. Before 1960, of course, a third plan will come into being, and unless some untoward misfortune discourages the planners, it may be expected to be even more thorough and more "ambitious" than the second. And as with the first two plans, the third will also be issued well in advance so that all opinions may express themselves freely on its details. I have already said that the Indian press seems to me in some respects the freest in the world—or perhaps, to phrase it differently, that it avails itself of its freedom more completely than any other press I know. The constant barrage of criticism which is kept up in the press and in parliamentary debate does not spare the economic plans or planners, and this, too, is in accordance with Nehru's ruling ideas. He is determined to leave India better off than he found it, but he is equally determined that this shall be done by persuasion and consent, in the fullest exercise of those democratic rights and privileges which belong to the citizen of a free world. In declaring for a "socialistic pattern of society," as he did in 1955, he was careful to declare that this, too, must come about only by persuasion and consent, within the democratic structure. Thus all the methods of violence which inhere in dictatorship are renounced in advance; there will be no confiscatory or punitive measures; the "private sector," that part of the planning which belongs to private business and enterprise, is to be coördinated but not coerced; India will pull itself up by work and sacrifice, if it consents to do so, but never, never under the knout.

So far as this process has already gone it constitutes an original contribution to mankind's material problems and it has aroused the keen interest of almost all the newly independent countries of Asia and Africa. If India can indeed do what it has set out to do, and if successive development plans can raise the living standards of a very depressed mass, there is an object lesson for East and West alike. So far as Asia is concerned there seem to be only two valid methods of planned development, of catching up with material progress, and they are exemplified more and more by China and India, two vast question marks across the future of the world.

None of this is specifically in Gandhi's language but it is, I suggest, an extension or further development of his language. It is Nehru's language—which, as Gandhi perceived, was at heart his own. "He will speak my language after I am gone."

The welder is the son of the potter.

III *The Enchanted Valley*

NOTHING IN THE STORY of India since independence has been more vexatious and controversial than the "Kashmir question," as they call it in the United Nations. A lovely mountain valley, renowned for its beauty during centuries past, stands almost as a symbol of the dire results of partition, the heritage of violence and acrimony. Relations between the governments of India and Pakistan have been poisoned for a decade by their conflict over Kashmir, and it is largely because of Kashmir that both countries feel compelled to maintain defense establishments larger than economy or necessity could otherwise justify. More: on the international stage, in all those questions of foreign policy, war and peace, in which India has a distinctive point of view and a contribution to make, the effectiveness of its effort is blurred or blunted by the recurrence of a "Kashmir debate" in the general forum, or even—such is the irony of circumstance—by the mere mention of the word Kashmir. A very large element of public opinion throughout the world regards Kashmir as a contradiction to the broad, general lines of Indian policy. This may be unfair; I think it is; but nobody could deny that such is the case.

Not long ago Mrs. Vijayalakshmi Pandit, Nehru's beautiful and talented sister who has represented India in the United Nations and at three of the principal capitals, was speaking to an audience of military cadets in England, where she was High

Commissioner. She was expounding the principal tenets of Indian foreign policy, its aims and methods, with that emphasis on peaceful solutions which is the ruling consideration. At the end of her talk, when questions were welcomed, there came cries from various parts of the audience: "What about Kashmir?" I have no doubt she extricated herself from this difficulty with her customary skill, but the point is that it happens too often—in fact, all the time—and can be said to be the stumbling block for India's course in international affairs.

Similarly, the costliness of the Kashmir imbroglio, its effect on military expenditure and its way of squeezing the last rupee out of the Indian Treasury have had a depressing effect inside India itself and upon many of its citizens. The Five Year Plan, too, and many a cognate or correlative scheme of development, have felt the consequences. Many a man in India today feels weary at the mere thought of Kashmir: "I'm sorry that such a place even exists," one such said to me. It has cost too much, at home and abroad.

And yet—and yet . . .

The truth of the matter seems to be that the fate of the mountain valley involves India so deeply, not in a material sense but morally and psychologically, that there can be no further compromise in the matter. It goes to the root of things, the fundamental theory of the Indian state, its secularity, its essential state function. Similarly the two-nation theory upon which Pakistan is founded (that is, that religion makes the nation, and Pakistan is the "Islamic state" for the Mohammedans of India) is gravely imperiled if Kashmir remains Indian. Theory may seem at times to bear little relation to practice, and yet these theoretical principles are at the very bottom of the foundation of both India and Pakistan: take away the theory and there exists practically no reason for the existence of two separate nations. Partition is an economic absurdity. It was justified by its proponents as being socially necessary, and by the British, reluctantly, as a way of avoiding civil war, but nobody has ever pretended that it was in itself likely to yield a good result. It had to be, as they say—on this there is quite general agreement now—but to any observer it must appear one of the most regrettable necessities our century has provided.

For my own part, with perfect good will toward both Pakistan and India, I have never felt in the least degree happy about anything involved in the Kashmir discussion, either in the actual occurrences or in the arguments based upon them afterward. In spite of having visited India repeatedly during the past twelve years, usually for months at a time, I have never felt clear enough in my own view of the matter to deal with it in any form—or even to go up into that enchanted valley. Last year was the first in which, somewhat grimly, recognizing the fact that the question cuts across the whole fabric of Indian history today, involving every single aspect of the material for this book and all others in the field, I saw the necessity and did my best to cope with it. That is, I did visit the enchanted valley and learned what I could there in a limited time, but I also went back over its entire story since India became independent, and reread the debates, notes and documents as if for the first time. It is only now, after twelve years—in spite of long acquaintance with the debate as it took place meanwhile at the United Nations and between New Delhi and Karachi—that I begin to see with some coherence what the entire Kashmir story has meant to those involved in it. Although the passions stirred up during this period have been extreme, there are many now who regret them, many who would go far to avoid rekindling such destructive fires. And of course in my own country there are many more (the largest number, by far) who never have understood what was at stake in Kashmir all this time and why it has turned into the sort of subject on which reasonable discussion seems to have become impossible. If some of these might go along with me in an examination or survey of the story and its implications, pausing a moment here or there to see whatever we can, to observe, associate, recollect, perhaps somehow or other we can get to a comprehension of why Kashmir acquires, for India and Pakistan and for the world, its extraordinary significance. For there is not much doubt in anybody's mind that the mountain valley today—the entire state of Jammu and Kashmir, but particularly the little Vale of Kashmir—is somehow immensely significant. We may not succeed in setting forth the reasons. These things which everybody feels to be true are sometimes the most difficult to understand or explain. Not to try, just the same, would be evasion—an evasion of the principal political difficulty which has faced the new republics created out of old, undivided India. Try we must.

2

The visitor to Kashmir comes down out of the clouds into a country which bears no resemblance to any other he is likely to see in Asia. If it resembles anything in the general experience it would be (as has often been said) some part of Switzerland, but I do not find in my own memory any strong similarity. It is a lush and watery mountain valley filled with flowers, with an air which is perpetually conditioned by the snowy peaks of the high Himalaya around it. The moment you arrive—at the very first step out of the aircraft—a sense of difference assails you. Where, you say to yourself, where are we now? Kashmir indeed! A valley on the moon, rather. It seems far from both India and Pakistan and unrelated to either. The first impression is durable: the hours and the days confirm it.

This is, probably, the thing I had to go to Kashmir myself to find out. The political, historical, and above all the polemical information about Kashmir can be obtained anywhere. The United Nations has printed quantities of argument, the governments of India and Pakistan have printed more, and the government of Kashmir has spawned a literature of tourist delights. All this one can read as easily in the New York Public Library as in Delhi or Karachi. But the one thing I had never read anywhere was that Kashmir had its own extraordinary distinctness from all other places, that one never for a moment could feel one's self to be in either India or Pakistan, and that the inhabitants of the valley quite naturally took this for granted. "When are you going back to India?" they will ask you, or else: "Have you just come from India?" They all speak of India as if it were France or Germany, and of Pakistan as if it were Timbuctoo. Within a single day in Srinagar, the dreamy capital of the little state, I came to understand more of the peculiarity of the Kashmir situation than would have been possible—than had been possible—by the study of a decade's debate.

Let us get this quite clear: it is not a political matter but a matter of instant, undeniable impression afterward confirmed. I know as well as the next one how idiotic is the notion of an "independent Kashmir," since the lovely valley cannot even keep alive without its neighbors across the mountain passes. What I mean is that the sense of Kashmir's distinct personality is immediate and lasting, that it is borne out by everything its own people say, that it is constantly confirmed by the snowy ring of mountains rising on all sides above its green beauty, and that, regardless of politics, you find yourself saying when you depart that you are "going back to India."

This separateness accounts for much in the history of these ten years in Kashmir, as well as for centuries past. The country —by which I mean the valley itself, not the whole state of Jammu and Kashmir—has never really been part of any larger unit and it is not part of India today. It enjoys a special status which corresponds to the special consciousness of its people. They have their own flag and government; their constitution is not that of India; they have "safeguards" for their land, religion and local customs; their prime minister is the only one in India who bears that title outside of the Prime Minister of the Indian Republic. (The other Indian states have premiers too, but their title is "chief minister.") One may not know these facts or their meaning during the first hour or so in Kashmir, but any traveler of average perception will know very early that they are a natural inference from the separate being which he can feel about him.

There are reasons almost without number for the separatism, if we may call it that, of the Kashmir valley. It is walled in by high mountains and has a climate utterly unlike that of historic India; its people are of a different racial mixture; it has had very long periods of independence both in the Hindu eras and after the Mohammedan conquest. It is only in modern times (1846) that the state of Jammu and Kashmir came into being when the British took over the valley and gave it, in consideration of some $1,500,000, to the Dogra chieftain called Gulab Singh. His domains, acquired by one means or another, included the populous state of Jammu (in the upper Punjab), which is unmistakably Indian whatever its religious mixtures, and outlying territories to east and west, including the mountains of Ladakh on the Tibetan side, predominantly Buddhist, and some Mohammedan tribal fastnesses (such as Gilgit) up toward Afghanistan. It is, or was, a composite state, held together for a century by nothing more substantial than the Dogra dynasty founded by Gulab Singh. They were rapacious sovereigns, governing without regard for the welfare of their scattered subjects, and the British paid little heed to them; the sprawling, mountainous kingdom subsisted by the apathy of its inhabitants and the cruelty of its rulers. Any great storm was likely to shake it apart again, as has happened now.

For the composite state is effectively broken up today, and there seems little practical probability of sticking it together again even if it were desirable to do so. A reunion of all the Jammu-Kashmir territories under one political regime would seem, to a foreigner, the last thing to be expected. It could occur only if larger and equally unlikely events took place first—such as, for example, a reunion of Pakistan and India. And any child in that part of the world can tell us how remote this is.

So, as a matter of fact, most people nowadays, when they say Kashmir, mean simply this beautiful mountain valley, the heart of the old Kashmir-Jammu state. Jammu itself, south of the high mountains, cannot be distinguished from the Punjab plain of which it is a part; the northwestern sheikdoms and feudatories, as well as the western end of Kashmir, are controlled by Pakistan; the northeastern mountains of Ladakh continue to be ruled chiefly by their monasteries, like the neighboring lands of Tibet, with a nominal control from Srinagar; and the word Kashmir has returned to its original historic application. It is the name of the lovely, fertile valley, only 120 miles long and less than 80 miles wide at its widest, around which the patchwork state of the Dogra chieftains was assembled. And although nobody concerned in the argumentation of the past decade would care to limit the question so drastically, it is really only the valley itself that has aroused so much passion. Jammu would have been Indian in any case, and the far-off

Himalayan regions (Ladakh, Gilgit, etc.) stir no pulses; but the Vale of Kashmir exercises an influence amounting almost to magic over those who, from within or without, have been concerned with its destinies.

This has something to do with its beauty and its romantic history, of course; the very name has carried a sort of poetry to Indian ears—and even to Western ears—for many generations. Jawaharlal Nehru's attachment to the valley has often seemed to be heavily conditioned by its beauty, and he has written of it almost rapturously at times in the past. To this must be added the strategic consideration: the valley is in the center of a momentous frontier, of interest to Pakistan, Russia, China and Tibet, as well as India. It is the source of one great river (the Jhelum) and the gathering place of two others which are vital to the whole Punjab. Economically it has no particular value—indeed, under present conditions it takes more than it gives—but the future may assign it more weight in that respect than it possesses at present.

Still, adding all these material, military and other considerations together, we do not get anything like enough motive power for the stubborn struggle which took place over the valley twelve years ago and has aroused acrimonious debate ever since. To find that motive power we have to go deeper. Pakistan and India feel—from opposing points of view—that the valley involves their existence, but in neither case can this conviction be traced to territorial ambition. Both countries already have more territory than they need and greater populations than they can feed. Kashmir offers nothing in a material sense to either of them and has already been costly to both. They cling with the utmost tenacity to their opposing points of view from motives which we may call ideological, philosophical, theoretical or moral, because it is in the tangle of such forces that the partition of India became necessary and Kashmir is the crux of partition.

3

And why was partition itself necessary?

If two religions make two nations, then larger numbers of creeds would make larger numbers of nations, and most of our Western states would be divided up into smaller units. That is the instinctive response of a Western mind, but it does not take into account the nature of Indian religions and their historic power. Religions are not only religions in India, as the late Mohammed Ali Jinnah used to say: they are also society, they are a way of life. The caste system rules Hindu life, law and economics. "The Hindu worships the cow and I eat the cow," Jinnah used to say. "What do we have in common?" The fierce monotheism of Islam and its detestation of idolatry made it, from the earliest Mohammedan conquests, a religion of forced conversions: great Hindu populations in centuries past were Islamized by the sword. The Persian conquerors were themselves somewhat Hinduized by the passage of time, and the religious conflict subsided, but nobody could say that it ever disappeared. The coming of the British made little difference except that there was now a third force, an arbiter whose impartiality was sometimes swayed this way or that by the primary consideration of British rule, which was to remain in power, collect taxes and maintain an army.

As this century beheld the great awakening of Indian nationalism under Gandhi's leadership there were tendencies toward collaboration between Hindu, Muslim, Sikh and Christian, although these last two communities have never been numerically comparable to the others. Gandhi himself, universalist in most of his thought (as is Hinduism itself in its higher reaches), did everything in his power to encourage the tendency toward partnership of the communities. He worked hard for the Muslims and at some periods, such as that during which the Islamic caliphate was a rallying cry (around 1920), his popularity among them was far greater than that of their own leaders. The British, by dismembering the Ottoman Empire and abolishing the caliphate, had thrown this great opportunity to the forces of Indian union, and Gandhi's genius made the most of it. Great numbers of Muslims joined the Indian National Congress at that period and many became trusted leaders in the movement. Gandhi was ever mindful of their claims and thrust them to the fore, hopeful of union and peace for many decades, until the woeful necessity of partition had been accepted by all the other leaders in the country and he could struggle no more.

It is a relatively recent demand and grew into a political reality only during the 1930's. Mohammed Ali Jinnah, a great leader of the Muslims in the Indian National Congress, withdrew from it and founded the Muslim League, taking with him a number of Congress notables who were to become prime ministers of Pakistan or members of its government after partition. The word Pakistan, made up of initials for Punjab, Afghanistan, Kashmir, seems to have originated at Oxford in 1936, among some Mohammedan undergraduates, and originally referred to the idea of a state for the Muslim northwest. It was rapidly expanded to refer to the notion of a separate state for all the Muslims of India, taking in not only the regions which are now Pakistan (east and west) but a band across the north of India, including Kashmir.

As the British made it more and more clear that they were determined upon giving India constitutional government and eventually independence, these separatist forces gained strength rapidly under Jinnah's leadership. The concepts of "Pakistan" and "Hindustan" were introduced into the talk of every Muslim village. A sentiment for the division of India into two parts was not hard to arouse among the Muslims. The difficulty came in saying what this division was to be and where its lines might run. Up to 1947-1948 the two communities were almost inextricably mixed throughout the north and in many regions of the south. There were Muslim majorities in some provinces or districts and Hindu majorities in others, but large, healthy minorities existed alongside them in almost every case. In the experiments at constitutional government which characterized the 1930's the Indian National Congress tried consistently to placate Jinnah and meet his demands, only to run into his stubborn insistence that he and his Muslim League must be recognized as the only representatives of the Mohammedans of India. What this did to all schemes of electoral districts and representatives may be seen at once: it was already a form of partition within undivided India. Jinnah's stand, which is comprehensible if one accepts his premises, was that only his party and his candidates could represent the Muslims, and any Muslims put forward by the Congress were in fact representatives of the Hindus. As the negotiations went on from year to year his claims increased, and at the end of the period (1946) when an actual chance at the union and independence of all India was immediate, he had settled upon equal representation for Muslims and Hindus in government as being his minimum terms. This principle, coupled with his insistence that the Muslims adhering to the National Congress could not be counted as Muslims, made nonsense of any democratic system of elections.

We do not need to go into the story of the successive negotiations between the British, the Congress and the Muslim League. Gandhi, Nehru and Rajaji all struggled hard to save the principle of Indian unity, but it seems obvious in retrospect that Jinnah on the other side had already made up his mind to create a separate Islamic state, even before this became his declared intention. As we have said above, his concepts of electorate and representation amounted to partition anyhow, except that it would be carried out all over India without territorial definition. It was, so to speak, a kind of horizontal partition, which was soon to be made vertical by means of artificial frontiers based on "predominant" majorities, without regard to the niceties of geography and economics. Thus, in the end, the Punjab and Bengal were cut in two, and the new state of Pakistan was created in two halves separated by a thousand miles of India.

Without dwelling on the exhausting negotiations which led to this result we may see that for the British and even for the Indian National Congress it was a matter of making the best of things. The British were determined to get out; having been so urgently invited to go for so many decades, they were not inclined to stay upon the order of their going. The last Viceroy, Earl Mountbatten of Burma, played a vital part in this final phase in accordance with his instructions from the Labor Government in London; his patience, tact, skill and forbearance will long be remembered in India. Both in the tragedy of partition and in the extremely delicate matter of pacifying the princely states, his personal contribution was immense. By an irony of history, the British, who have so often been accused of being pro-Muslim in the past century and a half, ended their Indian experience with a ruler who, impartial though he was, enjoyed the confidence of the Hindu leaders and incurred the dislike of the Muslim dictator.

The British and the Congress made the best of an impossible situation, or tried to do so; but the Muslim League was not altogether happy over the outcome either. Jinnah had considered some link between the eastern and western halves of Pakistan essential, and had thought to achieve it partly by means of Kashmir. Every detail of the division of Indian government property, archives, the rolling stock of the railways, etc., etc., became at once an excuse for bitter disputes. The frontiers, especially in the Punjab, were impractical and were almost immediately subject to revision by local commanders. The government at Delhi was already in being—Jinnah's refusal to join it had given Nehru an interim government which he could continue on into independence—but that at Karachi had to be improvised from scratch. I shall never forget that when I first visited the new establishment (Karachi, 1947) there was only one typewriter in the whole Foreign Office. Jinnah moved into the governor's palace and kept up a pomp and ceremony suitable to a viceroy, but there was no rule book for relations with foreign embassies, for instance, and no staff for most of the ministries. Partition and independence, when they came after so many years of turmoil, seem very nearly to have been a surprise.

But there was worse, far worse: civil disorder on a vast scale. It had started the year before and was worst in Bengal, worst of all in Calcutta; it spread; the Punjab was in flames by 1947; it produced horrors in Bihar and Assam. Hindus were assailing Muslims, and Muslims assailed Hindus; the Sikhs were on the warpath in their own Punjab regions. There is not much point in attempting to say who was responsible, who started the carnage, or who might have prevented it by doing thus-or-so in time. By actual date, the Muslim onslaught on the Hindus of Calcutta (August 16, 1946) came first, and may well have been in response to Jinnah's call to arms a fortnight before. "This day we bid good-bye to constitutional methods," said Jinnah in Bombay on July 29th; there can be little doubt of what he meant. Yet in the nature of this kind of strife there could be no circumscribing its limits or its responsibilities; if the Muslims massacred the Hindus in one place, being stronger in numbers or arms, the Hindus massacred the Muslims in another for the same noble reasons. This went on through the autumn of 1946 and all of 1947, and during the entire first part of the outrages Jinnah spoke in public only to threaten more. "Pakistan is the only solution," he said, over and over again, and "India stands on the brink of ruinous civil war."

By the spring of 1947 the Viceroy, plagued by the imminence of his assigned date of June 15th for the independence of India, was forced by the situation to consider partition: it was accepted by the last of all, Mahatma Gandhi, on June 4th after all his friends had already yielded. The date of independence with partition was pushed off to August 15th and took place on that day in the midst of panic and bloodshed beyond comparison in modern times.

It is said that upward of ten million persons were on the roads in that terrible autumn, moving from India to Pakistan or from Pakistan to India. A refugee problem of great magnitude was immediately presented to both the new governments. Along with this there was murder, arson, rape and abduction on a scale never known before. Nehru recalls that they kept a regular war map in his office with pins to show the centers of gravest disturbance, and the slender resources of the police power had to be shifted hither and thither to meet it. Delhi itself was the scene of cruel violence against Muslims just at a time when the madness was dying out elsewhere. The whole nightmare has left a gruesome imprint upon the minds that survived it, and has, even to this day, overshadowed the relationship between India and Pakistan with fratricidal suspicion.

Against this appalling situation at the height of its horror there came the invasion of Kashmir, followed by its accession to India and occupation by troops of the Indian Army.

Those events are differently viewed in accordance with one's point of view, but at least the time sequence is perfectly plain.

They came in the order I have stipulated: first the Vale of Kashmir was invaded from the northwest by Pathan tribesmen from Pakistan, then the terrified Maharajah signified his accession to India, and finally (October 27th) the Indian Army sent its first troops into Kashmir by air.

By early September of that year (1947) the Pathan tribesmen had been converging on the borders of the Jammu-Kashmir state and the western part of Jammu (the Poonch area) was soon in their hands. In mid-October they began the infiltration of Kashmir proper, armed with modern equipment which could only have come from the Pakistan Army. Their very transport from the Northwest Frontier to Kashmir was arranged for them, either by local Pakistan authorities or in some cases by the local Muslim League organizations. With gasoline scarce and severely rationed, with communications all disrupted by the shock of partition, they could not have moved at all otherwise. The invasion of the Vale of Kashmir, down the highway from Muzaffarabad to Baramula and Srinagar, was in full tilt after October 20th and could indeed have proceeded with great speed if the tribesmen had not halted at every opportunity to loot, burn, rape and kill. The Maharajah's accession to India (October 24th, made final on the 26th) and the dispatch of the first Indian troops (October 27th) were not only next in order, but were the direct, inevitable consequences of this invasion. So far as the dates and facts are concerned there can be no dispute.

A word about accession may not come amiss, at least for Western readers with short memories. The word refers to the alternatives presented to semi-independent Indian princes at the moment of India's independence, accompanied by partition. The princes could accede to either India or Pakistan, as they wished, with due regard for common-sense considerations such as geography; or they could, if they wished, remain apart from either of the new states and make their own terms with them. Mountbatten made it very plain to them that whatever they did, they could expect no assistance from the British—the "paramount power"—because at the moment of India's independence, Britain's "paramountcy" would lapse.

There were no less than 262 of these semi-independent principalities in India, from small self-governing estates to great territories like Hyderabad, Mysore and Kashmir, larger than all but a few European nations. The British had cajoled, nursed and threatened these princes by turns, keeping them quiet by wealth and honor as much as by fear, but never extending to their territories the administrative structure of British India. For decades many persons of eminence had predicted that any effort toward Indian independence would be thwarted by these princes, who would, in defense of their thrones, lay all India waste by fire and sword. In point of fact, almost all of them rapidly acceded to either India or Pakistan, depending on geography, and the few cases which presented difficulties did not long hold out. There was conflict when, as in Hyderabad and Kashmir, the ruler was of one community and the majority of his subjects of another. By and large, however, the problem of the princely states, once thought to be an insuperable obstacle to Indian nationalism, was resolved with skill and success. The rulers were indemnified or pensioned and their powers passed to the new nations they had joined.

Kashmir was quite a different story because its ruler, a Hindu of the Dogra dynasty, could not make up his mind. There is the strongest probability that he, like so many Kashmiri before and since—if we may call him a Kashmiri—thought the mountain state might remain independent. He and his family had enjoyed its revenues without let or hindrance for a hundred years and regarded it as their personal property—a theory of the princely function which was widely accepted in other states as well. The Maharajah of Kashmir was not unique in considering that his state revenues need not be spent on schools or roads or telephone wires, if it suited him better to use them for jewels or palaces; this was the attitude of many or even most princes, and the British had interfered with it very little. Honorable exceptions there were, naturally: the ancient house of Mysore had been in the vanguard of progress for three generations at least, and Travancore was not far behind. In an earlier generation Baroda had given a good example; so had Bhopal. But among the great states it can be said with assurance that Kashmir was the worst, doing least for its poverty-stricken people and most for its irresponsible tyrants.

The Maharajah, Hari Singh by name, could have joined either Pakistan or India on the day of independence, August 15th, or at any time before then, without bringing on his hapless country the miseries which were to ensue. All he had to do was to signify his will. Mountbatten visited Srinagar in June, 1947, and advised the Maharajah to join one or the other of the new countries (Dominions, as they were then called) by mid-August. The Viceroy bore with him the assurance of the government of India, the interim government headed by Mr. Nehru, that it would not regard it as an unfriendly act if Kashmir joined Pakistan. The one thing the government of India did not view with favor was any attempt to set up an independent Kashmir; weak, misgoverned and adrift, such a state would have been an invitation to trouble from all sides.

Mountbatten recalled all this in June a year later on his return to England. "Ascertain the will of your people," he had told the prince, which was probably enough in itself to frighten that dignitary out of his wits, "and join whichever Dominion your people wish you to join by August 14th of this year." Later, in a speech to the East India Association, Mountbatten said:

"Had he acceded to Pakistan before August 14th, the future Government of India had allowed me to give His Highness an assurance that no objection whatever would be raised by them. Had His Highness acceded to India by August 14th, Pakistan did not then exist and therefore could not have interfered. The only trouble that could have been raised was by nonaccession to either side, and this was unfortunately the very course followed by the Maharajah."

From August 15th to the end of October, therefore, Kashmir was in an anomalous and doubtful position, and every day's delay made it worse. The main routes of egress from and ingress to the mountain kingdom were the waterways flowing into Pakistan, and cheap commodities had no other. Air traffic from Delhi, five hundred miles to the south, was and still is the main link with India, although the road over the mountain passes can serve in summer. The Maharajah negotiated a Standstill Agreement with Pakistan, at the moment of independence, whereby the supplies for his landlocked valley were guaranteed, but he soon found himself without them. It is difficult not to suppose that Pakistan blockaded the valley as a means of political pressure, although it is also true that all communications were in a very bad way at the moment of partition and soon afterward. Both in India and in Pakistan the anxiety over Kashmir and its destiny was rising, and one is tempted to say now, in retrospect, that it might have been better if one or the other of them had taken some decisive step during those first six weeks to bring the state into line without bloodshed. Perhaps it could have been done; I do not know.

At all events the six weeks between August 15th and October 1st passed in turmoil; massacres, looting and destruction were having their way in many parts of both the new nations; in Jammu, the Punjabi part of the mountain state (that is, south of the mountain passes) the Hindus and Sikhs drove out Muslims in enormous numbers with numerous outrages. The Muslims fleeing to Pakistan told their dreadful stories and excited the rage of their co-religionists to new heights. It was downright inevitable, I suppose, that in a population like that of Pakistan, with the whole Northwest Frontier Province tribal and warlike in custom, violence should be the result. It was not, however, inevitable that this violence should be countenanced, patronized and supported by the civil and military authorities of the new nation.

It is a vexed question. Many in India believe that the Pakistan government called the tribesmen to arms, equipped them, transported them and commanded them in the invasion of Kashmir which followed. This has been denied; indeed for one whole year, until the evidence of Pakistan Army participation was overwhelming, the Pakistan government pretended that it had nothing to do with that invasion. It is now well known that the commander and some officers of the invading tribes were regular army officers of Pakistan, and of course from the very beginning the equipment used was that of the regular army.

However, I have always thought that one element in the situation was fear of the tribesmen on the part of those who governed in Karachi and Lahore. War with India was impossible; the high command of the Pakistan forces was all British, and informed Mr. Jinnah that they would resign to a man if he made war on India. Short of war, the new government, harassed and bitterly angry over many things, could injure India and save itself only by deflecting the ire of the Northwest against Kashmir. For anybody who has ever been on the Northwest Frontier knows that the tribesmen have contempt for all city dwellers, including those of Lahore and Karachi, and when their ire is up they think of nothing but murder and loot. Even in the most peaceful times they live in blood feuds; looting is a pastime; the gates of Peshawar are closed and manned at sundown. It was a tangle of motives, no doubt, which led to the invasion of Kashmir, but among these I have no doubt that Karachi's fear of the aroused Pathans, consciously or unconsciously, played its part. Only a few months later (March, 1948) I was to hear in tribal villages of the Northwest words like this: "When we get through with Kashmir we'll take Lahore and Karachi." Half in joke, perhaps, but containing a truth.

The horrors which accompanied the tribal invasion have often been described. They contain elements unknown in the West—such as wholesale abductions—as well as rape and looting on a vast scale. It is worth mentioning that there was no strictly communal basis for the depredations of the tribesmen: they murdered and looted their own co-religionists in many places as well as the Hindus and Sikhs. In Baramula they slaughtered the Christian missionaries. It was their long halt in Baramula—a town of much loot—that gave the Maharajah time to send his terrified telegrams to India and obtain help.

These are sorrowful things, best forgotten, but they have to take their place in the chronicle. Mr. Nehru probably had the most difficult decision of his life up to that time when he was faced with the Maharajah's telegrams. There were multiple strands of historic consciousness in his decision, as we have seen, and yet I do not doubt that in the crucial moment a very great part was played by his own love for the magical valley, its beauty and its appeal to the poetic imagination. He could not bear to sit by idly and watch it be destroyed by fire and sword. After consulting the military chiefs and the Viceroy (now called Governor-General) he ordered the flight of an airborne battalion of the Sikh regiment to Srinagar.

There were only 330 men in that detachment which, as we can now see, saved Srinagar from destruction. The tribesmen on that day were not far away: their advance parties were five miles from the capital. The whole invasion from Pakistan was far better armed, organized and equipped than the Indian government had believed at the time of the fateful decision. It became necessary to fly men and arms to Kashmir from Delhi in a steady stream for the next three weeks until the tide of assault could be turned and a great part of the valley cleared of the marauders. There ensued a desultory warfare for about a year and a month (dying down for long stretches) until, at the request of the United Nations, both India and Pakistan proclaimed a cease-fire with effect from January 1st, 1949. The lines upon which that cease-fire took effect have remained substantially unchanged in the decade since then: Pakistan has the Poonch area and the northwest, about a third of the Kashmir-Jammu state, and India retains the other two-thirds and most of the valley, along with the Tibetan-Buddhist country of Ladakh.

We have telescoped, abbreviated, foreshortened. Yet it must be plain that great suffering accompanied and followed these events. Along with that suffering in both mind and body there was an international debate which at times dominated the proceedings in the United Nations. It was India who appealed to the international tribunal (December 30, 1947) on the ground that international peace and security were endangered by a continuance of this situation. The appeal was made under articles 34 and 35 of the Charter, that is, under "Pacific Settlement of Disputes," Chapter Six, rather than under Chapter Seven on "Acts of Aggression." For this reason the United Nations for ten years has persisted in regarding the Kashmir problem as a situation in dispute: it has never put it into the frame, or under the light, of an act of aggression.

This may be due to a technical error on the part of the Indian Ministry of External Affairs. I think it is. They ought to have claimed aggression at the very start, if that was to be the basis of their complaint for all these years. My dear and respected friend Sir Girija Bajpai, now dead, was then directing the Ministry under Mr. Nehru, and if there has been a technical error it must have been his doing, aided by his advisers in the service. I can testify that Mr. Nehru twelve years ago, when I first saw him, was downright astounded that the United Nations never expressed a word of reproof for the aggression against Kashmir, and in all the years since then he has not changed. To his mind it is quite monstrous that the invader should have been treated as equal to the defender juridically and morally, giving Pakistan and India the status of equal claimants to a piece of real estate. In Nehru's mind, as in the minds of most Indians, this is a gross misconception of what happened and what is at stake. They do not give sufficient weight to the fact that their own original appeal to the United Nations presented a situation in dispute, and not an aggression. That may be a technicality but, after all, the United Nations is a deliberative body composed mainly of professional diplomatists who are trained to technicalities and who find safety only in obeying their own rules.

In the terrible turmoil over Kashmir (as well as within it) during 1947-1949, many suspicions came to the surface in India. It was thought, and not by the uninformed either, that the destiny of Kashmir had become enmeshed in considerations of power politics—that is, of the balance of power between the Anglo-American-French nexus and the empire of the Soviet Union. It was suspected that "oil"—what a word, oil!—was involved in it somehow: American experts were said to have found secret wealth in those mountains, and therefore wanted the mountain state to go to Pakistan, as being more amenable than India. (Not a word of truth in any of it, so far as I could find out then or since). The mere word "oil" was enough to start off a whole cargo of suppositions. In addition to this, the British Foreign Office, aided by the remains of the India Office and the Commonwealth Office and God knows how many others, was supposed to be pro-Pakistan and anti-Indian in this matter. Mr. Philip Noel-Baker, a conscientious Quaker and Socialist, was assumed to be the tool of these interests or their spokesman at the United Nations. Even Sir Girija Bajpai, a thoroughly civilized human being, was not altogether devoid of such suspicions when I returned from India in the spring of 1948 and found the Kashmir debate in flood.

It is worth recording that it was the representative of Nationalist China (that is, of Chiang Kai-shek on Formosa) who actually came forward, over and over again, and amended the Kashmir Resolution from its original form into one which, by acknowledging the freedom and sovereignty of India as well as of its command over its own armed forces, became acceptable to Mr. Nehru. Dr. T. S. Tsiang, the Chinese representative on the Security Council—an old Waichaopu man from Peking, really—did a loyal service to Asia and the world on that occasion. If he had not obtained these amendments it is doubtful if Mr. Nehru would have remained as Prime Minister of India: he had already said he would resign if the resolution passed in its original form. Mr. Noel-Baker said, several times, that he did not understand the sense of these amendments but that if the Chinese delegate regarded them as essential he would accept them. The Americans at this stage of the debate (1948) merely tagged along, so to speak; they did whatever the British did.

Now, of course, I was very close to this debate and I never did see why everybody was so suspicious of everybody else. Between India and Pakistan the issue was as plain as the nose on your face: they both wanted the same thing for different reasons. But the Russians at that time had no position; it was the period when they maintained that Gandhi was an "unconscious reactionary" and Nehru a "running dog of imperialism." They had no clear position at all about Pakistan. The Americans had no defined position either, so far as India and Pakistan were concerned. Over Kashmir, as a matter of fact, bewilderment seemed to be the predominant feeling in the Security Council so far as I could tell, and I went to the debate every day. It was out at Lake Success in those days—a wearisome trek, I must say—and I never will forget my astonishment in the middle of the process when one day a delegate, in whose motorcar I was a guest, pointed out to me a dim body of water under the spring rain and said that this pond was the actual lake named "Success." I never have seen anything which less resembled its cognomen.

In spite of this bewilderment there were plenty of men in India and in Pakistan, too, who saw "power politics" in the behavior of the Security Council. Pakistan was hugely encouraged, diplomatically and polemically, by what seemed to be a British inclination toward their view of the matter. Sir Mohammad Zafrullah Khan, the first Foreign Minister of Pakistan—and, as I remember, he was out of the country almost constantly for his first year in office—had a field day at Lake Success when it was discovered that under the Indian appeal (a situation in dispute, remember, and not an aggression!) he could bring in almost anything he chose to mention. By the time I returned from India that year I found that he had piled up a mountain of evidence, or at least of accusations, which had little or nothing to do with Kashmir, including one of genocide, that is to say, of wholesale racial murder, against India. He was referring, of course, to the dreadful events of the preceding months in both countries, but the word "genocide," with its associations from the Hitler mania, was either totally inapplicable or was applicable equally to both sides.

In this awful state of affairs, while hostilities were still going on in Kashmir between the Indian Army and what was soon to be acknowledged as the Pakistan Army, everybody seemed to suspect everybody else of skulduggery. Men I had known well for a number of years (Sir Girija Bajpai, Mr. Noel-Baker and others) were subject to this species of influenza. I must say I found Dr. T. S. Tsiang the halest and heartiest delegate with whom I had any conversation, and I shall always think his work during those spring months averted an even more disastrous result than what in fact ensued.

But the curious and interesting thing about all this is that the atmosphere of suspicion which was abroad in the world had some effect also on Mr. Nehru at this time. He, too, felt that the Kashmir debate at Lake Success was bogged down into a side issue or concomitant of larger maneuvers. It infuriated him (and still does) that nobody paid any attention to the fact that there had been an armed aggression. He believed that the Americans were following the British, more or less blindly, and that the British had been informed or prejudiced (as you may choose to express it) by certain pro-Pakistan officials. When I saw him again in that next December (1948) he was really quite sharp in some of his phrasing. It was a moment when the West—as we call it: anyhow the grouping of powers which the Franco-Anglo-American trinity hopes to inspire—was making one mistake after another, bolstering up defunct colonialisms and imperialisms in every corner of Asia. I could not find it in my heart to demur at anything he said about Indonesia, in particular, or Southeast Asia, in general. We were not being very intelligent about anything at that moment; and of course one can scarcely bring one's self to speak of our doings in China. But it also dawned on me, in the midst of this rather acrid conversation or monologue (it was at lunch), that the Prime Minister had something else underneath all this: it was Kashmir.

It nearly always is Kashmir.

Now, over eleven years later, many of these misunderstandings and resentments have vanished. It is perfectly obvious to everybody in the world who has given it a moment's thought that the United States was instrumental in setting Indonesia free. It is clear that the American position throughout the former colonial imperial world has been, up to the very brink of rupture with old friends, favorable to freedom. Our links with Great Britain and our historic debts to France, as well as our sincere attachment to both of those nations, inhibited us strongly for some years after the end of the Second World War, but not permanently or fundamentally. Our task in foreign policy has been to maintain our friendships, tried and true (the main ones, anyhow), while endeavoring to aid in the transition from colonialism to autonomy for the peoples of Asia. The Americans are anticolonial and anti-imperial by nature; it is not only our tradition—a thing we learn in school with the alphabet—but it is also our physical and material condition. To this crisscross there has been added in the past decade a sense of peril from the Communist world, which, of course, aims at conquest and always has, finding in us the principal obstacle to this objective. All this is plain in 1960, but it was not so plain in 1948. We were then suspected of conniving at schemes for the maintenance of colonial empires, which, indeed, in their final moments before liquidation, maintained themselves upon American arms and materials which had been supplied to their European centers under the Lend-Lease Act for the winning of the war against Hitler.

Nobody today knows this better than Mr. Nehru. But in

1948 it was not clear to anybody, not even to him. At that period he had never seen America, even from a train window, and could have had no idea of how utterly self-contained it is. He may have thought, I imagine, that we desired various emoluments and privileges along the lines of those which formed the historic development of England, entraining, as they did, the subjugation of other peoples. Mr. Nehru's mind was formed in England at least as much as in India, and for a great part of his life he has been accustomed to imperial concepts. I imagine that until he came to America he had no idea of how little it cared about or needed the rest of the world, how happy it would be to rest in its own busy, technological peace. A small island like England cannot really give an adequate idea of the United States, although it is obvious enough that the one engendered the other. Mr. Nehru in 1948 had not, I think, yet made these distinctions, and our foreign policy at the time was of no assistance to him in doing so.

It was, therefore, more or less fated that he should become, for a time, sharply critical of "the West." (As he says, this is a misnomer, too: when you say West and when you say East, it depends entirely on where you are standing.) We owe this largely to our own mistakes, but it is also due to the curious obtuseness and insensitivity of the Anglo-American-French attitudes and expressions about Kashmir. He thought he had a perfectly clear case and was confronted, to his utter amazement, with a coldly judicial impartiality between aggressor and victim. It was at this very time that the Dutch in their successive "police actions" were using American Lend-Lease materials against the Indonesians, as the French did against the Indo-Chinese. Vast quantities of the same American materials were being poured into the custody of Chiang Kai-shek, from which they rapidly passed into the hands of the advancing Communists. Kashmir became, or seemed to become, a part of a general imperialist-colonial pattern, which, although blatantly wrongheaded and untimely, contained the possibility of delaying emancipation for some years and was thereby resented in India as much as anywhere in Asia.

All this, of course, goes on the assumption that Pakistan was more amenable to Western influence than India: that Pakistan was favored by the Atlantic powers as a sort of willing protégé. The illusion persisted, and was not dispelled by the creation of the Baghdad Pact and the gift of war materials to Pakistan which followed. For my own part I never have felt that Pakistan was notably more friendly to the United States than to any other nation; I have felt that it was simply more cynical about the receipt of benefits from such an illusion. Perhaps, by now, this has come to be perceived even in Washington.

4

The point of view held with varying shades of meaning or intensity in Pakistan during this same past decade is relatively simple: it is that Kashmir, as a predominantly Mohammedan region, belongs to Pakistan by nature. The K in the fabricated word Pakistan stands for Kashmir; Kashmir was always a part of the new nation which Indian Muslims (some of them) wished to make in the 1930's. Nobody in the Muslim League, least of all Mohammed Ali Jinnah, ever supposed that it would go to India. In Jinnah's dream of a band or bridge across the top of India, connecting the western and eastern parts of his new country, Kashmir was the most vital link. One runs into this concept constantly even today, and it often goes beyond any mere thought of a "bridge." I have often heard, in private talk in Pakistan, that the Muslim state should properly contain a wide and deep slice of northern India, that its proper and natural capital is Delhi itself, and that in the fullness of time all this must come to pass. Like most concepts of "manifest destiny," as the American phrase had it fifty years ago, this ignores the great distance between the cup and the lip.

Still, there is no doubt of the sincerity of Pakistan's disappointment, resentment and subsequent bitterness over the fact that most of the Jammu-Kashmir state went to India. From the point of view of the makers of Pakistan, the ruling principle of partition was that of "predominant" majorities. There were great wrangles over what constituted "predominance," a word which, like a number of others harnessed to politics, was overworked in India. The percentages of Hindu, Muslim, Sikh and

Christian were the basis of calculation, but where no one community clearly predominated over all others combined, economics and geography had their say. The Jammu-Kashmir state was predominantly Mohammedan and the valley of Kashmir overwhelmingly so. To Jinnah and his immediate followers, as to most Pakistani today, it has always seemed beyond question that Kashmir belongs to Pakistan by right, by nature and by the principles of the partition.

If we were to accept the theory of the theocratic or religious state, strange and difficult as it might be to minds trained in democratic liberalism, it would follow that every Muslim in India was a citizen of Pakistan from birth, and every Hindu, Sikh or Christian a citizen of India. But such radical cleavages are not possible in a country where all the communities have lived for centuries in the same towns and villages, where all are of the same race and, area by area, speak the same main languages. Many millions of Mohammedans are attached to their native soil, in all parts of India, and have no desire to exile themselves to the strange Northwest or the teeming jungles of East Bengal. There are thought to be somewhere between forty-five and fifty million Muslims who are citizens of India today: it was over forty millions at the time of partition. What of these?

The government of India takes its stand very firmly on equality of the citizens, whatever their race, religion or language. In this view, cruelly tried as it was during the communal civil war that followed partition, there is no correspondence at all—no relation, no resemblance—to the view that a religion of itself makes a nation. That is what we are up against, nothing more nor less: a disagreement which arises from the terms of foundation of the two countries. It is next door to impossible, and it may even prove utterly impossible, to attain satisfactory working arrangements when the opposing views have no common theoretical root.

Nehru tried. After India and Pakistan had accepted the cease-fire line of January 1, 1949, which stabilized the lines as they stood on that day, he suggested to the Pakistan Prime Minister, the late Liaquat Ali Khan, that this form of *de facto* partition become permanent. It was a solution which would have pleased neither side, really, but might have worked as the larger partition of all India worked, for lack of anything better. It is difficult to find, in the realms of common sense, a more viable road from the dilemma. Mr. Liaquat, who was a highly intelligent and moderate man, might have been willing to come to terms on such a basis, but his own followers would have none of it, and although the cease-fire lines do, in practice today, constitute a sort of partition of Kashmir state, they are not regarded as permanent. They are subject to all kinds of petty violations and infringements, with the tensions and disquiet which ensue.

Pakistan holds about 5,000 square miles, including the Poonch area (called "Azad," or Free, Kashmir), Gilgit, Northern Ladakh and Baltistan. The rest, some two-thirds of the whole, is a part of the Indian Union but is administratively a good deal more autonomous than any other Indian state. The disputes among Kashmiri leaders have contributed, along with Pakistan's discontent, to keep the status of the country wrapped in clouds of doubt, so that after eleven years of so-called peace, at least of the cease-fire, it is still suspended in a climate of uncertainty. There might be trouble again any day (or so everybody there seems to think), and in such an atmosphere the recent events in Pakistan, placing that country under military dictatorship, have not had a calming influence. When I was there last spring all was beauty and order; there was not a single untoward incident that I saw with my own eyes or heard with my own ears; and yet I came away with an impression of edgy nerves and undefined anxieties. The enchanted valley is sensitive to an extreme; it has a neurosis.

5

The two great leaders of the Kashmiri people in this period have been the Sheikh Mohammad Abdullah and Bakshi Ghulam Muhammad, men of similar origins and diverse talents, who were once close friends and are now implacable enemies. It is "Bakshi Sahib" who rules Kashmir today, under the Indian connection, and "Sheikh Sahib" who is in jail, but it is perfectly possible that the whirligig of fortune might, as things go in Kashmir, reverse this situation and install the Sheikh Abdullah again someday as Prime Minister of the mountain state.

Abdullah was a romantic figure and still is. While there is the breath of life in him he will retain some special appeal to the Kashmiri people and to others outside the valley: he beguiles or stirs them, at will, by the extraordinarily attractive personage he presents to their eyes and ears. He is the "Lion of Kashmir," as they have been calling him for a long time. I confess that I do not find any notable intellectual content in such of his speeches as I have read, but his appeal is not to the intellect. He is such a bold, dashing figure, such a big, handsome man, with his Kashmiri cap (generally of unborn Persian lamb) askew over his liquid eyes, and with such natural gallantry of movement and gesture, that he really does not have to say anything original. His fire and fury take the place of intellect, and a certain instinctive bonhomie, a forthcoming and unsuspicious manifestation of nature, keeps the flamboyance from excess in most relationships. Abdullah seems never to have been afraid of anybody or anything (I say *seems*, because one can never be sure of what he feels). This very simple and obvious bravery has a special appeal in the fear-ridden valley, but it made its impression also in the committee chambers and hotel rooms of New York when he visited the United Nations over a decade ago. In short, the man is naturally endowed with such physique and personality that he might have been born to carry all before him, as indeed he did for quite a while. Up to 1953, anyhow, which means for five or six years after independence, his will was law in his own country and his charm prevailed outside it. No doubt this fortunate situation may have weakened his sense of measure, his estimates of forces and necessities: he probably came to believe that he could do anything he chose to do. His downfall would appear to have resulted precisely from that supreme self-confidence, that utter romanticism reckless of result, which in his heyday constituted much of his irresistible appeal.

Ghulam Muhammad, the "Bakshi Sahib," is another character altogether, and it has always seemed to me amazing that they should have worked together so closely for so many years. Bakshi Sahib is a realist, a practitioner, not a speechmaker: he can run a party machine and keep its joints oiled, he can administer, he can judge his situation and time his strokes. He seems to me—underneath a cordial affability of manner—to be constituted chiefly of iron or steel. Like Abdullah, although in lesser degree, he is also big and handsome. Both seem physically stronger than most men of the valley, more decisive, more obviously intended for action on the stage of the world. Bakshi Sahib has no visible quality of the dreamer, although obviously he must once have been some sort of dreamer for Kashmir or he could not have helped Abdullah lead the forbidden nationalist movement in the days before independence. What one sees in him today is a determination and down-to-earth practicality which may tack and veer but never lose sight of a goal. Abdullah seemed stronger than he was; Ghulam Muhammad is, I believe, even stronger than he seems, difficult though that may be.

It would be foolish to take this manifest strength of will and intention, this man-of-iron quality, for Bakshi Sahib's only gift. He knows his Kashmiri people through and through, and although I find no softness in him he is superbly capable of those demonstrations of kingly kindness which are traditional in that country. Once a week, on Saturdays, he is at home to all comers—like Evita Perón in Argentina, I reflected!—and at very nearly any hour of the day or night he can find time to receive petitions of a strictly personal nature. Those petitions, by the way, asking for jobs, salary rises, pardons for criminals, or almost any other boon, were once fairly common even in India and they have survived in Kashmir or even increased in the present period; I shall revert to them. Bakshi Sahib makes his present appeal to the villagers of the valley, and even in other parts of the state, through this systematic generosity, and the legend is widespread that he can and will redress all wrongs when his attention is called to them. His popularity is therefore, let us say, a structure rather than an emotion. It is no less real for that. When he found it necessary to rearrest the Sheikh Abdullah last spring, while I was there, not a finger was lifted in Srinagar and not a shop closed; my ears could not catch even a whimper of protest. The man does not have Abdullah's obvious advantages—the thrilling voice, the film-star presence, the wild and inflammatory gesture—but he has others of his own which are probably more durable. They have entrenched him, it seemed to me, without regard to those other circumstances, such as the support of Nehru's government and the presence of the Indian Army, which Abdullah also had in his day.

Bakshi Sahib has one further advantage over Abdullah which I hesitate to mention, since it involves a purely personal evaluation, but the whole affair is so personal that one takes the plunge more easily on this subject than on others: to wit, the advantage of intellect. I liked and admired the Sheikh Sahib for years but I never did think power or originality of mind were his primary characteristics. With Bakshi one feels the mind instantly—the mind behind the eyes, I was about to say; for the fact is that Bakshi's eyes are steady and penetrating to a remarkable degree, while Abdullah's were liquid and often dreamy. Bakshi has concentration and logic when he deals with a subject; the Sheikh Sahib was often digressive and contradictory. They are probably both well aware of all these personal differences, since they have known each other so long and well. I was with Bakshi Sahib in Srinagar on the night after Abdullah's last arrest, and he asked me point-blank, early in the conversation, what I thought of the Sheikh.

"A romantic," I said.

"I am the realist," said Bakshi instantly, taking the words out of my mouth. "Who do you think was running the party and the state while Abdullah was working his charms in Delhi and London and New York? Who do you think did the work all these years?"

In such expressions Bakshi shows not only his estimate of his rival's character and his own, but also, I think, some element of the jealousy which must naturally arise between the components of such a team. The realist and the romantic in harness together must some day pull apart, as they did. The political history of Kashmir since independence has been very largely the history of the relationship between these two leaders, their divergence and its aftermath. Such partnerships and divergences are well known elsewhere: we might mention dozens of them in American and English public life. Sticking to India, the example of Nehru and the Sardar Patel comes to mind. They were partners in the national struggle but disagreed on a number of questions during the first years of independence.

But Kashmir is small, politically immature, very recently emancipated from an unmitigated tyranny. In such a country the personal divergence of the two leaders has assumed an importance it could not have in India or in the West. It has in fact become the entire political life of Kashmir in the past decade, quite apart from relations with India or Pakistan. If there is a political life in Kashmir—that is, a realm which can legitimately be called "politics"—it arises from, and gravitates about, the personalities of the Sheikh and the Bakshi, their jealousies and their struggle for power.

This is another thing I had to go to the valley to find out. I had assumed, along with the rest of the world, that the quarrel between the two leaders had something to do with India and Pakistan. We all thought the Sheikh Abdullah had turned against that Indian Union of which he had once been a strong upholder. We tended to think that Kashmir politics, that is, inside Kashmir and without regard to the United Nations or Pakistan, were concerned exclusively with the question of how completely the state was to be integrated into the Indian Union. And we further assumed, I think now on insufficient evidence, that the two tendencies were represented by the two men. Under this view, while neither of them advocated union with Pakistan, the Sheikh Abdullah was or had become an autonomist, and in that sense opposed to the government at Delhi, while Bakshi Ghulam Muhammad was in favor of integration and therefore supported by the government at Delhi.

This puts an ideological aspect upon what was essentially a personal contest for power, and I never realized how personal it was until I went to the valley. In their ideas of how Kashmir should be administered, and in their actual practice of administration, there is little to choose between Abdullah and Ghulam Muhammad. Abdullah has, of course, given tongue far more freely and more picturesquely; it is in his nature to do so. He has talked to newspaper correspondents from afar—such as Kingsley Martin of *The New Statesman* in London—about some rather nebulous form of independence for the Vale of Kashmir itself, and of the "little Switzerland" that it could become, a sort of paradise for tourists, remote from political entanglements.

Ghulam Muhammad has not used this language: indeed he firmly adheres to the Indian Union in every public utterance.

Now, at the risk of stepping on everybody's toes, I must say that this appears to me to be essentially a verbal and temperamental difference, a difference of terminology or, at most, of rhetoric. Both Abdullah and Ghulam Muhammad are autonomists. With all his proclaimed belief in integration with the Indian Union, now and forever, Ghulam Muhammad retains for his state government all the special privileges which were written into its constitution by himself, Abdullah and their friends before they parted company. Kashmir has constitutional legislation providing safeguards for religion, language and land tenure. In this last respect Bakshi himself said to me, "I am an Indian citizen and I can acquire land or property in Bombay if I wish. A citizen from Bombay cannot acquire land in Kashmir." Kashmir has its own flag and its own assumption of nationality (to put it mildly) separate from that of India. What is more surprising is that central control, from Delhi, is shadowy in the extreme. During the past decade India has made liberal grants to the Kashmir government for development schemes and administrative assistance, partly allied to the Five Year Plans and partly separate from them; great sums have gone to the valley; and until I was there this past spring no accounting had ever been made to the Auditor-General of India. From now on there will be an audit of the sums India grants to Kashmir—only of those sums—and the state finances otherwise will not be subject to inspection. The same is true in all fields except foreign affairs and defense.

Ghulam Muhammad is dictator of the valley just as Sheikh Abdullah was before him. Is this not autonomy? And, by studying the speeches made by the Sheikh Abdullah between his release in January, 1958, and his rearrest in April, one cannot discover any way in which Abdullah would accentuate it further. In his public speeches, at any rate, he concentrated entirely on an appeal for a plebiscite—that is, that the people of the valley, which was his constant subject, not the state as a whole but the valley itself, should be called upon to vote their own status, even under the present abnormal conditions. In demanding this,

Abdullah of course realized that they had already voted, and if the elections were not wholly free, who can now say they would be any freer in a new vote?

In short, the two opponents have a verbal or terminological disagreement which looks like genuine opposition of ideas. The opposition is genuine, all right, but it is not in ideas: it is in persons. I do not believe, until proof is forthcoming, that Abdullah ever has wanted to unite Kashmir with Pakistan: whenever I talked to him in past years he was not only dead set against the two-nation theory, but also regarded it as contrary to the simplest material interests of Kashmir. Obviously the troubled and unhappy country of Pakistan cannot help Kashmir much; it can scarcely govern itself. No: Abdullah's dream has been of another order—a sort of enchanted valley indeed, with no connection to the outer world except to receive its generous, dollar-laden visits.

And I do not see that Ghulam Muhammad's feeling, although it is far more hard-headed than Abdullah's, is much different. Allegiance to India, yes: but was ever anybody more determined upon allegiance to India than Abdullah a few years ago? Can anybody be positive in asserting that Ghulam Muhammad will never change his mind altogether or in part? He will, I hope, forgive me for saying that although his assertions today seem to me as sincere as they are necessary, and I could not possibly doubt it, the political carrousel is constantly throwing everybody into different positions. Politics is, indeed, the region of successive sincerities and they are not always the same.

Across this curious story of the partnership and subsequent quarrel of Abdullah and Ghulam Muhammad, forming substantially the history of their mountain satrapy for a decade, there is constantly, inevitably, as we might say fatally, the shadow of Mr. Nehru. It is common knowledge that Abdullah was his devoted friend and follower for many years. It is known that he made overtures for the resumption of that friendship just before he was rearrested last spring. It is suggested that Ghulam Muhammad has supplanted him not only in the government of Kashmir but in Mr. Nehru's personal regard and esteem. A quarrel which was highly personal anyhow is made even more personal—more distinct from larger issues and ideas—by this constant introduction of Nehru's name into any discussion of the two Kashmiri leaders, and by the further assumption that what has taken place was by Nehru's will or intention.

This does not accord with my impressions either this past year or for the preceding decade. I am not party to any state secrets, but from what I have seen of the persons involved it appears to me that Nehru has consistently tried to mitigate the quarrels of Kashmiri leaders. Of course he wants Kashmir's accession to India to remain a solid fact: that is primary. But the quarrel between Abdullah and Ghulam Muhammad (1953) was not of his making, and the idea that he could quite coldly dismiss or imprison the one and install the other in power is, to me, fantastic. To suppose this, we should have to suppose that he regarded these leaders of Kashmiri nationalism as mere puppets, which is contrary to all the known facts: he has accepted a degree of autonomy for their successive administrations which would be impossible in any other Indian state. When Ghulam Muhammad rearrested the Sheikh Abdullah in April, 1958, there is reason to believe that the decision was his own and that Mr. Nehru acquiesced in it, as he does in many other anomalies of the region. If Abdullah, during his five previous years in jail, evolved toward some new idea of Kashmir's fate—or even if he cast his eyes in the direction of Pakistan—it would be a denial of his own deep-held convictions for the past thirty years and more. All he had said in public was that he wanted a vote. And in December, 1958, at the outset of his trial, we find him claiming the benefits of the contemporary revised laws of India—not yet extended to Kashmir—which is in itself a claim involving not less union with India, but distinctly more than has yet come into being.

All this tangle within the state has woefully confused the issues, even for Indians, and far more so for observers from afar. It is like a sort of peritonitis supervening upon appendicitis: it makes everything worse. There are times when we wonder if the patient can survive.

6

Now, of course, if you go to Kashmir as a tourist pure and simple, you might never notice anything out of the way. The capital, Srinagar, is annually visited by a large number of tourists, both Indian and foreign, during the months from April to September, and the revenue they bring in is very important to the state. The British Raj introduced two of the distinctive delights, trout-fishing and life on a houseboat, which have attracted generations of newcomers. Nobody could deny the charm of these attractions for the holiday maker, and the Kashmir administration has gone vigorously into the tourist business in recent years. The trouble is that newspaper reports of disorder—or even of political disagreements—frequently discourage the prospective visitor, and there were a good many reservations canceled last spring for this reason alone.

For those who ignored the newspapers, or perhaps had not read them, there were the usual pleasures, untouched by the tremors of politics. In the bar or the dining room of the Palace Hotel, out on the Dal Lake—converted from the former Maharajah's palace—where Americans in particular are much in evidence, it seemed to me that the general atmosphere was about what might be found at St. Moritz or Cannes or Venice. During the little time I could spend in such places I never chanced to hear a word, not even one word, about the difficulties of the state of Kashmir. The Mogul gardens, the mountain resorts, the Kashmir rugs and embroideries, the jewels in the bazaar—all this combined to keep the tourists' interest alert. It would be the ideal result for any Kashmir government, no matter who controlled it, to bring about a state of affairs in which this disregard for local affairs could become permanent. In fact one of the reasons given for Abdullah's arrest in April was that his speechmaking had a bad effect on the tourist trade just as the season was opening. So far as I could tell, the visitors I saw had never heard of him, but there were no doubt a good many others who had. Thus, as so often happens, his own activities had a bad effect on the very purpose he was supposed to have in mind, i.e., the segregation of Kashmir from power politics and its happy future as a paradise for tourists.

Switzerland may indeed be said to have achieved something of the kind, but it took a good many centuries to do so. To ask such blissful neutrality of a country tried as Kashmir has been in recent years would, so far as I can see, be impossible.

What, then, is to come out of all this? On the international stage there is a debate or discussion which shows no sign of ending, and within the country itself there is anxiety. Furthermore, there is actual fear of war, and who can say it is unfounded? A country under military occupation, however necessary it may be, cannot easily forget such things. It should be said that the Indian Army, although quite visible on the roads and in cantonments outside Srinagar, is as unobtrusive as possible in the capital and quite invisible in the mountain resorts. Its mere presence, even though for defense, does inevitably recall the bloodshed and terror of the recent past and summons up the idea of another army, not so far away, which might one day attack again.

The trial of the Sheikh Abdullah and some of his friends on charges of conspiracy against the state has been going on, in this atmosphere, for many months and shows no sign of coming to a conclusion. By June, 1959, eight or nine months had been passed in legal hair-splitting, arguments about procedure and the like; the charges themselves have not yet been reached. The procrastination is deliberate, of course. It is to the interest of India and of Kashmir that there be no disorder aroused over the case, and the longer the lawyers quibble the less chance there is for popular emotion to get out of hand. And in the meanwhile the peacemakers have been visiting both Abdullah, in his mild imprisonment, and Ghulam Muhammad in his capital. The aim of such visitors is to bring about a reconciliation between them so as to unite all factions—and thus, essentially, to abolish politics—in the troubled state. We may be forgiven for doubting that such a feat can be accomplished.

One new element in the situation, and only one, has played some part in the thinking of recent months. That is, of course, the anxiety aroused in India by the Chinese Communist absorption of Tibet, bringing the vast Chinese Army to the Indian border. Such anxieties may be justified or not, but they exist, and they are also shared in Pakistan. A notable softening of tone has been the result between India and Pakistan, which were no longer so antagonistic in the summer of 1959 as they had been for years past. There is even a very strong likelihood of agreement between India and Pakistan on the difficult question of the water supply for irrigation—that water which, flowing in the rivers from Kashmir, is a necessity of life for both countries. If this question can be settled, there is even some possibility that the Kashmir argument may also come to an end sometime, by an acceptance of the present partition—a solution which has been possible all along for the past eight or nine years.

In other words, an external threat of great magnitude against India would seem to be felt also in Pakistan. I am not saying that such a threat exists or that the Chinese Communist regime has any hostile intentions with respect to India: it is enough if many Indians *feel* threatened, whether they really are or not. It is common sense for the Pakistani to consider that their own country would not, could not, be dissociated from the fate of India in such a case. Thus a wave of troubled reflection, of worry and self-questioning, seems to have affected many men in both India and Pakistan since the Tibetan revolt of March, 1959, and its aftermath. The instinct of self-preservation, one of the deepest of all, may in due course diminish the suspicions and antagonisms which have flourished for a decade between India and Pakistan, bringing good out of evil: and in such a pacification, if it ever comes, Kashmir, too, may find peace.

IV *The Pursuit of Peace*

NEHRU'S IDEAS in foreign affairs were developed during the long years of study and reflection which preceded his advent to power. We should be quite safe in saying that many of them were evolved in jail, where, all told, he spent some nine years of his maturity. He was an incessant reader then—he has little time for anything but official papers now. During most of his periods of confinement under the British Raj he was treated with relative leniency and could receive books, periodicals and even letters (not always). When he was in solitary confinement we may be certain that his mind was active—and, as a matter of fact, his body too: it was in prison that he learned from a book, and developed into a daily practice, those simple exercises of physical yoga which he has never abandoned. When he was confined in the company of other leaders of the Indian national movement their discussions were incessant and served also to sharpen the wits of the participants.

This has some importance, psychologically speaking: it gives a greater detachment than is possible in the full turmoil of life. He may possibly owe to these innumerable hours of solitude, as well as to his own nature, some of the reflective quality which distinguishes him. He is capable of abstraction, even now, in the midst of agitated surroundings. It has been often noted that he possesses the faculty of withdrawing himself while others talk —Mrs. Roosevelt makes a point of it in her book, *On My Own.*

In his case one can actually see the mind take flight from its surroundings, but when it returns it generally makes a distinct contribution to the subject from which it withdrew. Once or twice I have even thought I detected this phenomenon in the midst of debate in the Lok Sabha. The Prime Minister is there, I remember thinking, but Jawaharlal Nehru is not.

It would be a rash man who concluded from this that he had not heard everything that went on during his moments of abstraction. One can only guess at the process, but I believe that when he so withdraws and allows his mind to collocate other things, either associated or dissociated, there is some part of his being which more or less automatically records what is being said or done around him. When he returns he has it all there, as if some industrious machine in a recess of his brain had just delivered it to him. It is a form of abstraction which, in other words, is more apparent than real.

At the same time it is a moral resource, a practical convenience and a highly characteristic aspect of his being, because he does obviously derive strength from these frequent withdrawals and returns. The unremitting hubbub of politics, the unending petitions and appointments, would be extremely difficult for a man of Nehru's temperament to endure if he had no such protection. Furthermore, I am tempted to throw out the suggestion that his entire foreign policy is, on the largest scale, a species of withdrawal and return, as if it were a vast shadow on the white screen of history—his own shadow.

A considerable number of words have been either coined or turned from their original uses to characterize Nehru's foreign policy. The commonest journalistic description of it is "neutralism," referring to the position of friendliness which India assumes with regard to both sides in the "cold war" between Russia and America. It is not a good word because it states an untruth: India is not neutral, and has in fact deployed an incessant activity for twelve years, besides constantly voting on the questions in dispute when they reach the United Nations. What this deplorable word really means is that Nehru has steadfastly refused to commit himself in advance—by means of treaties, alliances, blind pledges of this or that kind—toward the activities of other nations.

Hence we get another word in current use for the past four or five years: "uncommitted." It was Adlai Stevenson's word originally, I believe, but has been absorbed into contemporary journalese with avidity, as being less negative and therefore less offensive than "neutralism." This word does contain the truth that India and a considerable number of other free countries in Asia and Africa stand for, but it has always the danger of suggesting that older negative, "noncommittal," with which it is sometimes linked in print. India is no more "noncommittal" than it is "neutral," and it is only "uncommitted" up to the time when it commits itself, as it does on each question when it arises.

In other words, India's central and consistent claim in foreign affairs is the right to make up its own mind on every case, both in accordance with the merits of the case and of India's national interest, without regard to what other nations or combinations of nations may say or do.

We may see this mitigated a little, here and there, by considerations of special friendship—as, for instance, between nations of the British Commonwealth to which India belongs—since neither India nor any other country can operate in a vacuum. All sorts of considerations have their play and interplay in diplomacy, and personal friendships also count in negotiation: they make it easier or more difficult from time to time, and it is possible for them to color judgment. But so far as it can be done in human affairs, India has attempted to make up its own mind, choose its own course and stick to it.

This has sometimes aroused criticism, impatience or downright hostility in the press and public of the United States or even of Great Britain. Waves of feeling for or against India and its Prime Minister became quite common at one period in America, notably around 1951 and 1952: when Nehru (who had voted for the American resolution on Korea, be it remembered) demurred at the crossing of the 38th Parallel, for instance, there was an anti-Indian wave, to be followed at the time of the Korean armistice by a pro-Indian wave. It is also to be noted that the Korean armistice followed the lines which had been proposed by India a whole year and a half before, and which, if accepted in time, might have saved many lives. When the armistice finally came it was a detachment of the Indian

Army which had to supervise its most vexatious terms, those concerned with the prisoners of war held by both sides, and the success of the operation determined a new wave of friendliness on the part of the Americans. Thus it goes: one could point out a number of such instances in which our own emotionalism has prevented us from seeing that India's course in both categories—those acts which displease us as well as those which please—has been logical and consistent. And of course, whichever emotion happens to be topmost in the United States at the time, favorable or the opposite, is centered upon Nehru. I have been present at dinner-table conversations in which one might have thought him a candidate for our own presidency, so hot was the debate. A more equable view seems general at present, but it might vanish again in the temperature of crisis which so often recurs in our time, and Nehru again—depending on his course of action—may be hero or villain for an anxious hour.

It seems curious that this should be so in the United States because his foreign policy, which has a logical line and purpose, consistently applied, and can hardly fail to be of benefit to us, is precisely the same as that which formed and developed our own Republic. Under the influence of Washington's Farewell Address, American foreign policy set itself against "entangling alliances" for almost a century and a half, and the large number of interlocking alliances which have been created during and since the Second World War must be regarded as a tremendous novelty in our history. The novelty may be justified indeed—we may consider that no other course was open to us any more—but it does seem strange that Americans grow impatient with others for doing and believing what we did and believed for most of our existence as a nation.

Washington's words may have been written by Alexander Hamilton, but they clothed his own well-known ideas. Some of them are singularly in line with Nehru's thought and feeling. The phrase "entangling alliances," which is of recent coinage—a favorite of the American isolationists for several decades—does not occur in Washington's stately farewell, but the idea is there. Thus he enjoined the new American nation, on September 19, 1796:

"Observe faith and justice toward all nations. Cultivate peace and harmony with all. . . .

"In the execution of such a plan nothing is more essential than that permanent inveterate antipathies against particular nations and passionate attachments for others should be excluded and that in place of them just and amicable feelings toward all should be cultivated. The nation which indulges toward another an habitual hatred or an habitual fondness is in some degree a slave. . . ."

Later on he says that "a passionate attachment of one nation for another produces a variety of evils," and that the mere existence of a favorite nation is dangerous to judgment. (The reference to pro-French and anti-French agitation in previous years is only implied.) Then:

"It is our true policy to steer clear of permanent alliances with any part of the foreign world. . . .

"With me, a predominant motive has been to endeavour to gain time to our country to settle and mature its yet recent institutions and to progress without interruption to that degree of strength and consistency, which is necessary to give it, humanly speaking, the command of its own fortunes."

In these passages the advice given to the American people in their national infancy might be Nehru's to the Indian people: it may no longer be applicable or valuable for the United States, but it can be seen to fit the situation of India in the world today. And earlier we find another passage which also applies to Indian foreign policy, which has been, as everybody knows, conspicuously shy of any benefits or favors with "strings attached." This excerpt reads:

". . . constantly keeping in view that 'tis folly in one nation to look for disinterested favors from another—that it must pay with its independence for whatever it may accept under that character. . . . There can be no greater error than to expect or calculate upon real favors from nation to nation."

The world has so much changed since Washington's day that a strict adherence to all that he advocates would be impossible, and yet his warning rings true on many counts. When due allowance is made for the interdependence of nations and groups of nations in this century, much of what he says is still salutary for a country in India's position, entering upon an international scene governed by vast antagonisms. Sometimes it has seemed to me that the Farewell Address, by some weird historical metamorphosis, has come to define an important part (not all, but an important part) of Indian foreign policy today as it did for American foreign policy during a century and a half.

2

Nehru's own conception of Indian foreign policy is that it must adhere to three main, parallel lines, governed by three purposes. These are: nonalignment, the pursuit of peace when possible, and the national interest of India itself.

Nonalignment means "no entangling alliances" and above all no military pacts, although treaties of *principle* are acknowledged to be desirable. The celebrated *panchshila*, or five principles of mutual respect and noninterference, have formed the basis of agreements with Communist China and other countries. Military treaties are by their fundamental nature a form of alignment hostile to some other alignment and containing at the very least an apprehension, if not an anticipation, of war. On the simplest material basis—geography for one—India is in no position to think of war in such terms: war would be a disaster to India itself, so that the first purpose (nonalignment) is closely allied to both of the others.

The second purpose, the pursuit of peace when possible, has determined the very considerable activity of India on the world stage in the past decade, at the United Nations and in various conferences or negotiations dealing with the successive international crises (Korea, Indo-China, Suez and the like). It has also strongly influenced India's course with regard to Kashmir, although this critical situation is closer home and involves the third purpose deeply.

In the third declared purpose there come a variety of considerations ranging from internal development under the Five Year Plans to unity, independence, defense and integration, all the problems of making a new great nation, in which what happens inside and nearby must inevitably have some influence on the actions taken far afield. The unification of India within its present frontiers is well advanced, but is contradicted by the presence of one foreign enclave, Goa, as a leftover of colonialism. This has no importance compared with the greater preoccupations, but it may serve as an example of how national interest may naturally, inevitably flow in upon an otherwise disinterested view. India's friendship for the Western countries, which I think well established, suffers a setback when those countries go out of their way to patronize the Portuguese claim that Goa, in India, is "a part of Portugal."

These three purposes—I repeat them: nonalignment, the pursuit of peace when possible, and the national interest of India—were discussed at considerable length by Mr. Nehru in a private conversation with me on last May 18 in Delhi. His use of the words "when possible" indicates a modest sense of what India can and cannot do in the existing conflicts: it is a purpose mitigated by common sense and a certain humility. Mr. Nehru rejects with vigor any notion of a special mission for India in these respects. "Who are we," he asks, "to claim any mission at all?" All he has tried to do is to be of some service in the preservation or even perpetuation of peace, because that is consonant with the most widely accepted ideas inherited in India, along with the national interest.

"In other words," he says ironically, "a world war would not only destroy the world but it would upset India, too!"

Now, be it noticed that these three purposes, governing lines of conduct, are purposes only, or, as Mr. Nehru also said, directives. In their sense as directives they come straight from Gandhi, and it may be said that all Indian policy in this field was predetermined by the Mahatma. I suggested that previous centuries may also have had something to do with it. Nehru accepted the previous centuries with a smile, but insisted that specifically and precisely, in the present period, these overruling Indian directives came from Gandhi. He also insisted that no Indian government, of whatever conceivable political composition, would have been able to follow any other course.

The three purposes or directives have to be borne in mind whenever Indian foreign policy takes a positive turn this way or that: they are the key to what many persons, in the United States anyhow, have tended to look upon as a puzzle. They are not the total analysis: they have the characteristic of all declared intentions in that they ignore the cross-currents, the heritage of the unconscious, the memory of the past. Some parts of India's foreign policy, and at times some important steps taken as a result, come from this conscious and unconscious memory: they concern the rights of Asian and African peoples to shake off the remnants of colonial imperialism. To some extent they involve even pride, prejudice, illusion, resentment, suspicion. How could India, alone among groups of mankind, be exempt from such feelings? It would be a strange development if such a grand and wholesale purge took place in one mere decade.

This aspect of the matter was not even mentioned in my talks with Mr. Nehru this year, but during previous conversations over a number of years he has made it plain that he understands and to some extent shares the historical and psychological emotion. He is an implacable anti-imperialist and anti-colonialist; he knows how the oppressed races feel, although his own life, outside of jail, has been a highly privileged one; he would do anything within reason to help bring about conditions of freedom and development for others as well as for his own people. I should never describe him as a "racialist," but he clearly recognizes that the innumerable races of Asia and Africa, having been exploited for a century by the European "white" man, feel an instinctive distrust in that direction. The tendency of Asian and African countries, no matter how different they may themselves be in race, culture and political nature, to band together, consult together and vote together at the United Nations, is a concrete example of it.

Nehru's three purposes, therefore, are at times aided or influenced by an inherited complication which I should describe not as a purpose but as a *motive*. The Asian-African motive power is great even in the most enlightened minds of those vast continents. We have seen numerous examples in this present period, notably at the Bandung Conference in 1955, when countries widely at variance on method came together in a general agreement of Asian-African principle. In the case of

India and Pakistan, so deeply and painfully divided on many matters, a united front occurs whenever an oppressive racial measure, as in South Africa, arouses their common feeling.

Another effect of this feeling is the vivid interest taken throughout India in the fortunes of the American Negro. It is obvious and incontrovertible that every reverse in the long, slow struggle toward racial equality in the United States has a deplorable result in Asia and Africa: one bad thing, as usual, annihilates a hundred good ones. India has a much larger educated and politically literate class than most of these countries, but even in India there exists the universal tendency to generalize from the exception, and one situation like that in Little Rock during the past year outweighs all the orderly and unnoticed progress made in other places. This is plainly racial feeling, even though there is little in common between the races which feel it: they are united in their fear and distrust of the prepotent Caucasian. It makes a cross-current in political life and in the foreign policies of many countries. We who belong to the so-called "white"—or what H. G. Wells used to call the "pinko-gray"—race, try as we may, cannot altogether overcome this obstacle in the contemporary period. It takes more time than we have. We can only try to understand it with whatever sympathetic membranes we may possess, and if we do, we shall never be surprised when the winds of the past sweep across politics suddenly in racial form. It is like those spirals of sand and dust which appear in the desert from nowhere and swirl madly beyond the horizon.

These are ticklish subjects and hardly anybody dares to treat them honestly in public. The fashion of the day is to deny the existence of these deep, ancestral emotions. The fashion of the day is, as usual, idiotic. On all sides everybody repudiates "racialism." The plain truth which everybody knows, especially those who deny it, is that racialism is one of the principal facts of international politics in the present era. It might possibly, as the Russians since Lenin have thought, tip the balance between communism and non-communism in the dominion of the planet earth. Since this is so, the thing itself, a great reality in the subconscious of mankind and even, very often, in its conscious existence, may become a tool of ambition. That is, the ideological institutes of Moscow, such as the Sun Yat-sen Institute and the Lenin Institute, have taught for the past thirty-five years a thoroughly racial doctrine as a basis for Eastern nationalisms which, in their turn, according to Lenin's declared principles, must become a step toward communism.

The ambitions of Czarist Russia, as rephrased by Lenin, have at last become possible. Through racialism, anticolonialism and anti-imperialism it is at last conceivable that the Russians might rule the entire earth. This is precisely the vision of Czar Alexander I, the founder of the Holy Alliance, in obedience to what he called the will of God. For God the Communists have substituted "history."

The degree to which Nehru himself experiences any racial emotion is to me a subject of doubt. He has lived so much of his life with English people, and among them counts so many devoted friends, that I can hardly suppose him to regard them as being of a strange or hostile breed. He is himself English in the way that matters most, which is the language. (His fellow prisoners said he talked English in his sleep.) To him at the present time, or perhaps at any time, the resentments of the oppressed are a matter of sympathy (as they are with me) rather than of actual participation. He would probably put it on political, moral and historical grounds rather than as a matter of race feeling: and yet it is noticeable indeed that he has been a champion of the Asian and African races when opportunity offers. Any prime minister of India would do the same, or, if he did not, would incur the disappointment of his followers. The whole thing is a tangle of elements. What we can say with some assurance is that the anticolonial and anti-imperial principles are allied to a perceptible emotion of racial fellowship between the peoples of Asia and Africa, and that Nehru has a sympathy for that emotion whether he feels it directly or indirectly.

3

Declared purposes are one thing, inherited predispositions another; but Nehru's ideas in foreign policy are also personal, resulting from his total experience, including travel, reading and reflection. He has been intellectually concerned with foreign affairs for forty years and more. This could not be said of any other Indian leader—not even of Gandhi—and constitutes a high degree of preparation for his task.

In his memorable autobiography, *Toward Freedom* (1936), he gives some account of the earlier phases of his thought in these respects. He was, as we know, at Harrow and Cambridge for seven years, returning to India in 1912 at the age of twenty-two. There was little of politics in the Harrow years, of course, but the boy did make his first acquaintance with anti-Semitism, for example, just by school talk, and with the Italian struggle for liberation by means of a prize book. He was awarded Trevelyan's *Garibaldi* (one volume) for some good work, and took fire from the story of the Italian hero; he got the other volumes for himself and studied them. As he says, "Visions of similar deeds in India came before me, of a gallant fight for freedom, and in my mind India and Italy got strangely mixed together."

At the university there were more opportunities for the unfolding mind. He read a good deal (Nietzsche and Shaw) and engaged in a good deal of talk; he took part in the "Majlis" or parliament of the Indian students; he belonged to a college debating society. The news from India was exciting enough, for the national movement was just then (1907 and afterwards) getting under way. Most of the Indian students were "extremists," although Nehru remarks that practically all of them became staid and respectable Indian civil servants afterwards. When he got his degree at Trinity (1910, natural sciences) he spent another two years in London and on the Continent. Both Irish nationalism and the movement for woman suffrage attracted him; he visited Ireland in the summer of 1910. The Fabian socialists, the British Labor Party and all of the events of the day—including Count Zeppelin's first flight to Berlin from Friedrichshafen—were to be counted in the experience. On his return to India he had almost forgotten his native Urdu tongue and took his place in the national movement, at the Bankipore Congress, Christmas, 1912, as a writer and speaker of English. English was then, and was to remain for a long time, the real language of the national movement.

It was thirteen years before Nehru returned to Europe. They were years of immersion in the Indian revolution, of which he was, from the start, an acknowledged leader. He attracted the youth of the party and, in a general way, the "extremists" or the Left: a situation which brought him into opposition more than once to his own father and, in later years, to Mahatma Gandhi. He wanted, in a word, to go far and fast, toward not only a self-governing India but a social program for its development. His ideas were not to prevail for years, but they set up a current of activity inside the National Congress which that very proper organization—in its pre-Gandhian phase of respectability—had never known before. By 1918-1919 the Congress and the entire movement for national rebirth had passed under the influence of Gandhi's magical personality, which was to dominate it for the next thirty years, with an increasing reliance upon Jawaharlal as his principal lieutenant.

"I became wholly absorbed and wrapped in the movement," says Nehru, speaking of 1921. "I gave up all my other associations and contacts, old friends, books, even newspapers, except insofar as they dealt with the work in hand. I had kept up till then some reading of current books and had tried to follow the developments of world affairs. But there was no time for this now."

At the end of this momentous year, during which Gandhi seemed to have united India for the first time and cast a spell over all of it, Hindu and Muslim alike, the Prince of Wales made his famous visit to the country. The nationalists declared a boycott of all the ceremonies on this occasion and were arrested in large numbers—both Jawaharlal and his father among them. It was his first experience of jail. He was to know a number of jails well thereafter.

The illness of his wife, Kamala Devi, requiring some treatment in Switzerland, took Nehru out of India in March, 1926. The whole Nehru family was abroad that year and the next—Motilal, the two sisters, and Ranjit Pandit, Mrs. Pandit's husband. Jawaharlal spent most of his time with his wife up at Montana (she had tuberculosis) for some months. When he went to Geneva he was interested in the League of Nations and the International Labor Office. The General Strike in England aroused his keen interest and sympathy. Hearing of a Congress of Oppressed Nationalities in Brussels, scheduled for 1927, he asked the Indian National Congress to appoint him its representative, which was done.

The Brussels meeting gave him a first-hand acquaintance with numerous national leaders from Asia and Africa, as well as of British and other European labor leaders. There was a Communist tinge to that meeting—as I remember, it was organized by the Comintern. Nehru says, "There is no doubt that the gathering was friendly toward the communists, and, even though agreement might be lacking on some matters, there appeared to be several common grounds for action."

Thus early he experienced the phenomenon which has recurred so often since, in which Eastern nationalisms without a trace of Communist ideology find it possible to seek help from European communism, and, sometimes, to obtain it.

The Brussels Congress took permanent form as the League Against Imperialism, with George Lansbury at its head and Einstein, Romain Rolland and Mme. Sun Yat-sen as prominent members. Nehru took part in the organization of the League and in some of its committee meetings at that early stage; he was never able to do much for or with it afterward except by correspondence. He learned, to his amusement, that his way of doing and seeing things was more akin to that of the English and American members of these committees than to that of the Continentals. He was expelled from this League in 1931 for his part in the truce between the British government and the Indian nationalists (Gandhi's truce, leading to the two Round Table Conferences). The organization had in the meantime become more strongly influenced by communism and the Communists.

The principal event of this sojourn in Europe was undoubtedly a brief visit to Moscow for the tenth anniversary of the Russian Revolution. Motilal had come to Europe in the summer of 1927 and the two of them, father and son, spent three or four days in Moscow during the November celebrations. Both were impressed—particularly Jawaharlal, it seems—by what they saw and were told in Moscow. Neither of them knew much about communism, and to Motilal in particular everything was novel. As Nehru says, those few days in Moscow did provide them with some sort of background for their reading in future.

It was only later—during the prolonged jail sentences of the 1930's—that Nehru had time to read Karl Marx with care and to complement this with much other reading along the same lines. He was influenced but by no means convinced: his jail letters to his daughter Indira, published afterward as *Glimpses of World History*, reflect this progression and modulation. On his return to Europe in 1937, while fascism was gathering strength rapidly, he visited the Spanish Republic; this and other struggles of the day outside of India engrossed all the attention he could spare from the Indian movement. He was rapidly acquiring, if indeed he did not fully possess, a world-view by this time, one in which nationalism alone was seen to be an insufficient answer to the ills of mankind. In Indian affairs, from about this time onward, he tried to bring about a wider realization of the common nature of the human struggle, so that what took place the world over would be seen to be vitally connected with India's own efforts and destiny. His visit to China on the eve of the Second World War was part of this process: he was actually in Chungking, the guest of Generalissimo and Mme. Chiang Kai-shek, when Hitler invaded Poland.

Nehru was at this period a declared anti-fascist with a deep sense of the tyrannical and retrogressive nature of the Hitler-Mussolini alliance. The conquering myrmidons of Germany, Italy and Japan repelled him intellectually and emotionally: he could see nothing good in their victories and it is clear that he would have been glad to take part in their defeat. But at the same time he was incensed at the way in which Great Britain had put India into the war, on a simple declaration, without making any effort to consult responsible Indian organizations or leaders. His recurrent differences with Gandhi during this period arose from their variant notions of how to deal with the anomalous situation. Nehru would not willingly have undertaken any action to impede the winning of the war by the Allies; at the same time he could never give up his central purpose of independence for India. With Gandhi the second seems to have weighed more heavily than the first—or, rather, as a tactical matter, he thought that India's freedom should precede India's defense. Set India free and you will see how it will help to win the war—this is the general line of the Congress speakers at the time. It does not disguise a rather deep disagreement between Gandhi and Nehru on methods.

We all know the outcome: India was set free at the end of the war because its population demanded it ever more irresistibly, but also because the general world situation no longer made it possible for Great Britain to hang on to an outworn system. In the end of all, it was, so to speak, by agreement—or a series of hard-won agreements—between British and Indians, and over the conference table rather than in the streets, that India gained its independence with Jawaharlal at the head of its government.

He came to this after a development of thought in foreign affairs which I have merely sketched here. He had a mature view of the world, informed by reading, travel and reflection. Strong libertarian principles were native to him and if he had any natural prejudices they were in favor of the underdog. Otherwise his mind was singularly serene and clear with regard to the tangle of international relationships. He was "very far from being a Communist," as he remarks in his autobiography of twenty-odd years ago, and yet he recognized in communism one of the principal forces of the contemporary world, one in which many legitimate aims of the disinherited were at least voiced and sometimes attained. The achievements of Soviet Russia in industrialization and the conquest of illiteracy had impressed him deeply, as they do all Asians who face analogous necessities. He has never been blind, just the same, to the tremendous price Russia had to pay for these achievements—nor to the other fact, too often forgotten in Asia, that Russia is by nature endowed with colossal resources. The comparison between Russia and India, or between Russia and China, which is often made—suggesting that methods similar to those of the Russian Communist regime must produce similar results—does not beguile or deflect Nehru's judgment: he is well aware of the difference between a country which possesses everything in its own soil and one which lies, deforested and exhausted, at the mercy of a ferocious climate. A determined effort under almost any system of society and government could probably have developed the wealth of Russia: the effort came under communism, but the wealth was there to begin with. So far as science has revealed up to now, nothing at all comparable is likely to be found in India.

Most of all, Nehru's rejection of communism for India is based upon the violence and tyranny which seem inseparable from it. This view is cogently expressed in his letter to local Congress leaders (1958) to which we shall recur. He has not delved, and apparently does not wish to delve, into the theoretical maze (economic determinism, dialectical materialism) which the Communists have so amply developed; he might say that this is because he has not studied it enough, but my guess is that he instinctively feels it to be erroneous. On the Gandhian principles it is not necessary to consider these rather scholastic points of Communist theory: to Gandhi ends and means were inevitably of the same nature, and bad means cannot produce good results. Thus, since communism rules by violence and tyranny, which are themselves bad, it cannot in the long run produce a good result. If he feels this deeply, as I think he does, there is no need to theorize. He does want a "socialist structure of society," and he does oppose the exploitation of human beings by others for profit; but he would never pursue such aims except through the democratic freedoms to which he is vowed.

His attitudes toward the West are, as we have already seen and shall see in other connections, very much conditioned by what the West says or does, particularly in regard to India. A nationalist revolutionary who spent the greater part of his life in revolt against England, he never lost his friendly feeling toward the English people. English poetry and literature in general have lived in his mind since childhood; the House of Commons, too, has been a formative influence and remains a model. When there are thorny questions of parliamentary ethics or procedure, as during the debates over the former Finance Minister (Krishnamachari) in 1958, Nehru turns to this authority as a pattern to follow. And not only intellectually or theoretically, but in all the nonreflective, instinctual ways revealed by daily life, he shows what I see as a kind of kinship with the English. He understands them, gets along well with them, has a large number of real friends among them. They never surprise him very much—astonishment is rare within a family.

The same cannot be said of his relations with the Americans. He had little acquaintance with them up to the time of independence—a few missionaries, journalists and other specialized persons at most—and had never visited America. His one big tour of the United States took place in 1949, during the Truman administration, and his brief second visit (1957) was to President Eisenhower at Gettysburg. It would not be possible to say that either of these visits gave him any real acquaintance, on ordinary terms, with our huge and various country. But since the independence of India he has met large numbers of Americans engaged in affairs in India—diplomats, engineers, businessmen, experts and professors, even distinguished tourists—and has dealt with them on many matters, including some of the utmost importance. I think his widened experience has tempered his original views: he has even grown used to our accents and our ways of using the English language. (He is not averse to an occasional Americanism himself, if it comes in handy during ordinary talk.) There is no doubt, just the same, that he had some suspicions of American purposes during his first years of power—as we have seen in the case of Kashmir—and the vexatious matter of our military assistance to Pakistan revived them for a while. If I may generalize, it seems to me that American help in the Five Year Plan has done more than any other one thing to mellow Nehru's attitude toward us. (He might, indeed, deny that it has changed or "mellowed" in any way, and yet this is my impression.)

Nehru is not, by temperament, well suited to some of the American company he has encountered as Prime Minister. There is one story often told in Delhi; it has reached print also, notably in Moraes' *Jawaharlal Nehru*. It is to this effect:

During the Prime Minister's tour of the United States in 1949 he was the guest of honor at a dinner of financial and industrial magnates in the Waldorf-Astoria Hotel. At some point toward the end of the meal the man sitting next to him said, "Have you any idea of how much money is represented in this room?" The Prime Minister said no. The man said, "Twenty billion dollars."

It conveyed to Nehru a feeling that nothing mattered about these men except their possessions: that nothing was held to be of account except this number of dollars. Useful, salutary and desirable as dollars may be when rightfully employed, they can hardly take the place of everything else in human existence —or so we may imagine Nehru (or any other Indian) thinking at that point.

A certain amount of boasting about financial and military power does not disturb Americans; we are used to it. But during the period some years ago when various public speakers, dizzy from our monopoly of atomic weapons, used to state their estimates of how quickly we could destroy any possible enemy on earth, the same distaste was felt by Indians. No matter how true such statements might have been, at least temporarily, they could but repel and enervate the sensitive in other camps—and even, sometimes, in our own.

Nehru's feelings in such matters are not much different from those of an Englishman, being based upon taste and manners, but beneath all that there is an Indian distrust of open, declared materialism and I believe that he shares it to some extent, even unconsciously. There is an exactly similar revulsion, by the way, against similar boasting on the part of the Soviet Union.

To cut this short, we may say that Mr. Nehru has an instinctive and familiar relationship with the English—a sort of cousinship—only occasionally disturbed by such episodes as the expedition to Suez; he has a more quizzical attitude, certainly, toward the Americans, but it has softened a good deal in recent years—and, I think, specifically since Suez. Fundamentally he has a sincere friendship toward both, because no number of incidents or episodes could conceal from him the fact that they struggle in the main toward great ends which he values.

Toward the French, West Germans and Italians he has shown friendly feelings, too; they, along with the Swiss, have been welcomed into the development of the Five Year Plans. Of course, their part is smaller and they do not take up nearly so much time and effort as the relations with the other two Western powers. Difficulties of a diplomatic order have arisen with the French over colonialism, and it is enough to recall the mere names of Indo-China, Tunisia, Morocco and Algeria to see what the difficulties have been; we remember how the French delegates at the United Nations rose and left the room when Mr. Krishna Menon rose to speak on Tunisia a few years ago. The scene has been repeated. It still does not alter the fact that on other matters India and France have kept on friendly terms.

There is hardly a doubt in my mind that if the vestiges of colonialism were out of the way Mr. Nehru would find it altogether pleasanter and easier to deal with the Westerners (all of them) than with some of the difficult and suspicious representatives of Russia and China. The natural bent of his mind is toward our ways of thinking; he found it out on his first trip to Europe as an adult, and says so; freedom and good will signify greatly to him. In the personal power which he wields over Indian foreign policy, even more than over the rest of his government, the West has no reason for discontent.

4

If Indian foreign policy conforms in general to the foregoing sketch, as I think it does, nobody need be surprised to find that its most satisfactory results have been obtained in relations with the British Commonwealth, particularly with England.

This might have seemed a most improbable outcome to many observers during the 1930's and early 1940's. Thirty years of a determined nationalist revolution which periodically involved not only the political classes but the overwhelming mass of the Indian people—years of sporadic repression, police violence, jail sentences—built up an acrid bitterness which many might have considered beyond remedy. Hatred was certainly in the air at one time, particularly in the earlier stages of the national movement. For an imaginative presentation of this state of affairs, more vivid by far than any compilation of facts, we need only to go to E. M. Forster's masterly novel, *A Passage to India*, a monument to the unreason which prevailed in the pre-Gandhian and even the early Gandhian period. The society described in that novel, with an English directorate perched dangerously over a vast and ill-comprehended Indian population, was so unnatural that it blew up from time to time all by itself, without any assistance from political agitation. It exists no longer. In fact, during the two decades preceding the independence of India the process of "Indianization" in the civil service had gone very far, so that the English officials in administration over the country at large were a scattered few. This was what made the transfer of power possible—England had systematically trained Indians to administer the country and by 1947 they were doing so, even under the British Raj.

The society described in Forster's novel could not well survive the apostolate of Gandhi. Gandhi preached love, understanding and forgiveness, he was himself fond of England and the English, he counted some devoted English men and women among his followers, and his effect upon English people (even his adversaries, even his jailers) was always profound. Indians could not follow Gandhi and entertain feelings of hatred toward the British overlord; they may have had their difficulties in subduing natural resentments, but it was their Gandhian duty to try. And similarly the British themselves, with the political wisdom which seldom deserts them, realized in good time that the day of the empire was over and set themselves out to make friends where there had once been subjects.

The reconciliation which came after independence was, so far as I know, unique in the annals of imperialism. When we think of the virulent hatred which Indonesians feel toward the Dutch—or Indo-Chinese toward the French—we have some measure of England's achievement in India. True, the methods of British imperialism were always more beneficient than those of the Continental Europeans. When we read the letters of Wellington (as Sir Arthur Wellesley he was once governor of Bengal) or of Macaulay, when we see how even in the early part of the nineteenth century there existed a desire to improve conditions, to educate, to administer justice, much that has happened becomes more comprehensible. In *A Passage to India* the resentments and hatreds are on a small scale: they have to do with the sacrosanct English club, with social distinctions and prejudices, all of which make a focus of anger. Yet this local pettiness vanished quickly with its cause, and does not, to my best knowledge or observation, have any effect on Indian thinking today.

On the contrary it seems to me beyond dispute that the best-liked foreigners in India today are the British. The evidences are many. British businessmen are more numerous in the great centers (Bombay, Calcutta, Madras) than before independence, a consular official assured me; British banks, shipping and insurance have lost nothing (even in partial nationalization); the volume of business with Britain is still far beyond that with any other nation. The individual Englishman seems to me to get along with Indians by nature. It is not a question of "long experience" at all: the young man fresh out from England seems to do as well as any old India hand, perhaps better. The friendly relationship which obtains in the educated classes (in business, politics, journalism and the like) extends right through the country, and in my own travels I have often profited by the helping hand, the friendly assistance, which is extended to one whom the villagers take to be English.

Thus some kind of temperamental or sentimental basis does clearly exist, and on a very broad base, for India's friendly arrangements with Great Britain. A most vivid illustration was given in the autumn of 1957 when Harold Macmillan visited India. He was greeted in Delhi by a fantastic display of Union Jacks fluttering from countless windows. It hardly seemed possible that there could be so many British flags in India—indeed, a decade earlier that banner was anathema. I could give dozens of examples scarcely less surprising. In sum, here is a case where yesterday's bitterest enemy has become today's best friend.

Nehru must have foreseen this remarkable reconciliation, or at least discerned the possibility, at the very moment of independence. He had himself in his youth been an "extremist" with regard to the British rule, and along about 1930 the idea of membership in the Commonwealth made no appeal to him. By 1947 he had begun to see the advantages of some British connection, even though he still adhered to the principle of complete independence. The solution to which he and his colleagues in government came was new: the Republic of India, free, sovereign, independent, was nevertheless by its own choice a member of the British Commonwealth of Nations. Sovereignty resides in the people of India (not in the Crown), but for practical arrangements the Republic would work with the Commonwealth.

There were certainly extended conversations, even negotiations, during the 1947-1948 period on this point. The personal influence of Lord Mountbatten, the last Viceroy, the friendly counsel of Clement Attlee and Stafford Cripps, who were then in power in London, as well as the gentle, kindly voice of Gandhi, must clearly have been on the side of maintaining some kind of connection. There were numerous down-to-earth matters in which the connection was valuable as well. England owed India two billion dollars; problems of foreign exchange were so thorny that it was better from every point of view to keep this in the dollar pool in London, to be drawn upon at will. The transfer of power also presented a vast number of personnel problems, and for a time there were many points on the earth where the new Republic of India had to be represented by the regular British diplomatic or consular staff. A very few British officers had to be retained for a while in the Indian Army and Navy. The last of these left the Army in 1950, but it was only a year ago (1958) that an Indian became commander-in-chief of the Navy. In scores of relatively minor matters the existing British establishment was of service to the new Indian nation, and it is highly creditable to the retiring empire that such services were rendered with great good will. Indeed it may be said that England in the end set India free in the grand manner, with courtesy and respect as well as generosity, and every Indian in his heart knows it.

Thus, when the work of writing the Constitution of India began in 1947, there existed a good number of reasons for preserving a special connection with the Commonwealth. Some of the old-line Congress leaders, who had spent their lives struggling against the British, did not take to the notion easily, and of course the Communist minority has always been against it. Nehru defended his course very ably in a number of speeches to the Constituent Assembly.

"I wanted the world to see that India did not lack faith in herself," he said, "and that India was prepared to coöperate even with those whom she had been fighting in the past, provided the basis of coöperation today was honorable, that it was a free basis, a basis which would lead to the good not only of ourselves but of the world also."

And later on:

"We have to wash out the past with all its evil."

It was largely because of the Commonwealth connection, which Nehru could have maintained or abandoned at will, that *Pravda* baptized him, in that period, "the running dog of imperialism."

On the whole we see that the relation of India and England, however tenuous, has worked for the good of all concerned. Nehru has attended the Commonwealth conferences in London and, according to some of his British associates, has been heard with deep attention. One such associate told me that the wisdom and elevation of mind which Field Marshal Smuts used to bring to the discussions had now passed, oddly enough, to India's Prime Minister and representative. Certainly there have been questions (particularly those with Smuts' own country!) which called for wisdom and elevation of mind.

And at times, of course, the connection has broken down altogether. Such a time occurred in 1956 when the British and French made their expedition to Suez. India was not informed (nor were any of the other Commonwealth nations) and reacted sharply. For a period there was a great coolness, one result of which was that the British information dispatches were cut off from Mr. Nehru just when they might have been most valuable (on Hungary, for instance).

In spite of Suez and the acrimonious debate which followed, this part of India's foreign policy is still, in the minds of good judges, the most harmoniously and continuously successful when regarded as a whole. Such is the opinion of Mr. Krishna Menon, now Minister of Defense, who has represented Nehru as a roving ambassador in many negotiations. Krishna Menon draws no particular satisfaction from any of the various settlements in which India played a part, mainly, I gather, because they were all compromises containing the germs of further trouble. He does, however, consider that the relation with England and with most of the Commonwealth has been satisfactorily worked out, and he counts it as the principal achievement of the foreign policy in this decade.

I do not have the advantage of Mr. Nehru's concurrence in this opinion because, strangely enough, we do not seem to have discussed the matter; at least my own notes and diaries, such as they are, show nothing of the kind for the past twelve years. Mr. Krishna Menon was a strong advocate of India's adherence to the Commonwealth; he knows England well, lived there a great part of his life, and was at one time a member of the British Labor Party. I can have no doubt, on the public record, that Nehru agrees with him and that Menon's services in this respect—in the normalization of relations with England—have helped to form the Prime Minister's high regard for him. Nehru said in a broadcast to all India on May 10, 1949:

"I have naturally looked to the interests of India, for that is my first duty. I have always conceived that duty in terms of the larger good of the world. That is the lesson that our Master taught us and he told us also to pursue the ways of peace and friendship with others, always maintaining the freedom and dignity of India. The world is full of strife today and disaster looms on the horizon. In men's hearts there is hatred and fear and suspicion, which cloud their vision. Every step, therefore, which leads to a lessening of this tension in the world should be a welcome step. I think it is a good augury for the future that the old conflict between India and England should be resolved in this friendly way which is honorable to both countries. There are too many disruptive forces in the world for us to throw our weight in favor of further disruption, and any opportunity that offers itself to heal old wounds and to further the cause of coöperation should be welcomed."

And to the Constituent Assembly one week later he said:

"We join the Commonwealth obviously because we think it is beneficial to us and to certain causes in the world that we wish to advance. The other countries of the Commonwealth want us to remain, because they think it is beneficial to them. It is mutually understood that it is to the advantage of the nations in the Commonwealth and therefore they join. At the same time, it is made perfectly clear that each country is completely free to go its own way; it may be that they may go sometimes so far as to break away from the Commonwealth.

In the world today where there are so many disruptive forces at work, where we are often on the verge of war, I think it is not a safe thing to encourage the breaking up of any association that one has. Break up the evil part of it; break up anything that may come in the way of your growth, because nobody dare agree to anything which comes in the way of a nation's growth. Otherwise, apart from breaking the evil parts of the association, it is better to keep a coöperative association going which may do good in this world rather than break it."

At the end of the first Commonwealth conference in which Nehru participated (April 27, 1949, about a fortnight before these speeches in India) a declaration was issued stating that the Republic of India had chosen to remain in the associated nations—on its own terms, of course, presenting some political or theoretical novelties, but within the "mystic circle," as Churchill called it, just the same.

On this basis the Constitution was completed and the Republic proclaimed on January 26, 1950, the twentieth anniversary of the date fixed as Independence Day by the Working Committee of the Congress. It is now celebrated as Republic Day, the principal national holiday.

5

Aside from this regulation of an old account it would seem to most observers that India's pursuit of peace "when possible" has had some appreciable results in fields afar. With Russia, China and the United States, the other giant countries of the age, India is on better terms now than they with each other. At the moment of independence none of these countries had a settled policy or a reasoned attitude with respect to India. In Russia the Communist ideological attack on Gandhi and Nehru was at its height just at that time (1947-1948), reaching considerable extremes of insult and vituperation. China was coming out of a tremendous civil war with the mainland united under one regime (1949) for the first time in about four decades. The nascent Indian state recognized the Kuomintang regime of Chiang Kai-shek and exchanged ambassadors with it, only to switch when the Communists installed their rule over the whole country in 1949. The United States was, so to speak, "sitting back," and had not yet formulated a policy toward an area of the world where it had never needed one before. The British Indian Empire dissolved into successor states of varying tenor (Pakistan, India, Burma, Ceylon) and it took some time for the Americans, Chinese and Russians to get acquainted with the new situation, even to familiarize themselves with the characters of these new countries.

For, however obvious it may be, it always needs to be stated again that India was isolated from the modern world by the British Empire. It is indeed an essential condition of colonial imperialism that it must take the subject nation as an economic, military and political preserve; otherwise it is of no use to the exploiting nation. American business activities were not favored in India at any time up to independence. Russian interest in India, great or small, was viewed with the deepest suspicion by the British; Kipling's "bear that walks like a man" was always an enemy, even in the days when the home governments of Russia and England were allies. China was immensely remote, as it has been throughout history, and the towering Himalaya always made it necessary for trade or other relations between the two greatest Asian countries to pass the long way round, by sea. Britain excluded the world from India, and when independence came it was not at all surprising that the world in general had to improvise attitudes and aptitudes, thought and technique, just as India itself had to do.

The change in a decade has been at least as great among these interested foreigners (Russian, Chinese, American) as among Indians who have to deal with them. Most foreigners, even at the higher levels of education and information, had no idea how able the Indians really were. (The British knew but had not advertised the fact.) During the terrible days of partition and internecine strife, when the woe of the people seemed beyond endurance, many foreigners freely expressed their belief that the whole machine of government and administration was bound to break down, and soon. They were astonished that the post office and the railways, the buses and telephone systems, continued to function. They looked for collapse at any moment, the kind of collapse many of us had seen in China during previous years.

That was only in 1948, after all, and yet today the foreigner in India does not betray any such alarm. He expects the railway or the airplane to take him to his destination, as it does, and he expects the apparatus of life to operate normally when he gets there.

This change is an evidence of the respect which, through no fault of their own, the foreigners had never been permitted to entertain for India before independence. It is now quite generally understood that Indians know how to run their own affairs pretty well, and although there may be vexations, as there are everywhere, a certain amount of ordinary human flexibility can deal with them easily enough. In the most elementary matters facing a foreigner in India, such as, for example, the regulations concerning entry, customs, passports, police registration, etc., etc., the Indians have immensely simplified and streamlined all the procedures since 1948. They inherited from the British a cumbersome and paper-mad system suited only to a police state, and a very antiquated police state at that (everything in laborious handwriting, typewriters unknown). They have rationalized the whole affair now so that coming and going is smooth and easy—as much so as in London or New York—without sacrifice of efficiency.

Such relatively small considerations have wrought a deep psychological change in a decade. Indians seem to me to have overcome most of that "inferiority complex," as it is called, which the Empire gave them; at least the chip-on-the-shoulder attitude, as I should prefer to call it, gets rarer and rarer. The new respect they encounter from foreigners may be partly responsible—and by foreigners I mean chiefly the new foreigners, Americans and others—but it arises also from the consciousness of their own capacity to do the job, any job, in a viable manner. I am not pretending that Indian officials or other workers outshine others in efficiency, but they do get their jobs done more smoothly than before, and the whole thing goes coherently; the machine works. All those prophecies of disaster which the foreigners in India handed out so profusely in 1948 were conclusively proved, by 1958, to be balefully false and silly. India is much more a "going concern" today than it was at the moment of independence.

We see a variety of effects on the foreigners themselves, and all, I think, are salutary. It was uncommon, although not unknown, for Americans, Russians or others to devote any great study to Indian languages, society or culture in the time of the British Raj. They made great contributions to scholarship in Sanskrit, for example, but purely in the mood of the library. At the present moment the study of Indian life in all its aspects is encouraged by the governments represented in Delhi, and a whole new crop of knowing young men has appeared on the scene. A knowledge of Hindi, or, in its earlier form, of Hindustani-Urdu, has come to be accepted as valuable in most of the foreign services, even in the American State Department. I knew a young American on my last stay in Delhi who had worked out a simplification of the Hindi alphabet and spent some fruitless hours trying to teach it to me; such a phenomenon would have been unknown in our foreign service ten years ago.

The Russians, with their taste for extremes, have improved on this desirable evolution: they have sent some diplomatic officers to Delhi who can speak Hindi but no English. (I was told there were two such young men in the Russian Embassy.) This might be taken as a compliment to India, perhaps, but it could hardly be of much practical use in Delhi, where the ordinary language of government offices, even among Indians, is English.

What effect small things have on great ones is always conjecture, and perhaps all these rather wispy or subtle alterations of attitude do not amount to much on the scale of world politics. They may be effects rather than causes; but at all events they exist. In their aggregate they constitute a quite different relationship between Indians and foreigners—on the level of officialdom, diplomacy, society, journalism—than that which was usual when India obtained its freedom. Is it too much to suppose that some elements of this new mutual respect, this adumbration of true confidence, may filter back to the capitals from which the new representatives come? I only suggest it; nobody could prove it.

What we can prove by the calendar is that with all the

giants, Russia, China and the United States, Nehru's government has steadily improved its intellectual traffic, which may be called its moral position, during the decade after 1949. It has been an extremely ticklish undertaking to keep on such good terms with all these governments at once, because the Communist powers on the one side and the Americans on the other have a similar or identical exclusiveness: they all tend to say that "those who are not with us are against us." Nehru is suspect to the Americans because he believes in an orderly evolution toward socialism, or toward at least "a socialist pattern of society." He is suspect to the Russians and Chinese because he believes in civic freedom and political democracy, is associated with the British Commonwealth, and is friendly with the Americans. Neither side in the cold war takes readily to the idea that an honorable man of obvious good will can be candidly well disposed toward both. To accept this would be to entertain the notion (forbidden to all fanatics) that there might be some good and some evil on both sides. Cold wars, like hot ones, are best waged in the conviction of exclusive righteousness.

Nehru does not believe in exclusive righteousness, least of all for India. Often in these past years he has ridiculed that idea in conversations with me. "The gentle Hindu," as he says with an indescribable irony, has proved capable of just as much violence and wrongdoing as anybody else on earth.

But if, as he also says, India has "managed to be friends with more or less all the other countries," this is in itself an achievement which promises useful results and has, we think, already yielded a few. It is of some interest to see how this present position came about; it was not easily attained and there were many forces outside of India involved.

To start with, Stalinist Russia was unfriendly to the new India because of the moderation of its governing party ("running dogs of imperialism"). In a general way the Russian Communist Party, since Lenin's pronouncements in 1921, has supported all movements toward the liberation of colonies, all efforts against imperialism, whatever their nature. The most reactionary potentate in Asia, if he held the possibility of damaging or expediting an empire, was worthy of Communist support. Mustapha Kemal Pasha—Atatürk—was perhaps the earliest image held forth in this category, that is, of an anti-Communist who must have Communist support. For thirty or forty years the formula remained much the same: anybody and everybody who opposed imperialism, right on down to the Emperor Bao Dai of Annam, was good enough for the Communists. In this same logic they supported Gandhi, or at least did not oppose him, until India became independent.

An independent India governed by bourgeois, democratic elements, offering a good chance for stability and development along lines untenable by Communist theory, was a totally different matter. It presented Asia with a new and different possibility and ran counter to the vital currents centered upon the impending Communist victory in China. For this reason alone—there may have been others but this was enough—the Russian Communist attitude toward Gandhi, Nehru and the new India they had brought into being turned very sour at the moment of independence. Correct diplomatic relations were established and maintained, but the press of Moscow (even the Soviet Encyclopedia!) conducted a steady enfilade of contemptuous, doctrinaire abuse.

The bridge to a friendlier climate was provided by China, which had with India some common ground as a huge Asian country emerging from the struggle against imperialism. To tell the truth, the area they have in common is meager; the only true cultural link through the ages was Buddhism, but that great faith did not survive in India after its first eight or ten centuries, while in China, where it flourished, communism is in haste to get rid of it. Otherwise there was not much in the way of relations, either in culture or commerce or politics, between the two largest countries of Asia, and their simple acquaintance with each other—to put it on the lowest terms—was slight. India has historically been open to the West and Northwest, and China to the East, Northeast and South; they face in opposite directions, like the two heads of the god Janus, and only the present century could reveal a kinship between them.

But this century, as everyone knows, has been prolific of inventions. One of the most potent of these in political thought has been the concept of Asia as a force in itself, in all its parts, a continent disinherited and exploited by imperialism but capable in some future circumstances of action in common for common ends. Gandhi was imbued with this idea. I well remember his speaking to me of a certain French metaphysical theorist as being "a friend of Asia"—not of India only, but of all Asia, which is quite an undertaking. Nehru was early influenced by such ideas and keenly followed events in China as in lesser lands of the great continent.

I have a pretty shrewd notion that his earlier enthusiasm for Asian coöperation has cooled a little; obviously there are only a few rather limited fields in which sincere agreement is likely among nations of utterly different cultures—far more different than those of Europe. But within those fields, certainly, Nehru has labored mightily to bring about whatever agreement and even common action may be attained.

An opportunity to do so was offered first by the struggle in Indonesia between the nationalist movement there and the Dutch empire. The original All-Asian Conference (Delhi, March, 1947) came before India was independent; it was convened by the Indian Council of World Affairs and opened by Nehru, then head of the interim government. It dealt with general principles without much issue in practice, but it was a beginning. As Nehru said, it might divide the past of Asia from the future.

The second Asian conference was summoned specifically to consider the Indonesian situation (January, 1949), and constituted a formidable warning of Asia's kinship on at least the question of imperialism. That conference produced some interesting illustrations of the vagueness of political geography. Turkey, for example, did not accept membership (it sent an observer) on the ground that it was European rather than Asian. Australia sent a representative but New Zealand an observer. Egypt, which by the textbooks is in Africa, was an active participant. Even then it was to be seen that the representation of China would soon come into question: before the year was out India had broken with Chiang Kai-shek and recognized the new Communist regime in Peking.

This recognition had been decided upon in consultation with other nations of the British Commonwealth, and England was as prompt as India (or Canada or the others) in the matter. It was India, however, which found most cordiality among the Chinese Communists, not perhaps at the very first, but within a relatively short period of time. I know little of them, but it seems that the Chinese Communists, too, are very conscious of Asia as a separate force in the world, and for this reason were prepared to greet the Asian brother. Such concepts are neither Chinese nor Communist, really—to the history of China all foreigners are equally barbarians, and to the Communists all races and peoples are theoretically the same. Yet this pan-Asian sentiment, which it would be excessive to call solidarity, seems to exist among Chinese Communists. Whether it is a motive or a pretext, and whether, indeed, it is only a temporary tactical device, events will show. At the present moment and for at least five years past it has played a part in the relations of China with India and, subsequently, with all the other non-Communist or anti-Communist countries of Asia.

In June, 1954, Chou En-lai visited Nehru in Delhi, and in October, 1954, Nehru returned the visit in Peking. These events were accompanied by great demonstrations and a number of statements showing at least a desire on the part of the two governments, in spite of their widely differing systems, to find some common ground.

And during the 1950's it can hardly be denied that India's firmly friendly attitude toward Communist China has brought some results on the international scale. The Korean war (June, 1950, to July, 1953) tested the relationship, which was new and precarious, in a variety of ways. India voted for the American resolution in the United Nations at the outset of that war, since North Korea had quite obviously invaded South Korea. The Indian contribution to the campaign was not in troops, for there were none to spare, but in the form of a hospital unit. Later on, after General MacArthur's victories had pushed the North Koreans back into their own zone, Nehru, acting on advice from his ambassador in Peking (Mr. Panikkar), tried to bring about a cessation of hostilities at the original dividing line, the 38th Parallel, and failed. He then warned the American government that an advance toward the Yalu River would be, in Chinese Communist eyes, an aggression, and would bring Chinese intervention in the war in some form. He was disregarded, with the results which everybody knows. The war continued its damaging course until, in the end, both sides agreed to an armistice along the lines Nehru had originally proposed. A detachment of five thousand Indian troops was sent to Korea, under General Thimayya, to supervise the execution of the armistice terms.

Again, in the negotiations which brought about an armistice between north and south in Indo-China (1954), India's influence was felt even though Nehru had not been officially invited to the conference. And in the crisis over Quemoy, Matsu and Formosa in March and April, 1955, Nehru's correspondence both with Eisenhower and with Chou En-lai, which will someday be published, played a significant part in averting serious dangers.

All these results, and some others less spectacular, were made possible by Nehru's determination to keep on friendly terms with all the powers at the same time. As he repeatedly explained, he was not concerned with the internal affairs of any state, but only with its existence, its entity: in the past year he has even entered into diplomatic relations with Franco's Spain, which, for an old anti-Fascist, was a resolute application of the ruling principle. He has steadily advocated the admission of Communist China to the United Nations for the same reason, and holds that the absence of the Peking regime makes a good deal of U. N. activity illusory. In talk with me he points out, in some amusement, that state visitors to Delhi during the 1950's have included "kings and potentates, Communists and labor union people and dictators and feudal lords," people of every political, social and economic description.

China is, of course, a very special case indeed, and it has not always been easy to keep the even keel. The two Asian giants only really touch at one point, which is in the high Himalayan regions and especially in Tibet. The Government of India in the old days (British) always urged its claim to a special status in Tibet, if only on the ground that the high mountain country depended on India for most of its communication. At the same time nobody ever contested the fact that the Peking government had a feudal suzerainty over the monkish kingdom. This remains more or less the same in theory today. In fact, however, the Chinese Communist regime invaded Tibet in 1950 and has established a military and political control there which far surpasses any known to earlier history. India protested in 1950 and has kept an anxious eye on the mountains ever since. There are other important Buddhist lands up there which are dependent on India (either as an influence, as in Nepal, or a protecting power, as in Sikkim and Bhutan). Not one of them feels quite safe now that the Chinese Reds have openly annexed Tibet. The approach of the Chinese Communist power to the borders of India must arouse much disquiet, but so far there has been nothing to justify alarm. By a treaty agreement Red China permits India to trade with Tibet now, and this seems to be the only special right India has ever been able, historically speaking, to claim.

And yet nobody could deny that the situation in Tibet and in the entire Himalayan region causes deep anxiety and foreboding in India. Indians are accustomed to showing their feelings; they are a people given to demonstrations; it is not easy for them to keep quiet while the Peking regime moves its entire governmental apparatus and a huge army into the plateau of Tibet. Nehru's principle from 1950 to 1959 has been noninterference in the affairs of another state, but we need no special intuition to discern that this costs him a great effort. Tibet may or may not be the "roof of the world," but it is certainly the roof of India. Aircraft from the Tibetan plateau could dominate the whole of India, and the kindred states of Sikkim, Bhutan and Nepal, so near Tibet and so tied to it by religious custom, are gateways to the plains. These are things which every Indian knows and feels. The Prime Minister's efforts to dampen such feelings arouse sharp criticism in India, even among his own followers. The crucial events of late March and Easter week, 1959, are too recent to evaluate, but the deposition of the Dalai Lama and the elevation of the Panchen Lama are symbols of one certain policy: the integration of Tibet into China. Whatever China's "suzerainty" rights may be—and they have been different at different periods—they have now been vastly exceeded.

To what limit could an Indian government's interest in Tibet be stretched? That is the question which arises whenever Tibetans call upon India for help against China. If the Indian Army and Air Force were strong enough to give effective aid to a Tibetan national movement (a rebellion against Red China), would that aid be given? In principle, no. As Nehru has repeatedly said, the affairs of another state are not India's concern. The various treaties of *panchshila*, the Five Principles, of which the chief is with Red China, make this doctrine an international dogma.

But the fact is that the Indian Army and Air Force are neither numerically nor in any other way comparable to the vast war machine of the Chinese Communists, which is in turn supported by the vast war machine of the Soviet Union. This, from any practical point of view, makes the question academic and it is not only theoretically correct, but is actually practical, to return to the agreed principles.

The famous Five Principles appeared in the preamble of a treaty between China and India (April, 1954) on trade with Tibet, and were reiterated in June, 1954, in a statement by Nehru and Chou En-lai at the end of the latter's visit to Delhi. The Principles are:

(1) Mutual respect for each other's territorial integrity and sovereignty; (2) nonaggression; (3) noninterference in each other's internal affairs; (4) equality and mutual advantage; (5) peaceful coexistence and economic coöperation.

The fourth and fifth principles are of such a general nature that they do not come much into the pattern of events, but the first three are crucial, particularly with respect to the Himalayan regions. By 1954, when this agreement was made, China had formally and plainly declared Tibet to be a part of China, while India had with equal formality placed the border states of Nepal, Bhutan and Sikkim under Indian guarantee and was on record to defend all these northern borders as well as the borders of India.

The line, therefore, would seem to run along the southern borders of Tibet, which, if the present process is continued up to the point of total conquest by the Chinese in that country, would put the Indian and Chinese armies face to face in the Himalaya.

The notes exchanged between India and China in October, 1950, when Chinese Communist armies invaded Tibet, were sharply phrased. India deplored the invasion and the "resort to force," but China swiftly declared Tibet to be "entirely a domestic problem of China." There was also the accusation that India, in attempting to further a negotiation, was acting under "foreign influences hostile to China."

From the asperities of this exchange to the mellow idealism of the Five Principles is a journey which it took four years to accomplish, and to many persons (including a great many Indians) it has seemed that Nehru in accomplishing it had given up practice for principle, fact for theory. Whatever special rights India might claim in Tibet—vague, uncertain as they were—had seemed some kind of protection, now withdrawn. Such critics find it unpalatable to admit that without the use of force there could be no opposing China's policy in Tibet. It is still more unpalatable to reflect that under existing conditions the only choice is between a friendly and an unfriendly Chinese regime up there on the world's roof. The dilemma arises again in 1959 but will be dealt with, we may be sure, under the formulae of the Five Principles rather than along the lines of the previous policy.

In other words, whatever the provocation, India's attitude toward China must conform to its own principles as taught by Gandhi and as reiterated in various agreements, treaties and formulae by Nehru. The entire stucture would be wrecked, theoretically or philosophically, by any quarrel with China (even a debate) over the Himalayan regions. There is not enough historical justification for any claims, nor is there enough actual force in reserve to compel China to consider such claims.

At the same time a look at the map must show that the strategic position of India, always based on the high mountains to the north, becomes seriously weakened as China becomes more firmly entrenched in Tibet. An unfriendly Pakistan and a Communist dictatorship in Tibet—these are dangers which are the creation of recent years, new perils in the wake of independence. Either would be bad enough; both at once restrict India's freedom of action, no matter how accidental or fortuitous the combination may be.

It would seem that in this case there is no escape from a Gandhian remedy—such as, for instance, the principle that only increased friendliness can overcome unfriendliness. Those who think such principles dangerous should examine the alternatives permitted by geography and material fact. With China and Russia in such proximity, and with Pakistan sharing the great plain of the Punjab, India's pursuit of peace is not only ideological or philosophical: it wears the aspect of necessity.

6

The high point of Asian coöperation up to now was no doubt the Bandung Conference, in the beautiful resort city of Bandung in Java (April, 1955).

To this meeting twenty-five independent countries of Asia and Africa were invited by the sponsors—India, Pakistan, Burma, Ceylon and Indonesia, called "the Colombo powers" because of their previous meeting at Colombo. The Central African Federation (the Rhodesias and Nyasaland) was new and excused itself; all the others accepted. The array of representatives from countries so diverse was in itself fascinating, and I remember thinking on the first day that no congress of Europe could ever range so widely, either in dress or manners or language, as this one. You found yourself pondering over what there was in common between, say, the men from Ghana and those from Ceylon. As the conference went on it was apparent that one of the main bonds stretching from West Africa to East Asia was the English language, along with parliamentary procedures, habits of speech and the manners of democracy. And in spite of deeper cleavages these things are very consequential. They make communion possible to start with and assert a kind of contemporaneity of spirit, a sense of belonging to the same century.

The great novelty of the occasion to most of those present was the Chinese Communist delegation headed by Chou En-lai. He had come, it soon became apparent, in no contentious spirit, and in his first big speech he declared his desire for peaceful relations with all countries "including the United States of America." We had just been going through a very spiny crisis for the past month over the Chinese off-shore islands and Formosa. One of the last newspapers I had seen in crossing the United States to the Pacific had contained a prediction, by an admiral of the U. S. Navy, that we should be at war by April 15th. (The Bandung Conference opened on the 16th.) Chou's speech, with its assurances of good will in more or less all directions, was a surprise to that meeting, in which a great majority was anti-Communist. Altercations arose in the various committees afterward, particularly on the phrasing of a final declaration, but Chou's main emphasis upon friendliness between all these nations regardless of their differing regimes set the tone.

Mr. Nehru's activity before and during the conference was, I believe, largely in private or by correspondence, but he is widely credited with an influence upon Chou's conciliatory line. One of Chou's unwonted and unexpected amiabilities was the scattering of invitations, right, left and center, to visit Communist China. He made one such invitation in public, blanketing the entire conference and all the countries represented there, and then went on whenever he met an Asian or African delegate in private to repeat the same cordial message. Many such visits did actually take place during the next year or so and continued the general Bandung assumption of some common ground between all Asian countries. It is an assumption which, whether fact or fiction, possesses some political or psychological reality. Witnesses of the proceedings at Bandung could scarcely doubt it.

Divergences of view could not fail to appear, just the same, and the task of reconciling them made the final communiqué fairly innocuous. The same might be said of almost any other conference which has not been called to settle some specific dispute. At Bandung there was no dispute to settle; all was harmony and flowers; the only debate was on how to state this harmony, in the end, without compromise on any of the fundamental principles of widely variant societies.

Many observers at Bandung, and I for one, thought of it as rather a foreshadowing than a fulfillment. It traced out the shape of things to come, or so many of us thought. In the fullness of time there will be community of principle and interest between a great many of these countries. Just now, for all I could see, the thought had to be taken for the deed.

Mr. John Foster Dulles, after Bandung, saw fit to give the meeting credit for a calming influence on China. There was now less danger of war over Formosa, he said, as "the result of a number of causes, one of the most important being the Bandung conference where Asian nations had made it clear that they did not feel that the Formosa issue should be resolved by a resort to war by one side or the other."

This is no doubt the case, but my own feeling was that Chou En-lai actually *arrived* at Bandung in a conciliatory mood. What he found there did not diminish it, but his declarations at Bandung must have been settled upon in Peking before he set forth. To this mood a preceding correspondence with Nehru, who was also in correspondence with Eisenhower, must have contributed elements which the conference itself was to turn into recognized facts.

According to some of his friends, Mr. Nehru did not think of the Bandung Conference as being particularly necessary, nor did he consider its results very momentous. It was a period of his life when private correspondence seemed more efficacious than any sort of public meeting with all the concomitant dangers. This runs counter to an impression I retained, and have already stated, that the mere physical reunion of twenty-four independent Asian and African countries for the first time in history was in itself significant enough to dwell long in the memories of those who were there and to influence their action. It was the final "Asian conference" of the series Nehru initiated in 1947 even before independence. None has been held since Bandung.

7

Reconciliation with England, friendly relations with all countries, a willingness to be of use in trying to settle dangerous arguments, and, finally, a rapprochement of special character with all the independent countries of Asia—these are the aspects of Indian foreign policy I have discussed in addition to its three leading directives as Nehru defines them. All of it put together could hardly constitute ground for sincere criticism on the part of those who want to keep the peace.

And yet there is criticism, sharp and constant, at every step in the evolution. It comes from all sides in turn and sometimes even from all at once. In a period when so much of the world is aligned either with the United States or with Russia in a struggle of wits and sinews toward an unknown outcome—when interlocking military alliances have become a commonplace arrangement—India's refusal to line up with either complex has irritated both. In the result many well-meaning observers tend to lose patience and to betray simple bad temper when India's views are stated, as they must be over and over again in the operation of a foreign policy. Nehru has to answer questions on that policy in the Indian parliament; he has to instruct his ambassadors, reply to notes, make speeches; he must receive visits and return them; he has to have an opinion on every event that takes place in the whole field, even where no direct Indian interest is involved. If he does not speak up at once, but awaits further information—as he did in the case of the Hungarian rising in 1956—his silence is a grievance against him; if he is prompt to state a view, this, too, is resented. It seems to be inherent in the situation, and Nehru seems to me quite resigned to it.

"We do not like it," he said to me once with a wry smile, "but we must put up with it."

The crises over Suez and Hungary, coming so close together, subjected Nehru and India to a new wave of Western resentment. The expedition to Suez shocked a considerable part of English opinion, as well as the greater part of American feeling; it was not India alone that viewed the events with consternation. Nehru is convinced that the Russians thought this expedition was the calculated prelude to world war. They found it impossible to believe that the enterprise had been undertaken without American support and approval. And, as Nehru sees it, such an attempt to reclaim the ramparts of the past, if it had been supported by the United States, would indeed have brought a general catastrophe. The primary purpose of Indian policy, aside from self-preservation or as a part of it, is to avoid that catastrophe.

The bloody suppression of the Hungarian popular uprising was Russia's reply to the supposed threat of attack. Nehru deplores it as much as anybody could but he relates it to the war menace: the Russians were protecting their flank. He must have some good reasons for thinking so, arising from his private correspondence. There was one long letter from Bulganin, for example, at just that time, which set forth the Kremlin's point of view.

All those events in 1956, which brought the year to a gloomy end, were beclouded with suspicion and distrust. We need only remember how sharply the British and Americans reacted against each other to see that even the best friends may fall out when trust is absent. The Americans were incensed at being kept in the dark about the Suez expedition and its purposes, which so easily might have involved the United States in desperate consequences. Nehru was equally in the dark, and from both sides. He had cultivated the friendship of Gamal Abdel Nasser since his rise to power, and there had been a conference with him at Brioni (as Tito's guest) that same summer, but it appears that no indication was given of Nasser's intention to seize the Suez Canal. Yet in the high crisis which eventuated, it was obvious that Nasser counted on India to attain some kind of acceptable settlement.

Popular opinion in India was favorable to Egypt in every step of the crisis over the canal, but it was also strongly favorable to the Hungarian nationalists who had risen against Soviet rule. Nehru, with no ambassador in Budapest and no independent sources of information, did not express his natural abhorrence of violence quickly enough to suit his own public opinion or that of the West. On one occasion in the United Nations Mr. Krishna Menon actually voted with the Soviet Union, on a Hungarian resolution, because he had not received his instructions from Delhi; when those instructions came the next day, they were to abstain. Such things as this, and the curious, unavowed connection between the events in Egypt and in Hungary, subjected Nehru to more than the usual sharp talk in the West. It was said that he had one scale of values for the West and another for the Soviet Union (which might be true in that violence is more to be expected from a regime which reposes upon it). If the use of force was wrong in Egypt, where at least there was some sort of case for it, it was doubly wrong in Hungary: this is what many Westerners said, and with reason. Nehru's overriding concern for world peace—Suez as the immediate danger of war, Hungary as the deplorable but characteristic Soviet response—never received full consideration, and at the time it could hardly be stated in public. By the time he did express condemnation for the Soviet action it was too late to make much impression.

Thus India's "stock" in Western opinion goes up and down with the events. In 1956-1957 it was not high, and may have struck its lowest point in that winter. It might be added that the voice of India was sometimes expressed, during these crucial times, with rather more venom than we usually associate with universal benevolence and a desire for peace. Mr. Krishna Menon, an able and devoted servant of Nehru's foreign policy, only too often seems enraged by unidentified wrongs and insults when he takes the floor at an international conference or at the United Nations. That is, he does not seem to be thinking strictly of the questions at issue, but of larger and vaguer calamities which arouse his ferocious resentment. Thus his language and manner bristle with hostility when no cause for it can be discerned. He is capable of lethal thrusts in this mood, sometimes going far beyond what is customary in discussion. As an advocate of brotherly love or at least mutual forbearance he surprises, when he does not repel, those who often would prefer to agree with him.

Now, in this whirligig of present time, Western opinion, or anyhow American opinion, seems more pro-Indian than for some previous years. The spectacle of tangible successes in the second Five Year Plan has induced a good many influential Americans to come out strongly in favor of assisting it by outright grants or easy loans to cover the currency deficit. One important citizen, Mr. Walter Lippmann, has gone even further: he advocates a more radical and decisive action amounting to "all-out support" which would make India into a "show window" of democracy in Asia. There seems small doubt now that the Five Year Plan will be completed on time and as scheduled, thanks to American aid, with perhaps more to come—perhaps even Lippmann's proposal for the future. These are great advances over the attitude of a very few years ago. What we read now as the opinions of Senators Sherman Cooper and John Kennedy, or of Mr. Averell Harriman and others, would scarcely have been expressed, except by a handful of obscure journalists, in 1954.

The irony of the situation is that such pro-Indian feeling is most likely to be enhanced if India gets into any considerable difficulties with her immense northern neighbors, China and Russia. It is a kind of seesaw: when Nehru visits the United States he is disliked in Russia and when he visits Russia he is disliked in the United States. These ups and downs are part of the pattern. No true friend of India could wish to see any real difficulties arise between that country and its dangerous neighbors, but it is beyond doubt that such a misfortune would arouse the United States as nothing else could. We may deplore, but must duly note, that the pursuit of peace has less appeal to mass emotions than the danger of war.

Nehru is pledged to defend the borders of India against all comers. He has said so repeatedly, and in particular since the first crisis over Tibet in 1950 (the Chinese invasion). He has never renounced the use of force, and India used force both in Kashmir and Hyderabad; what he says is that force is a last resort, and that every possible means of peaceful negotiation should be tried first. In the case of Goa, where a tiny Portuguese enclave contradicts the unity of India, he has shown notable forbearance. It would be easy enough to take Goa but he refrains. Goa will come of itself in due course. In the Himalayan crisis, Tibet may have counted too much on Indian assistance, but Nehru never has promised more than his "good offices" for that country. The other Himalayan countries (Nepal, Sikkim and Bhutan) are under Indian protection and their borders are, for defense purposes, the borders of India. There, and on the frontier with Pakistan, are the only two concrete threats of war to India in 1960, and in both cases, as has been stated over and over, India will fight only if attacked. The right of self-defense, as even Gandhi recognized, is inherent and natural.

Nehru makes quite a point of promising nothing unless there is the fullest intent to fulfill the promise.

"You must not encourage others to rebel unless you are fully prepared to go in and assist them with all your power," is the way he puts it. He was referring, as it happens, to Hungary and other countries of eastern Europe, where some American propaganda (broadcasts in particular) seemed to encourage rebellion. The same thing would be true of India with regard to Tibet or any other part of the Chinese Communist realm. What America could not do in Hungary India certainly cannot do in Tibet.

To sum up: Nehru has made a constant effort, since he came to power, to seek peaceful solutions for international disputes. He is predisposed by nature, training and reflection to these courses, but regards them also as being imposed upon him by the legacy of Gandhi. He is no saint—far from it—and he can lose his temper as easily as the next one. He has resentments and fiery impulses, like everybody else. But he sees no health, progress or advantage for India in abandoning the course laid down by Gandhi, which he defines as "the pursuit of peace—when possible." If I may add a word of my personal opinion, it is that Nehru knows, better than most statesmen, what is possible.

V *Nehru As Politician*

THERE IS a well-nourished legend in India to the effect that the Prime Minister is remote from internal politics and takes little interest in political affairs. It is nourished by many stories and they have also traveled outside of India, giving, as it seems to me, a somewhat erroneous or distorted impression. They make Nehru out to be "above the battle," at least part of the time, as a matter of choice or of temperament, while various developments take place without his knowledge.

Certainly it is true that a prime minister has to devote most of his time to government, and party matters must take second place. The quantity of dispatches Nehru, as Minister of External Affairs, actually reads every day is great, and he is compelled also to spend a good deal of time in parliament. He is consulted by all the administrative departments; a vast number of appointments are referred to him for final settlement; he is the head of the Five Year Plan Commission. The amount of governmental work that devolves upon him is actually much larger than that which falls to most prime ministers. By choice or by necessity—and you will hear both versions—he is actively concerned with the business of the whole government. And in addition he has a schedule both of state visits and of public appearances which would discourage many a stalwart. Under these conditions it is obvious that the time he can afford for all the organizational and electoral problems of his own party, the National Congress, is not what it once was.

There were long years when, as secretary of the party or as its president, he was immersed not only in the national struggle—the fight for freedom—but in the entire life of the Congress. He probably knew as many local Congress workers as anybody did except, perhaps, the late Sardar Patel. When he was not in jail he was touring India without respite, and in any given campaign—whether electoral or social, such as the work for the farmers of his own province—he seemed to be omnipresent.

Those days have gone for good. Nobody in his right mind could expect such activity of a prime minister; he has too many other things to do in twenty-four hours. Granted, it is Nehru's nature to do too much: he could scale down some of his work and omit some of the public appearances. To do so, he would have to be a different person, which is not, all things considered, desirable for India. The very critics who think he wastes time on public appearances are well aware that these are a powerful contributory element to the unity of India and the strength of the national government.

The legend of remoteness from politics becomes a charge or an accusation when it is applied to party details. The Congress Party is said to be going to the dogs because Nehru does not pay enough attention to it. Corruption in the party, the jobbing of appointments, various financial peculations and combinations, abuses of political influence—all those vices of a party holding exclusive power for a decade—are attributed to this cause. If Nehru had more time to be vigilant such things could not occur, or so the theory goes.

A foreigner has to be extremely cautious about all these accusations of corruption which fill the air in India. You may hear them aired very freely indeed, and you may read them in general terms in the newspapers every day, but when it comes to pinning them down you find them pretty elusive. However, granting that there is a modicum of truth in all of this, and that the Congress Party after its long tenure of power stands in need of something like a Roman censorate, it is beyond reason to demand of Nehru that he assume such a task so long as he has to head the government. What he can do, and does, is act upon the facts when they are presented to him.

The Congress Party has lost a number of by-elections in recent years. Its majority was decreased in the last general election and its popularity in many regions has sharply declined. Whether this can be attributed to the stories about corruption, or whether it is the inevitable reaction against the party in power, nobody can say with authority, but the significant fact is that wherever the Congress loses the Communists usually win. The other parties are weak in the country at large, electing a representative now and then in some local area of special strength. The Socialists are divided and the Hindu right wing (the Jan Sangh, taking in the old Mahasabha and other Hindu traditionalists) makes little appeal. The Congress had a sweeping victory in the first general elections of India's history, during the winter of 1951-1952 (November to February), when over 160,000,000 men and women went to the polls. Five years later alarming weaknesses had developed in the Congress itself and the results were surprising in many districts. Congress continues to rule, with a safe majority somewhat reduced; but one whole state, to the astonishment of India, elected a legislature with one more Communist than all the non-Communists put together.

This was the new state of Kerala, made up of the old principalities of Travancore and Cochin—the beautiful Malabar Coast. In accordance with the Constitution, the Communist Party there proceeded to form a government, responsible to the legislature, which governed for two years and more. So far as I know it is the first time the Communists legally won a free election anywhere, and the first time they undertook to govern constitutionally. The anomaly aroused keen interest, along with anxiety, both in India and abroad.

In both these campaigns Nehru electioneered with great energy, and whatever caused the decline of the Congress or the emergence of the Communists, it was not lack of speechmaking or travel on his part. Even in a by-election he can be counted on to do his best for his party, and he made a whirlwind tour of Kerala only last spring in the Congress interest.

The difficulty lies deeper. Obviously the Communists have been busy building their organization for the past decade, reaching into every village, profiting by every local discontent. When they win, it is not by the votes of Communist Party members, who are nowhere numerous enough to matter. They win by going out for and getting the votes of people who are displeased with the government, for whatever reason, and thus some weird combinations of local interests have been brought about. So long as these are controlled by the Communist organization their inner discrepancies do not matter to the result. This is how Kerala's Communist government came into being, and how some impressive results were obtained in Bengal and elsewhere. A refugee or a landless peasant needs no great persuasion to vote against the government.

There may also be skulduggery beneath some of the apparent Communist gains: it has certainly been alleged. Voting rolls, residence lists and suchlike papers can be falsified rather easily in a monstrous city like Calcutta, for instance, where a considerable part of the population even in so-called "normal" times is without fixed abode. Now that the city bulges with refugees from East Pakistan and the overcrowding has become a real horror, it would certainly be very easy for a determined Communist organization to roll up fictitious votes. I was told there, on the highest authority, that such had been the case in the last elections, but I have seen no proof brought forward either in the legislature or the courts. It will probably be thought injudicious, for some decades to come, to peer too closely into the electoral processes because a quantity of irregularities would show up on all sides: with over 160,000,000 actual voters, a dubious census system, an overwhelming illiteracy and an inexperienced personnel at the polls, what else could be expected? What can be said is that the Communist organization, more determined and more unscrupulous than the other parties, is likely to take every advantage of the situation—including, it is said, voting dead people and persons who never actually existed.

Even allowing for this, the Communists have made a better showing in 1957 and in the by-elections since then than anybody expected. They owe it partly to their own relentless efforts, but also to the growing weakness of the Congress Party. Sometimes it seems that Gandhi's farewell advice, given on the day of his death to Sardar Patel, was the true wisdom. He said that the Congress Party, which had existed to achieve independence, no longer had a reason for existence as a political unit and should confine itself to work for social welfare.

2

The origin of this advice of Gandhi's and indeed of the entire structure of party politics in India is to be sought in the story of the movement toward independence, the national movement, the one thing which has really united Indians in the present century.

Congress was not originally a party of independence—far from it; and in sober fact it was not a party at all. It started out to be an annual convention of professional and upper-class Indians and its founder was a Scot named Alan Octavian Hume, a former member of the Indian Civil Service, who thought of the meeting as a way of bringing out Indian opinion. The absolute rule of the Viceroy in Council, plus the unlimited autocracy of the Indian princes in their own separate states, had robbed the educated and thinking tenth of the population of any way to express themselves. The All-India National Congress was a harmless, gentle way of supplying this lack.

The year was 1885 and the place was Bombay. We read that the proceedings began with "three times three" cheers for the Queen-Empress, Victoria. From that polite beginning the Congress evolved into a full-fledged nationalist movement, stage by stage and year by year, until only a few decades later it was threatening the foundations of the British Empire. By 1929 (forty-four years after the foundation) it was declaring the independence of India.

To this development many astute and devoted men contributed, most of them Hindus, to be sure, but among them a good many Muslims. One thinks of B. G. Tilak, the intrepid publicist and speaker who aroused his own native Maharashthra (in the west, that is) but also the whole of Bengal in the extreme east of India. Tilak believed in violence. So did Aurobindo Ghose, that wonderful phenomenon of the Indian consciousness who afterward became the silent, remote sage of Pondicherry. This was the period when bomb-throwing was not only frequent but was actually approved by the intelligent elders. They, like the Irish, did not seem to have perceived that woeful wrong, and wrongful woe, do not bring happiness. This period was 1906-1914.

The situation of Indian nationalism, its aims and methods, its ways of using brain and heart, altered from the time when Mahatma Gandhi returned to his own country from a long sojourn in South Africa. This was 1914. At first he did not take any part in public life or—least of all—in politics, but the country was already extremely aware of him because of his struggles in behalf of the unfortunate Indian laborers in Africa. He set up his colony or retreat near Ahmedabad and began to preach his gospel, on a small scale, to those willing to listen. His "political *guru*," G. K. Gokhale, had advised him to be quiet, and as silent as possible, until he could get used to his native land again.

We sometimes wonder at the strange antithesis between Tilak and Gokhale in those days which have begun to seem so incredibly far off. Tilak was all fire and fury. He is a sympathetic character, really, and one understands his impatience. At the same time his nationalism passed all bounds. He published an edition of the *Bhagavad Gita* in which he made the most extravagant claims for its antiquity, purely on nationalist grounds. So unassailable an authority as Professor Radhakrishnan, now Vice-President of India, has put the *Gita* at about 300 B.C., later than the whole body of the *Mahabharata*. Tilak wanted it to have the authority of immense age and proceeded to bestow this regardless. In the same way he welcomed imprisonment and exile (or "internment" in the Andaman Islands) for his "sedition." He was probably a necessary, and certainly a comprehensible, flame of life in the awakening Indian nationalism. Even today some of his words strike off flashes when we read them. He loved mightily, was ready to strike and also to die. Every nationalism must have, it seems, some such paladin.

But Gokhale was astute, thoughtful, cautious, fond of silence and meditation. He lived in the middle of the rising nationalist turmoil (he and Tilak were rivals for control of the Congress) but he knew how to shut it out of his mind. It was Gokhale who most deeply impressed Mahatma Gandhi on his return from Africa in the early part of this century, and it is Gokhale alone, who died in 1915, to whom Gandhi applies the term "my political *guru*."

To put it in other language, one might say that Tilak placed the *Mahabharata* in 3,000 B.C., for no reason at all, whereas

Gokhale, if he had been asked, would have truthfully said that he did not know. And it was Gokhale that Mahatma Gandhi chose to follow.

But the Congress to which Gandhi and Nehru came as members and ineluctable leaders was a very different body, just the same, from that which they made out of it. Gandhi was horrified at the sanitary arrangements when he first went to one of the annual conventions, and he spent most of his time digging latrines, with such aid as he could obtain. He was also shocked at the fact that nobody spoke any Indian language—everything was in English—and at the general comfortable, satisfied attitude of the members. The combination of frock coats, striped trousers and bad sanitation seems to have been enough to keep Gandhi out of Congress politics for several years.

Nehru had some of the same dissatisfactions but he does not seem to have voiced them. His own father was by this time so important a member of the Congress (and several times its President) that he could not have done so with much decorum. We do know from his autobiography that these middle-class gatherings of lawyers and doctors were not to his taste. We also know that on his first view of Gandhi, at such a meeting (1916), he found him "remote" and established no bond. We are perhaps better situated, at this distance in time, to understand what ailed them.

What both of them wanted, of course, was to make the All-India Congress into some kind of mass movement or mass party for the liberation of India. Neither Gandhi nor Nehru stated any such aim until much later but it must have been in heart and soul even during the First World War. When the opportunities arose (1918-1920) neither was slow to seize them. Gandhi and the two Nehrus found the Congress an annual convention of *arrivés*—in American, stuffed shirts—and turned it into a national mass movement. The actual instrument, the National Congress, was an assembly of imitation Englishmen. What Gandhi did was to make Indians out of them, with the most enthusiastic coöperation of the two Nehrus, father and son.

Specifically what started the national movement off in its final, or Gandhian, phase was the Rowlatt Act, a piece of repressive legislation at the end of the First World War which violated the ordinary civil rights of Indians, or other British subjects. Against this legislation Mr. Gandhi declared a *hartal*, or day of mourning, day of the cessation of all activity—something with the effect of a general strike. It worked with the most astonishing completeness and the world saw for the first time how one little man, simply by prayer, fasting and a word of advice, could paralyze an empire.

It went on from there, ever wider and deeper, year after year, until the liberation of India from imperial rule became, in 1930 and after, a matter chiefly of time and method. In the process Gandhi made an enormous expansion of the original Congress Party. Instead of an annual palaver of Anglicized Indians in frock coats it became a mass movement with its roots in the villages, with a network of organized workers, a religious and philosophical coloration suited to the Indian tradition, an irresistible appeal to youth and a power of unity based upon collaboration between Hindu and Muslim. This honeymoon of the Hindus and Muslims in the 1920's was due mainly to a British error, the destruction of the caliphate in Constantinople. Actually the British could have waited a short while and Mustapha Kemal Pasha would have done it for them. Gandhi became an advocate of the caliphate of Islam and brought into the Congress fold a great Muslim mass which had never been there before.

Gandhi's own social and economic innovations, the revival of the spinning wheel, the boycott of foreign cloth, the emphasis on asceticism and ethics, did not always convince every Indian of their necessity; Nehru rebelled in his mind more than once, and sometimes in public. The Mahatma's prolonged fasts and his way of calling off any public activity if it were marred by violence—his deeply religious nature, his "inner voice," his day of silence, his iron rules for his own immediate followers—all this made his personality distinct from that of any other leader of the century. He was, indeed, saint rather than politician, and we have amply stated that this is not Nehru's nature. The reverence with which he was regarded made his course successful in at least one of its aims, the liberation of India, and this alone, his constant rightness of judgment when seen by the results, was enough to give him dominion over those who might otherwise have doubted.

But the point is, on the subject which here concerns us, that it did not create a political party. In the decade of the 1920's Gandhi's unique personality impressed itself on the Congress in ways almost without number: the effect persists today. The wearing of homespun garments and the white cap, the "Gandhi cap," became universal among nationalists, and there were few among them who could not recite some of the main verses from the second chapter of the *Bhagavad Gita*. Dietary rules, pledges of behavior, "disciplinary resolutions" and the like became very common throughout the movement; fasting was prevalent, especially when the Mahatma himself was fasting. All these manifestations gave evidence of Gandhi's immense power over the Indian mind, but they were not, in any practical sense but one, classifiable as "politics."

The one political aim and result was, of course, independence. In all the realms of thought and desire aside from India's freedom, the Congress was not a coherent political entity. It contained conservatives, liberals and radicals all at once; the two Socialist groups were within it also; the Communists generally supported it and in the 1930's were even members of it, as a part of the world-wide tactical arrangement called the "Popular Front." In short, the Congress *was* India, in a good many ways, and had every right to speak for India as a whole, but it was far too comprehensive, too universal, for party politics. It came near to fulfilling George Washington's prescription for the newborn American Republic: Washington said, "If parties exist we must reconcile them."

This unwieldy and cumbersome universality of the Congress heritage—its catch-all and carry-all quality—has to be borne in mind even today when we wish to apprehend the peculiar characteristics, the individuality, of Indian political life. There were wide extremes within the Congress at the moment of independence and they still exist. Sardar Patel and Pundit Nehru, at the moment of Gandhi's death, differed widely on important political problems. Nehru's triumph in a doctrinal sense has been fairly complete, and since 1955 the Congress has been pledged to "a socialist pattern of society," but you find Congress members who interpret this pledge in widely different ways.

One fact stands out above all others in the Congress, which is its control of the central and state governments, its power over appointments, its hold on the purse strings, during more than a decade of independence and another decade of regional autonomy before that. It has been in power for a long time. Many intelligent men in India think that what it needs most of all is an opposition, some kind of political party which would keep it from lapsing into complacency and staleness. The Communist Party, although alert and noisy enough in parliament, does not qualify as a democratic opposition because its allegiance is too obviously elsewhere—it obeys external directives. And the Socialists, in spite of some admirable leaders (Jayaprakash Narayan first of all), have not developed as once was hoped. For some reason, possibly in their own party organization, the Socialists do not make a strong electoral appeal, even in areas such as Bombay where they once seemed likely to prevail.

No foreigner could make a safe guess about the outcome of the present disquiet in the Congress itself, its misgivings about its future, or the criticism to which it is constantly subjected. About a decade ago my guess would have been that a split in the Congress ranks was likely, with the conservative and liberal elements going their separate ways; and such a guess would have been wrong. When Sardar Patel died the chief conservative leader was gone and Pundit Nehru's sovereign personality had full sway. The emphasis upon the "welfare state" and the "socialist pattern of society," to which he has persuaded the whole Congress, right, left and center, is essentially a program of the moderate left, and in some of the Congress membership it gets only lukewarm support at best. A movement of division in the Congress between right and left, the two clearly perceptible tendencies, may still be possible, but nobody now considers it probable so long as Nehru remains at the helm.

He knows all this better than anybody else could, and although he may not have as much time for party politics as before, it is also true that he does not need it. His comprehension is wide and deep; in five minutes he can take in a local party situation and, if it is necessary, deal with it. He has had too much experience to need maps and compasses in such matters. My own feeling is that what his Indian critics call "remoteness" from politics is not that at all, but the inevitable result of the priority he gives and must give to government, foreign affairs, high policy. Certainly when he goes at it he is not only the best electioneer in India and the most indefatigable speaker, but a skillful organization man as well. If he cannot be all these things at once, twenty-four hours a day, it is because in the just balance of time first things must come first.

3

Speaking of the Congress Party's monopoly of central and state governments up to 1957 Nehru said to me, with a wry smile, "We were becoming almost monolithic." I could not quite decide whether he regretted the monolith or deplored it. Anyhow, for better or for worse, the Congress control is monolithic no longer.

The principal rift is down in Kerala, where a state government with a tiny Communist plurality (one, subsequently two and then three votes) ruled after April, 1957. This was the most striking upset in the elections of 1957, but was abetted by Communist gains in the lower house of the central parliament as well as in a number of state legislatures. The opposition that has come into being in these two years is therefore not a "loyal" opposition, in the old parliamentary sense, such as might have evolved if the Congress had divided into two parts. It is an opposition which is plainly aiming at what Communists everywhere want, a party dictatorship called "of the proletariat." The Indian Communists naturally put the soft pedal on all ultimate aims, since they are trying, in the present phase, to win non-Communist votes from any convenient discontented element. At the same time no Indian Communist could disavow the ultimate aims and still remain a Communist.

So we get a rather intricate tactical pattern in Communist activity, and contradictions which are only apparent and temporary are permitted to flourish, evidently with Moscow's approval. The Communist state government in Kerala was bound by the Constitution of India, for instance, and could not hold office otherwise, although that constitution is incompatible with Communist doctrine. The main consideration of the Communists in the present stage of their being is what will or will not bring them most votes—which seems remarkably like the thought of politicians everywhere. In Kerala they want to be reëlected in 1962; in other states they want to gain more seats in the legislature, as they do also in the central parliament. Their leadership has confidently predicted Communist majorities in two more states, Andhra and West Bengal, in the next elections; sometimes they claim even more.

For these objectives to be attained they must go through some temporary and apparent compromises with democracy, at least on the surface, while their party organization assiduously cultivates the combinations and bargains which, at the village level, may deliver them the votes.

The victory they won in Kerala was perhaps a pattern for those they hope to win afterward. They spread their net in the villages and plantations, among the untouchables and a special Kerala caste which is close to the untouchables; they combined with this some middle-class elements (even among the ancient Hindu clan of the Nayars) who were at odds with the Congress; they went into the fields to organize the landless and the most underprivileged. In public speeches and appeals to the general electorate—and the educated, who in Kerala are more numerous than elsewhere in India—they never ceased attacking the Congress state government for corruption, malfeasance and promises betrayed. A considerable vote in cities like Travancore and Cochin came from educated, middle-class men and women who were very dissatisfied with the Congress and registered their protest in this manner; I have spoken with some of them and know they voted for "good government" rather than for Communist government. Most of them were as surprised as possible when the votes were counted; so, I am assured, were the Communists themselves. They found themselves pledged, at least on the surface, to "good government" rather than to Communist government, which, under the Constitution, was not possible anyhow.

In their two years of power they did not make great

changes, but they exerted themselves to disseminate this impression of "goodness." Certain gestures of austerity—such as not using state motor cars—marked their early weeks and months. A year later they were being accused of using too many state automobiles for their work—I remember the debate in the legislature when I was there—although the detail seemed faintly irrelevant. They preach against corruption but it has not saved them from being accused of some curious transactions, such as a deal with the Birla interests in Bombay for industrial development. Their main clash with the central government was on a constitutional issue: whether they had the right to bring all private, parochial and church schools under some degree of state control in appointment of teachers, maintenance of standards, etc. Since the state pays heavily in grants for all these schools it did not seem strange to an American that they should want some control, but they were obliged in the end to modify their stand.

On taxation their position has been more orthodox. I was in Travancore when the budget of 1958-1959 was presented, and was struck by the fact that the new taxes proposed would fall most heavily on the poor (public bus fares, for instance). The Minister of Finance explained that he had no choice in the matter because direct taxation was reserved for the central government under the Constitution.

On some occasions—not when I was there—public order has been endangered by clashes between demonstrators and the police. The Catholics, Protestants, Muslims and even the Nayars have private schools subsisting largely on state grants, and they resented the Education Bill to the point of public demonstrations; the police are accused of considerable brutality. Misuse of the state police for Communist Party purposes is also charged in other connections and in both ways—i.e., permitting Communist street shows while suppressing others. And, of course, efforts to favor Communists in the state in all sorts of minor ways might be expected of a Communist administration. They have, it seems, occurred, especially in villages.

On the surface, just the same, nothing in Kerala seems to indicate a regime different from the rest of India. Travancore, by the sea, is the state capital, a beautiful city open for centuries to a variety of cultures. There is even some hint of Chinese (tilted roofs) in its special architecture. The high level of literacy here came originally from its accessibility to foreign missionaries, who long ago set up central schools and colleges in the city. The rulers were mostly beneficent; public works flourished; there are roads, schools and cheap electricity here and all the way up the Malabar Coast. Food is a perpetual problem to any administration because it must be imported in quantity from other states. The level in clothing and cleanliness often seems higher in the Malabar villages than elsewhere, although I saw little of the untouchable and the landless. The greatest medical center in India, one of the largest and most modern anywhere, has sprung into being during the past few years outside of Travancore. One would think the whole state of Kerala, Travancore and Cochin alike, to be better off than a good many other districts that come to mind. Even so, it is here that the Communists were able to win their first electoral victory of any importance in the world.

Mr. Namboodiripad, the Chief Minister of the state, was frank to tell me he was surprised at the elections. "We thought we might win," is the way he put it, "but we did not expect it." He also was perfectly candid about the inability of his administration to operate on a Communist basis so long as it was obliged to keep within the Constitution of India. He thought the discontented agricultural workers provided the bulk of his vote in 1957 and looked forward to being reëlected, mainly, I gathered, on the basis of having provided "good" government in this period of trial. No doubt his government would never pass up a chance to strengthen the Communist organization from the roots up, but he did not say so: he took a straightforward constitutional position for the moment without giving up any of his long-term Communist aims or beliefs.

It is a strange position indeed, and without access to the secrets of the Communist Party organization or any other, it seemed by common sense to be untenable for long at a time. I remarked something of the kind and Namboodiripad laughed in a way which indicated agreement. When I assumed (fishing for response) that he and his colleagues had never had any of the conspiratorial, underground experience of their coreligionists in Europe he laughed again, this time uproariously. He started counting up the number of years he had spent underground and the number in jail; they seemed to come out about even.

"But I was in jail more often as a Congress Party worker than as a Communist," he added with glee.

Such are the anomalies in the lives and minds of these "constitutional" Communists, a new breed in politics. They do not, and cannot, believe in what they are doing but evidently think it might lead to what they do believe in. The spectacle must induce a rare state of confusion among their voters, mostly non-Communists, and no doubt that is one of the things they want. The clear-headed nucleus of the organization, by taking advantage of the caste system and other misfortunes, can bring out a combination of the muddle-headed in their support. Namboodiripad is a Brahmin of the highest rank known in those regions but has gone to great lengths in his efforts to use the lowest castes and the out-castes for his purposes.

It is a little strange, too, that nobody seems to have foreseen, up until these past five years or so, what an instrument the Communists would find in the manipulation of caste grievances. By bringing backward castes forward and combining them, under a system of universal suffrage, it is possible to get a disparate "protest vote" big enough to become a majority. So far as I remember nobody took this possibility into consideration until it was proved in Kerala.

4

The whole world became aware of the problems presented by the State of Kerala during the summer of 1959, particularly during the seven weeks which preceded the final assumption of authority there by the central government on August first.

The world misunderstood completely, utterly, thoroughly, as almost never before. It was assumed through the greater part of the world that some kind of "Communist revolution" was going on in Kerala, and headlines to that effect appeared in even the most reputable newspapers. It was hardly possible for the voice of sanity to be heard in the uproar of journalistic nonsense. We who were in India at the time looked on in utter bewilderment while the outside world manufactured a revolution which had never existed. Any fledgling journalist who could find blood on an old woman's sari was convinced that this was Armageddon.

It was, in fact, almost precisely the contrary to what the outside world supposed and proclaimed. That is, there was no "Communist revolution" in Kerala. The legally elected Communist government had so alienated a good part of public opinion that it was opposed by strongly entrenched and organized bodies such as the Roman Catholic Church, the Nayars, the Muslims and the disgruntled Congress Party. Deplorably enough, these forces, professing their faith in democracy, endeavored to overthrow their legally elected government by street demonstrations, without any legal process whatsoever. It is one of Gandhi's precepts, as it was Abraham Lincoln's, that the people have the right to "dismember and overthrow" a government they do not like. Only a few weeks ago a member of the central parliament in Delhi said that the right of the people to indulge in "civil disobedience" (or passive resistance or whatever it may be called) was sacrosanct in India because it came from Gandhi and would never be forgotten or surrendered.

In my own opinion, and I am far from a novice in such matters, the Communist government of the Kerala state could have gone on for a long time—at least until the next general elections—without arousing any wholesale popular protest if it had not been for external events. That is, the Communist administration in the state was hamstrung, as I have explained several times, by the Constitution of India, under which it could not introduce any specifically Communist legislation of any kind. Its innovations were devious or invisible (favoritism to Communist puppetry in villages, etc.) except on the rarest occasions when police action was employed for partisan purposes. It was about as harmless as any Communist administration could possibly be—merely, of course, because it had no power to be anything else.

It could do nothing about taxes, property or the judiciary, little about the police, less than nothing about civil liberties or the free press; it was forbidden to touch anything fundamental, with one exception, which was education. Education is a state prerogative or responsibility, as it is in the United States. The Kerala Communists produced an education bill which would have brought the entire conglomerate school system of that state under some degree of central control. In effect it would have established the principle that where the state pays the bills the state must have the right to choose teachers, audit the accounts and supervise the curriculum.

This is very old hat to Americans or English or French people. We went through all that a century ago and more, and we do not call ourselves Communists. However, state control of the churchly schools was immediately and bitterly opposed in Kerala —that is, a year and a half ago and more, when the proposed law was first introduced. (It has never been put into effect, by the way—another thing the outside world omitted to notice.)

Emotion is the determinant in mass movements, of course, and some emotion might be generated by the idea of state control of the subsidized schools. Some. Not, in my opinion, enough to explain the outburst of anti-Communist feeling in Kerala. I traveled all over the state a year before and discussed the education bill with all sorts of persons: many were against it. I never met anybody who wanted to make a "revolution" about it.

Well, what happened? What was new in the summer of 1959? What made men, women and children go out into the streets and lie down in front of buses and tram cars, or defy the police by forbidden demonstrations, or offer themselves for punishment in other ways? Merely because of the schools?

I think not. I am convinced that it would not have been possible to arouse the anti-Communist ardor of so many ordinary human beings in Kerala by the education bill (which is, in itself, fairly reasonable) or by anything else the Communist administration has tried to do since 1957.

The ardor of the anti-Communist population was aroused, not by anything the Communist administration did or omitted to do, but simply by the fury of indignation which shook all India after March, 1959, when the Chinese Communists absorbed the autonomous country of Tibet. All India was enraged and still is enraged; sometimes it seems to me that India's anger is deeper and bitterer than that of any other country, partly, I suppose, because it is materially impotent. No Indian of my acquaintance is the same today as he was before March, 1959.

Now, if this wave has swept the whole country, as I am quite certain it has, what do you suppose an Indian who is a citizen of Kerala, living under a Communist administration, must have felt? He, and he alone, is governed by those whom he now considers to be his country's enemies. His anger and his bitterness are immensely multiplied by the fact that right there, in his own home state, the devil's henchmen are in power. So, being an Indian and steeped in the Gandhian tradition, he joins organizations of protest, offers himself in voluntary sacrifice, parades in the streets, makes up slogans and defies the police. These are the methods Gandhi used to obtain freedom from the British, and they were used in 1959 to overthrow the elected (Communist) administration of the State of Kerala. By the end of July it was apparent that public order could no longer be maintained under these conditions, and the central government took over the state administration pending new elections.

Mr. Nehru came to this decision reluctantly, since the precedent thus established is dangerous to the democratic principle. If a legal government can be overthrown at any time by organized demonstrations in the streets, the theory and practice of elective representation are gravely weakened. What is more, the Communist Party of India has thus had presented to it, on a silver platter, a perfect technique for their own purposes: they can use the same methods against legal governments elsewhere, and have already tried them in Bengal. If they had more adherents, or enough adherents to put up a simulacrum of mass movement, they could be toppling over their democratic opponents in one state after another—if, that is, Kerala is to be a precedent.

However, the Communist Party of India is itself in the doldrums just now, so far as any extension in the masses is concerned. The C.P.I. contains some brilliant intellectuals, and some of its representatives in the central parliament are skillful to a degree, but the anger which India as a whole feels about events in Tibet and relations with Communist China cannot be overcome by clever argument. The entire C.P.I., and the Communist administration of the State of Kerala in particular, have paid dearly for the aggrandizement of China.

As the summer turned into autumn it became evident, indeed, that relations between the governments at Delhi and Peking were getting worse every day. Mr. Nehru steadfastly maintained and maintains his desire for peace and for friendly communications with all powers. He can do no other: it is his basic principle. Yet even his heroic determination has been sorely tried by the stubborn arrogance of Chinese claims. Perhaps the worst thing he has had to bear is the contempt with which the Peking doctrinaires receive representations from the Government of India. Sometimes these representations are not even acknowledged; often they are acknowledged without being really answered; generally they are contested as being untrue or unfounded. It may be said that nothing but the patience of a saint could endure the kind of humiliating and vexatious treatment to which Mr. Nehru has been subjected from Peking since March, 1959. Mr. Nehru is not a saint, of course, and his patience is not inexhaustible. If worst came to the worst he would defend the frontiers of India by any and all means in his reach: anybody who thinks otherwise knows nothing about him.

The Tibetan nationalist rebellion against Chinese military occupation (March, 1959) was followed by the romantic escape of the young Dalai Lama, the "god-king" as the newspapers call him, from his Himalayan fastnesses. When the Dalai Lama reached safety in India, he was of course made welcome by Nehru—no other course would have been consistent with Jawaharlal's principles—and has been protected ever since. The Peking regime declared promptly that the Dalai Lama was "under duress," and that the national rebellion had been contrived by foreign imperialists and "Indian interventionists." Chauvinism and xenophobia are easily aroused in China—indeed the ordinary Chinese character meaning "foreigner" contains within it the symbol of a devil: we are all "foreign devils" to the Sons of Han. And yet nobody on earth has tried harder to make friends with the Chinese than Jawaharlal has. Even when his doubts were strong he still tried, in accordance with Gandhi's principle. "If a man betrays you, trust him again," said the Mahatma, "and if he betrays you again, trust him again." This was perhaps a little easier for Mahatma than it is for other human beings.

At all events the People's Republic of China has become increasingly rude, crude and insolent with respect to India all through 1959, and incidents on those icy frontiers of the High Himalaya have shown that it respects no boundaries. When you add to this the incessant attack on Indian trade with Tibet, Indian traders, Indian currency (all guaranteed by treaty); when you consider further that public insult has become a settled part of Peking policy; and when you perceive that the Himalayan principalities of Nepal, Sikkim and Bhutan are actually threatened with military aggression at every moment, it becomes nothing short of wonderful that any semblance of diplomatic civility can still exist between India and China. If things go on like this, a severance of diplomatic relations can hardly be avoided.

Now, of course, all this has been deeply offensive to Indians of all parties, classes and races. A bitterness has been created which obliterates other distinctions and unites those who otherwise have few points of agreement. Jawaharlal's incredible skill, his immense prestige and the love the people bear him have all been hard pressed these last months because he alone, very often, seems to stand for peace with China at almost any cost. When he is forced to speak out against the pretensions of Peking (particularly on boundaries) he is cheered to the echo; and when he advises moderation, patience and restraint, his own followers are restive and ill at ease. It has been a development fraught with misery, and the end is not yet.

Politically speaking, the India-China relationship of the late summer and autumn of 1959 seems very nearly to dominate the mind of India. It certainly dominates every other consideration in foreign affairs. With Indian friends I have often noted a tendency to blame Jawaharlal at each step in the development, without any compensating suggestion of an alternative. Sometimes I have asked point-blank: "What do you want him to do? Do you want war?" Oh, no, of course not: nobody wants war! Well, what is there, short of war, which will contain the expansive megalomania of the Communist Chinese? And, supposing war comes, what are the respective strengths of China and India?

These are stark, grim matters. China has at least eight million men under arms, thus, in numbers only, being sixteen times as strong as India. Angry and bitter as the Indians may be, they have to remember such unpleasant facts.

So, as to the State of Kerala and the activities of the C.P.I., as to foreign affairs in general and a considerable number of internal matters, the passionate resentment against China which inhabits the very air of India today is a political reality of the greatest importance. It flows in upon almost every other consideration, even the most distant; it pervades the intellectual and emotional climate of the hour. It has required every resource of Nehru's personal supremacy to ride out this storm without disaster, and it casts the chilliest and most somber fog over the future.

5

Nehru's attitude toward the Communists of India has always been clear enough. They are a legal party; all parties and shades of opinion are legal. If they win enough votes they are elected. But whenever they threaten public order, the laws, the Constitution or the public interest in such matters as food supply or communications, he comes down upon them with severity. He accepts their interruptions and attacks in the central parliament as part of the day's work, and has developed a considerable resistance to those personal slings and arrows with which they assail him. This is all part of his deep belief in parliamentary democracy.

What threatens the food or life of the people is a different matter. The Communists, through their influence in the railway unions—influence, not membership—made a disruptive effort of some gravity in 1949-1950. If they had carried out their intentions there might have been a strike which imperiled the food supply of some provinces (now states) which are always running short. Reserves of food are permanently very low, often for no more than about three weeks in advance, in many parts of India. At that period and for some time thereafter a large number of Communists went to jail under the Preventive Detention Acts. The figures were not published in detail but I was told there were about 12,000 of them in prison in 1950.

In certain states, from time to time, Communists throw their organizational weight in favor of some disruptive movement which is not Communist, or even not political, in any intelligible sense. They do it for the sake of disruption and disorder, to increase a climate in which they hope to flourish. Such a movement was rife in the country districts of Hyderabad just after India took over; there was a lawless agrarianism akin to banditry, and the Communists saw advantages in giving it leadership. There were public disorders in Maharashtra not long ago when the same thing happened. The quarrels were over language, essentially, which has nothing to do with Communist doctrine, but it was a chance to make trouble and it was taken.

Generally speaking, direct action by the police maintains public order and the Detention Acts are a powerful weapon against those who would upset it. The law provides punishments for infringements after they have occurred; the Detention Acts prevent their occurring by incarceration of the ringleaders.

There is no use denying that preventive detention offends most of our democratic principles and there are few observers, Indian or foreign, who take kindly to such methods. Those directly involved in the maintenance of public order think differently. They believe that a country in the making, a country new to self-government and unity, needs special defenses against those who would disrupt and destroy it. The Chief Minister of Hyderabad had just signed four preventive detention orders when I went to see him one day last year. They were against four known Razakars (remnants of the Muslim guerrilla bands which had terrorized the state before integration).

"I am not ashamed of it and I do it when necessary," he said. He was young, incisive, sure of himself. "I know that if they had their way and went free there would be destruction and deaths."

In this same way and in this same spirit the governors and chief ministers of the Indian states have sent thousands of Communists to prison—not as Communists, but as menaces to the public order. I do not myself like this way of dealing with their activity, but when asked point-blank what else to do, I have no practical reply. Obviously there are a good many cases in India in which the full application of all the civil liberties known in England and the United States would endanger the life and livelihood of the people. In our countries we do not have famines, and there they do: that is enough to make the critic think twice.

Preventive detention orders are not absolute, of course. The state government has to "show cause" within thirteen days, but it usually can do so. A trial is entailed, dependent upon the law's delays, but often the persons detained in prison are released by executive order before any trial takes place. The judicial branch often has no chance to pronounce.

This is not at all appetizing to those who believe in the separate and independent powers of executive and judiciary in a democratic system. I know that Jawaharlal Nehru does not like the method any more than I do. He uses it or avails himself of it because the emergencies of a nation aborning are so great, the stresses and strains are so violent, the necessity for union so imperative. Under the federative system of India these special powers belong to the separate states, but obviously the Prime Minister could encourage or discourage their use: his wishes generally prevail when he chooses to express them. He has not discouraged preventive detention.

All this indicates one way, maybe the chief way, in which the Communists are kept in order—or at least from revolution—in parts of India. The method is arbitrary but reposes upon the supposition that the chief ministers of the states, who use it, and the magistrates, who keep an eye upon it, are honorable men with a just view of the state's necessities. They have to judge, sometimes within a microscopic measure of time, when the activities of known rebels will be disruptive to the state, and then to put those known rebels into jail with all celerity. They must do so without arousing too much protest, either, since, as these decades have more than proved, Indian opinion can get extremely vociferous when it is aroused.

These procedures may be distasteful to persons born in Illinois or California (or, for that matter, Devonshire or Normandy). However, it is not our problem. As observers we can see that the procedure works without any real disturbance to the ordinary population and without a sense of tyrannical excess. It has nothing to do with the Gestapo or Cheka method we have known elsewhere, which strikes in the dark and has no issue. Here all is open and known and, in fact, temporary. The governor of the state usually regrets having to use these emergency powers (invented by the British) and would curtail the detention, or soften it, whenever possible. Often the dependents of the detained person are allotted sustenance. Sooner or later the detained person is released, none the worse for wear, to resume his former activities or to refrain from them as the case may be. There is no secrecy about any of it and no human being simply vanishes without a trace, as they did so very often in Hitler's Germany and Stalin's Russia.

Communists, being by definition hard-boiled, do not make much fuss about these procedures which often confine thousands of them to jail. They know they will get out again. They also know, without a doubt, that these methods are very gentle and soft as compared to the methods they would use if they ever attained the supreme power.

When it comes to foreign affairs they are at a great disadvantage with Nehru, because he always speaks for the national interests of India and they too obviously cannot (unless, that is, you concede that the national interests of India are those of Communists everywhere, including the Soviet Union, Red China, etc., etc.—a nonsensical proposition on the face of it). Their internal argument has force with unhappy and underprivileged people: in effect they say, What has the Congress government done to destroy poverty? Where is that chicken in every pot on Sunday? The government can reply that poverty is immense, that it takes a long time to abolish it, and that great steps have already been made in that direction; but such responses do not always counteract the easy yell of protest.

In foreign affairs the Communists do not have much to offer, aside from pointing to the material achievements of the Soviet Union, along with stereotyped or mimeographed diatribes against the "imperialism" of the Americans. They can oppose the British or any connection with the British: this has gained them some votes, no doubt. Nobody knows very much about the Americans and the hullabaloo the Communists make against "American imperialism" does not signify a great deal to the people. (To the present day, travelers in out-of-the-way places in India, if they happen to be Americans, face the problem of explaining what that means: most Indians take them to be British.)

But there are numerous questions on which the Communists are at a great disadvantage in foreign affairs. They cannot possibly condemn anything done by the Communist governments of Russia, China and the satellite states. Many of the things so done are repugnant to Indian feeling, especially when wholesale brutality and violence are concerned. Russian actions in Hungary in 1956-1957 were a terrible shock to Indian opinion—worse by far, I think, than the shock given by the Anglo-French expedition to Suez.

Worst of all, naturally, is the "rape of Tibet," as the *Hindustan Times* called it (March, 1959). The Chinese invasion of Tibet in 1950 had aroused strong protest, which went into abeyance afterward with the "Five Principles" and the Chinese promise to respect the autonomy and customs of the Himalayan theocracy. When, in 1959, all pretense vanished and the Chinese troops undertook to conquer the entire Tibetan territory, Indian opinion was on fire. Mr. Nehru tried to calm it down, of course, since nothing could be done to eradicate the cause, but he also expressed the natural concern of India at the course of events. He furthermore welcomed the Dalai Lama not as a refugee, but as an honored guest of India.

The Communists in this juncture behaved in accordance with their over-all directives and ultimate aims: that is, they hailed the action of their coreligionists in China and attacked Nehru.

He replied with energy, and in terms which may cost the Communists a good deal in the coming years. He said they were "not Indians." He did not know what they were; they had non-Indian superiors and mentors; they sought non-Indian purposes. It was enough for him to say that they were "not Indians."

Episodes of a similar character have occurred before, naturally, and with all his desire to respect every shade of opinion Nehru has been forced to flame out at them. Once during the election campaign of 1952 they paraded in front of him with an array of red banners bearing the hammer and sickle.

"Why don't you go and live in the country whose flag you are carrying?" he shouted at them.

"Why don't you go to New York and live with the Wall Street imperialists?" they shouted back.

Since Nehru has not the faintest desire to live anywhere but in India, or to be anything but Indian, these taunts are meaningless. When he, on the other hand, says the Indian Communists are "not Indian," there is not a peasant in the country who will not ponder his words. He has behind him a lifetime of devotion to the country's interests, and his independence toward "the Wall Street imperialists" has been proved as often as his independence toward London and Moscow. When the Communists attack him, at any rate in foreign affairs, they are beating against an impregnable wall. They are not at all independent and he is. Strange to relate of a country so largely illiterate, this is well known in all parts of India.

6

When I am told that Nehru is "remote from politics" in the sense of internal party squabbles, I think of a long series of episodes in the past twelve years in which the contrary has been proved to me. He no longer has the time he once had for party matters—I have nagged on that point because it is all-important—but his interest never fails. He watches every by-election and every regional or provincial fight. They are many. His sense of communion with and responsibility for the Congress Party is greater today, I think, than it was about twenty years ago. He electioneers with fury and at times yields to the dominion of his party against his own wish, instinct and judgment.

Such a case occurred in the spring of 1958 when he wished to resign his office for a trial period—a period of thought and refreshment—while others tried their hand without him. The uproar in the country and even abroad was great; it looked as if everybody thought the entire machine depended on Jawaharlal. He thought this exaggerated and persisted in his intention. (I think he was supremely right.) The parliamentary party, which means the Congress Party representatives in the central parliament, held a meeting in the courtyard there and sought to dissuade him by every argument they could bring forward: duty, honor, country, of course, but underlying all this and added to it was the concept of party loyalty. The truth is that the party was frightened at the thought of having to get along without Nehru even for a trifle of time (three months had been mentioned).

I was not at the parliamentary party meeting because I was waiting at the Prime Minister's House for Mr. Nehru. His daughter Indira, Mrs. Feroze Gandhi, who has the beauty and intelligence so lavishly bestowed on that family, whiled away the time with me; we talked of remote parts of India which each of us had visited. The Prime Minster eventually came in, not from the ceremonial entrance which most of us use, but from the other side, and I could tell at a glance that he was spiritually and perhaps physically exhausted. No doubt he had totally forgotten that I was waiting for him, but it came back to him the moment he saw me (he never really forgets anything), and he began to speak to me of a book containing his remarks about democracy.

"Is it any good?" I asked.

"That is not for me to say," the Prime Minister answered in a tired and rather ironical manner. "It does contain everything I have ever said on the subject. He has put it together."

He did not tell me a word about the grueling meeting from which he had just come. I learned it an hour or so later from the press representatives who had been present. But I really did not need to be told: I knew from his manner and his words that he had again, as in so many other cases, yielded to the wishes of the majority.

He has done this a large number of times for a very simple reason, because he believes in it. He shares this political simplicity with Abraham Lincoln and Winston Churchill, both of whom used their authority to the utmost but at the same time were willing to give in when a majority had spoken. In this I do find one overwhelming difference between Mahatma Gandhi and Mr. Nehru: the Mahatma would rather retire, fast, pray, take care of lepers and educate children, than go along with a majority opinion in which he could not concur. He did so often. In a sense, he did not believe in democracy: he believed in the good and the true, with—far behind—the beautiful, which he could understand only as a function of the good and the true. If his "inner voice" had informed him that such-and-such was the good and the true, all the hundreds of millions in India could never dissuade him. Rather he hoped, by God's aid, to persuade them to his view.

Franklin Roosevelt was also one who yielded to the majority, as we saw in the case of the Supreme Court. These are believers in democracy, persons who believe that sovereignty resides in the people and that the majority of the people might, conceivably, be wrong, but must eventually come right, in the fullness of time, with the working out of the consequences. A faith in the people is probably the indispensable mainspring of political action among men who have governed great democratic states: even when they disagree with the majority's errors they will accept and serve them in the hope of ultimate correction. Even if a corrected course should never come, the believer in democracy yields just the same because he thinks that this course is far preferable to the evils of its opposite—coercion, dictatorship, tyranny.

Nehru has yielded to the majority of his party and of the country (more or less the same thing) in the same way and for the same reasons. For example, the question of languages and of linguistic states caused him much suffering some years ago, because it seemed a disruptive tendency, something inimical to the unity of India which he holds so dear. It was what the Mahatma would have called "fissiparous," using that word which, rare in the English-speaking world at large, is quite common in India. Mahatma did not live to see the demand for separate linguistic states or its fulfillment. Nehru lived through it, did not like it, and yielded to it simply because it was the wish of the majority of the people. To see India all chopped up in accordance with the linguistic differences was to postpone for a century, or perhaps more, that ideal communion which might come through a national language. And yet Nehru yielded.

One could name many other instances. He has campaigned against popular causes, such as cow protection, with vehemence, and acknowledged defeat without changing his own views. "Cow protection" is the name given in India to the laws under which, in certain provinces, the diseased and starving cows, many of them belonging to nobody, are allowed to roam at will on the ground that they are sacred. It is forbidden to slaughter them but it is not forbidden to starve and maltreat them. Jawaharlal's method of cow protection would be to round them all up and let the fittest survive, as has been done in the state of Bombay; he is interested in the improvement of breeding; he knows what can be done if science has its way. He would breed more and better cows and give the cities milk; but he has had to yield on this, hoping for a better time. (It should be explained that such questions are for the separate states, not All-India, and the campaign in which Nehru opposed the majority was in his own state of Uttar Pradesh, the former United Provinces.)

It is well known in India that some hideous villains, guilty of the exploitation of child labor and all labor, as well as unavowable transactions on the stock market and in politics, have gained merit in the eyes of an illiterate Hindu public by cow protection. It should also be noted that no reasonable human being could object to the ancient thought, deep in Hinduism, that the cow as the "foster mother of the human race" is worthy of all respect and should be cherished. The cow may even be sacred if one wishes to consider it so. However, to regard it as sacred and then leave it to decay of famine and all maladies, infecting human beings as well, is sheer nonsense and Nehru has said so. The Swami Vivekananda, apostle of Hinduism to the West and founder of the Ramakrishna Mission, agreed with him completely sixty years and more ago, although I do not know if Nehru, so penetrated by Western culture, has been aware of it.

The Prime Minister respects all the beliefs of all of the people, whether they are religious, political or social. He has no patience with superstition and has had to gulp hard many, many times when he faces it. When he went to Kerala last spring he was perfectly courteous to the Chief Minister there, Mr. Namboodiripad, the Communist leader responsible for many of the worst attacks on Nehru and his government. It must be said that at least Nehru knows what the Communists are doing and what they are after: they do not mystify him. There are elements in Indian life, which means also politics, that do mystify him and there is nothing he does in public life which arouses my admiration more than the way he deals with them. Whether it is Hindu, Muslim, Buddhist, Christian or pagan, he sees the belief and takes it for what it is, a social reality—indeed, a political reality. Such things are eminently consequential in India.

On one occasion he took me with him to Calcutta (spring, 1949) to receive the relics of the beloved disciples of the Lord Gautama Buddha. These two young men, Mogallana and Sariputta, followed the Lord Buddha in his old age and what he said to them, as well as what they said afterward, is deep in Buddhist lore. Some small bones of the young disciples were preserved in the ancient Buddhist *stupa* at Sanchi, in the principality of Baroda, where they were discovered by Sir John Cunningham in the early part of the last century and removed to the Royal Albert Museum in London. On the archaeological evidence about Sanchi, which had not been disturbed until Cunningham got there, these are almost certainly the oldest relics in the world.

After the liberation of India it occurred to the British Government, headed by Clement Attlee and Stafford Cripps, to send the relics back to India in the battleship called the *India*, which was to be given as flagship to the Indian Navy. It was an astute combination of material generosity and spiritual comprehension, for, as a matter of fact, the transfer of the relics caused a wave of intense emotion throughout the Buddhist world. They remained for an entire year in Ceylon, being venerated by the populace, and paused also for acts of worship in Siam and Burma. They were ceremonially received at Calcutta by Jawaharlal Nehru, transferred by him after three days to a Buddhist monastery, and eventually restored to the depths of the great *stupa* at Sanchi, where they will remain an object of pilgrimage while mankind endures.

The entire Buddhist world, which means most of East Asia, was represented at these ceremonies. For two days the relics were exposed in the throne room of Government House at

Calcutta, not far from the imposing, oversize portraits of King George V and Queen Mary, and just underneath the golden throne. When I got a chance I used to sit there and watch the Buddhist princes, monks and politicians at their worship. There was an atmosphere of utter sincerity. I remember well the Maharaj Kumar of Sikkim (an Oxford man) and the incommunicable devotion in his eyes as he gazed upon the small reliquary. He and the other Himalayan princes—not the Dalai Lama: he was not there—were the ones I recall best because of their worshipful submission. The monks, some of them mere children, who had come from Ceylon, Siam and Burma to sit there in attendance, had not anything like the same concentration. The political representatives—cabinet ministers and the like —came and went more briskly.

But Jawaharlal Nehru was the phenomenon of the occasion to me. He had a schedule which began at seven each morning and ended each night with some sort of official dinner—ambassadors, governors, cabinet ministers. That dinner might end when it ended, not late, of course, but long after my own poor old bones were longing for bed. During the day the string of motorcars would start out at seven or shortly afterward; there were speeches, dedications, ceremonies; we were back at Government House for lunch but then started out again. The crowds in the streets and for miles outside of Calcutta were suffocating. Even though the police stood arm to arm along the way, the mobs often broke through them in the hope of touching Jawaharlal or seeing him close. Sometimes I was actually frightened, not for me of course but for him, at these tumultuous demonstrations. I was generally placed in the car immediately following him, with the security officers and the aides-de-camp, and there were many times when the crowds had broken through with such insistence that we could make no progress at all and almost lost him. And yet he would be standing up in the open motorcar waving his hands at them or making *namasthe*, the prayerlike greeting with two hands joined. It was during these days that I decided he was to the Indian crowds what Antaeus was to the earth—the native son deriving strength from contact with the mother.

These were public and political things, of course. There was the mass meeting in the Maidan of Calcutta, half a million people perhaps, when representatives of all the free Buddhist nations spoke and Nehru finished. There were also more private and strictly religious ceremonies.

The one of these which will remain in my memory forever is the scene in the small Buddhist monastery where Nehru consigned the relics to the monks. There were not a dozen persons present. It was cool and dark. The Prime Minister sat on the floor in the middle and half a dozen monks in saffron robes encircled him. The relics were brought; he presented them; the monks prostrated themselves before them. There were some brief chants and prayers and it was over.

We had come into this place, up some stairs, from the streets boiling with an almost uncontrollable affluence of people. I had been actually dragged through the mob by the security officers in the wake of Jawaharlal. The silence and serenity of that monastic room were a startling interlude.

His behavior both in public and in private during this episode was marked by an instinctive elegance and delicacy which few men can attain when they are in touch with the intimate beliefs of others. Nehru has no attraction to relics; he is not a Buddhist; he is not given to forms and ceremonies. I think I take to all these things more naturally and easily than he does, by which I mean that I feel them without thinking, without questioning. Jawaharlal feels them humanly, that is, with relation to those other persons there present, so that he cannot be indifferent to their beliefs or hopes, but must share them for the moment. He is sympathetic not to the august tradition here worshiped, but to the human beings who feel, worship and love. He would never say one word or do one thing to injure that exquisite integument between a man and his god, whoever the man or whatever the god.

Let us be plain about this: the Prime Minister is a thoroughly rational human being. The relics of the disciples Mogallana and Sariputta no doubt meant to him precisely what they meant to me: the oldest relics on earth, venerated by some hundreds of millions of human beings. He was well aware of the importance of this occasion to India and to the Buddhist world, which means a large part of Asia. That to which he paid reverence, and to which he bowed very deeply (although he never prostrated himself), was the *faith* of mankind, not the occasion of its faith.

No doctrinaire could behave as Nehru does in such contingencies. The particular occasion was rare; it will never occur again; but it indicates the soul of the man. He certainly knew the political advantages of his course with regard to the Buddhists. This may even have had some weight in his decision to go to Calcutta and receive the relics with such reverence. But once he got into the thing his responses were all true, unsought and unthought, the instinctive answer of a son of Asia to one of Asia's greatest sons.

Buddhism makes a distinct appeal to Nehru, of course, as it did to Gandhi—not the Buddhism of the innumerable sects, but the Lord Buddha himself and his pure doctrine, or what is left of it. Many are the Indians who have regretted the conquest of Buddhism by Brahmanism centuries ago. But in contemporary fact Nehru has had more occasion to champion the Muslims—and has done so—than the Buddhists. There are few Buddhists in India now, and what he does with respect to their towering faith must affect persons outside of India more than his own people.

But the Muslims are a huge part of the population. There may be fifty-five millions of them by now. They regard Nehru with trust, affection and a species of awe. He has been their friend all their lives and they cannot think what it would be like to get along without him. They know perfectly well that he does not share their beliefs but they realize that he would go to any length to protect their right to believe as they do. He has constantly struggled for them and his most fundamental statement about India—the "secular state"—reposes upon his confidence in them. He will protect their festivals, their ceremonies and their mosques, wherever the civil power is competent to do so, and they know it.

I remember Nehru's house and garden in York Road, in New Delhi, in the bad days of 1947-1948, when horror was abroad. Even in New Delhi, usually more or less like Washington, which it physically resembles, there was fear everywhere and there had been murders in the streets. In Old Delhi, too dense with humanity, the situation was much worse. Nehru's house and garden were crammed with persons taking asylum. Every inch of the garden was occupied. He had made the army put up tents for the people who came to him; they mushroomed all over the grass. In his own house he had many. Every room was filled and they put army cots in the corridors. These were fugitives from every sort of outrage the time provided. I know that some of them were Hindus from the Punjab. I also know (and every Muslim knows) that many were Muslims from Delhi itself.

Furthermore, even in Pakistan it is understood that Nehru has befriended the Muslims whenever and wherever it was possible. They may say he does it for political reasons (I have heard brash young Pakistani say so), implying thereby that it is insincere action. I have seen enough of politics to realize that combinations of motives occur oftener than not; and I do not think any the less of Nehru's natural, instinctive and life-long friendship for the Muslims because it also happens to be good politics.

But the point is, so far as the subject of the present chapter is concerned, that it *is* good politics. It is a kind of good politics that the Communists cannot begin to touch, because it concerns a realm of being which they are, for doctrinaire reasons, obliged to treat with a contempt they can scarcely disguise.

The Muslims of India support Nehru, by and large, although communism is said to have made some inroads among their university students. The Muslims of Pakistan tend, on the whole, to put more trust in him than in other Indian leaders. These two things are vast political realities in the most practical domain; not in "religion" but in common sense. A Pathan on the Northwest Frontier, a great bearded primitive who leaned his rifle against the wall of the house while he noisily inhaled his tea, said to me in the spring of 1948, "Tell Jawaharlal that if he is in any danger we will send Pathans to Delhi to protect him." It was supposed to be a joke, of course, especially since the struggle in Kashmir was then going on between the Pathans and the Indian Army; but it was one of those jokes which point to an underlying element of truth. The Pathans would never send riflemen to Delhi, and could not if they tried; but they would want to do so. They may not precisely like "Hindu Raj," as they call it, but they regard Nehru as its least objectionable feature.

These, mind you, are primitives of the Northwest Frontier, culturally akin to Bedawin of the desert—and Professor Toynbee even calls them savages. How much more appreciative of Nehru are the city Muslims, the educated and the middle class, who have had occasion to know his concern for their welfare! Among them I doubt if he fails to win every election, although the majority may vary in their voting according to the local candidate, local situations, etc., etc. They are a very significant part of the electorate, roughly an eighth or ninth, which, however vastly outnumbered, must always make itself felt.

So far as Buddhism is concerned the political advantages of Nehru's course are not to be counted in votes inside the Indian Union; there are few Buddhists left in the land of the Buddha. But outside of India the echoes are great. They count in the Buddhist countries all around India to the north and east, especially in the Himalayan kingdoms, in Tibet and in Burma. Even as far off as Japan Nehru is regarded as one who understands and protects the Buddhist faith. This, on the rebound, has considerable effect among religious Hindus, who, without abandoning Brahmanism, have long revered the Lord Buddha and often have devoted study to his doctrine.

Here it behooves us to make another contrast between Gandhi and Nehru, who have done so many of the same things for such different reasons. Gandhi was profoundly sympathetic to Buddhists, Muslims and Christians because to a very considerable extent he, like other Hindu sages, participated in their beliefs. Many Buddhists think of him as a Buddhist, and actually once on the American radio I was trapped into an unfortunate argument with a missionary who contended that Gandhi was a Christian. The Muslims do not go so far as to believe he was one of them, but they have revered him for decades in all parts of the world. You would have found some kind of fly-specked photograph of Gandhi, generally in color, in almost any rebel nest of Muslim Asia during this century, whether it was the Algerian mountains or the mud huts of Kurdistan. Gandhi's death brought forth religious commemorations of a mass character in the Buddhist countries of Asia. He had earned this regard because he was Buddhist, Muslim and Christian, as well as being supremely Hindu. He could rationalize all of this: he had read the scriptures of all the religions and in each one he found his own beliefs reflected, boldly and beautifully stated for other peoples in other lands. Thus the Beatitudes, in the Sermon on the Mount, became a part of his nature; the resolute equality of all men before God was what he found in the Koran, and he could not even reject the doctrine of "holy war" as it was austerely expressed by the Prophet Mohammed (Upon Whom Be Peace!) As he pointed out, "holy war" was a last resort, the result of much fasting, prayer and meditation, and was historically extremely rare. As for Buddhist doctrine (that part of it which we can be fairly sure of), it was more or less what he had believed all his life anyhow.

Gandhi's religious attitude toward these psychological realities in the world was essentially different from Nehru's. Nehru respects all the beliefs without, as it seems to me, sharing them. He is aware of their separate merits and their decisive part in the evolution of human history, but I doubt if he has ever had time to read their scriptures with care or to contemplate their several truths. There is, as in everything he does, an element of sheer good manners, something of taste and breeding, something of *grand seigneur*, about the reverence he pays to the gods of others.

And a very lucky thing it is for India, I should say!

Returning, then, to this alleged "remoteness from politics," I should say that it does not exist and that those who bring the charge are in reality thinking of something else. After watching Nehru from near and far for the past twelve years and more, it would seem to me that he possesses real political genius. This does not consist merely in a grasp of his own party organization, although he has it when he needs it. It consists in a grasp of all the political realities, including a very considerable number which are beyond the comprehension of the party hacks. He believes in democracy and yields to it when he cannot persuade; he is quite capable of the necessary compromises between irreconcilables; he even makes appointments on a purely political basis when necessary. Nothing could exceed the respect and decorum he displays in the parliament, toward its members and toward the Speaker of the House. "Sir, if I may say so . . . !" How often have we heard him preface a remark with this bow to the Speaker! He endures interruptions and attacks in the House, even of the most personal nature, with a demeanor which seldom reveals the resentment or anger he must often experience. And, finally, toward the new problem presented by the Communist successes in 1957, his course is quite clear: they are on the same basis as any other legal party up to the point where they may endanger the security of the country, its constitution and its laws. When they do that, as they sometimes have done, they go to jail.

Aside from party matters, elections, parliamentary procedures and all the rest, Nehru's political power in the country really does transcend electoral democracy. It comes from dozens of extrapartisan matters which I have attempted to indicate. It comes also from plain and simple popularity, which never has been a party matter in any country. The man appeals to the people and what is more, he fascinates them. They would all rather talk about him than almost any other subject. The delicate adjustments I have mentioned, as with Muslims, are in a different category from this simple, straightforward popularity. Whenever he shows himself, which is often, we see the evidence. I think he has been in more parts of India (meaning, in the past, undivided India) than anybody else except probably Gandhi. With a smile and a wave of the hand he can throw oceanic crowds into wild enthusiasm.

Last year I sat with him at the folk dancing in the big National Stadium (formerly the Irwin Stadium) and he explained some of the dances to me. This festival is now an annual part of the celebration of Republic Week (the week around January 26). He seemed familiar with the choral dances of the villagers from every part of India. I wondered aloud: "Have you been *everywhere* in India?" He considered the question with a thoughtful smile.

"Depends what you mean by *everywhere*," he said. "If you mean every village, certainly not. No life would be long enough. But if you mean distinctive parts, areas, regions, I should think I had probably visited them all at some time or other."

Anybody who does not regard popularity of the simplest kind as a power in politics has forgotten Roosevelt, Churchill and dozens of other democratic exemplars. It may be a natural phenomenon, but it takes hard work to attain and retain. We see it at its purest form with children, soldiers, sailors, villagers, the nonpolitical, the prepolitical and the apolitical. With all of these Jawaharlal has a magic touch; I have seen it many times.

Take, for an example, the children. One of the commonplaces of campaigning in all democracies is the attention the candidates pay to children, the "baby-kissing," as we call it in America. It has become a more or less routine joke at election time; we had a thorough exhibition of it during the New York elections of 1958 when Mr. Harriman and Mr. Rockefeller were opposing candidates.

This kind of thing is simple nature to Nehru. He loves children and always has done so; they bring forth his friendliest smile; he notices them before anything or anybody, wherever he is. By instinct he wants to pat them on the head and say "hello." If they give him *namasthe*, the greeting with hands joined before the face, he solemnly gives it back to them, and if they say "*Jai Hind!*" he says it back to them again. I have watched him a considerable number of times with children so young that they could not possibly know who he was. It is quite extraordinary how they smile and beam at him. I have never seen a child who showed the slightest sign of fear before him. He has some knack of making them all, singly and collectively, accept him instantly as a friend. Once in Calcutta we went to a school for girl refugees, not, let us say, a very happy gathering by definition, but the same thing happened at once.

His affection for children has made him yield, on their account, to one or two things which are against his own rather fastidious rules. He does not like to see his own name plastered over public monuments, streets, institutions and the like. He refuses permission. Otherwise, I suppose, there would be as many streets and buildings called Nehru as there now are called Gandhi. There are two exceptions which I have seen, one in Madras and one in Kashmir, and both are playgrounds for children. In the same way the public insistence on making a national festival out of his birthday used to worry him; he has solved the problem by appointing that day (November 14th) as "Children's Day," which is now celebrated throughout India.

Say what you like, such things are immensely popular, and although they are not politics they affect politics deeply. Some of Nehru's political critics in Delhi who say he wastes time on children's art exhibits or children's hospitals or children's parties when he might be attending to the cesspools of party politics are ignoring the facts. Nehru's personal popularity is the leading political fact of contemporary India. His party profits by it exceedingly, and ought to have sense enough to realize that it transcends the party system.

With soldiers and sailors, who are as a rule not interested in politics at all, Mr. Nehru has the same personal power. They beam upon him; they love to talk about him; they listen to him with rapt attention. Once in a while they may yell "Hear, hear, sir!" in the best accents of Sandwich, but that is the only breach in their eager silence. The Indian Army and Navy are not ascetic any more than they are political. I heard a very high officer once, long ago, refer to some Congress Party ministers as "chaps in white caps." Prohibition, for example, is not applied to the armed services, and religious distinctions, although scrupulously honored, do not have the same acuity as in civil life.

All things considered, one might not expect Nehru to make the same appeal to officers and men of the armed services as he does to civilian India. He, too, is a "chap in a white cap," which nowadays means mainly the Congress Party, although it once meant nationalism. Although he is not ascetic or religious, Mr. Nehru does not drink alcohol or eat meat, out of deference to Hindu feelings in these matters. He is a cabinet minister—something which most soldiers and sailors everywhere regard as a deadly bore—and a politician. What, then, is the secret of the magic he holds for Army and Navy?

To me it appears that it comes from one very broad, deep layer of his being, which is nationalism. It is not his highest level but it is very strong, strong enough to support all the rest. The soldiers and sailors feel it, and since he, like St. Paul, is all things to all men, it is from this level of being that he speaks to them. Instinct, intuition, call it what you please: he communicates with these men on the electric channel of their unifying faith, which is in India and the future of India.

Once in the Punjab I was present at an army dinner (a regimental mess and an anniversary) when all these things were vividly apparent. After dinner he spoke at considerable length, improvising as usual—reminiscing in a rambling manner about his attitude toward the Army from his earliest days; recalling his father and what his father had said to him. "One day, you must always remember," Motilal had said, "it will be *our* Army, even though it may be British today." The sense of the Army as India's shield was put forward in these unprepared, easy, somewhat disconnected remarks more cogently than could have been done by any prepared oratory. I saw tears glistening in some very martial eyes. To these men and their like since then, Nehru's word is the law and the prophets. Again it is one of those nonpolitical facts which are stronger than politics.

To sum the whole matter up, Nehru may be somewhat less of a politician than the late Sardar Patel, who held the nationwide party organization in the palm of his hand. And yet even Patel knew the facts: "They come for Jawahar, not for me," he said of the immense crowds once in his own Bombay. It is also true that Nehru does not have time any more for the details of party work every day. But by and large there is no man in India with a keener political sense, as he has repeatedly shown in emergencies, or with a deeper sense of responsibility toward his own party in the democracy. If he finds wider and deeper sources than the party machine for his own strength, it is because his nature, and the people's, would have it thus: such sources are older than parties and will outlast them. In turn he supports his own party with all the energy thus acquired, and it has every reason to be grateful to him. What may happen in his absence is another matter, but so long as he is there the political equilibrium will be maintained.

VI *Sovereign States and Mother Tongues*

WHEN INDIA achieved independence in 1947 it contained not only the great unit known as British India, with a unified civil administration and democratic institutions well started on their way, but also 562 separate states linked to the British crown but not with each other. The central government at Delhi exerted a varying degree of influence or authority over these states, depending on circumstance. There were also special "agencies" for frontier districts, northwest and northeast, and for specified tribal areas remote from the center and from the general life of civilized India. We can say *grosso modo* that the country to which Great Britain yielded total freedom in 1947 contained about six hundred units of different sizes, shapes and characters. This is not counting Burma and Ceylon: it refers only to the old, undivided India, now Pakistan and India.

Leaving out the special agencies for tribes and frontiers, the two new countries into which the superpeninsula was cut had to come to terms with the 562 princely states. These were all technically sovereign but bound to the "paramountcy," as it was called, of the British crown. The wealth, powers, capacities and intentions of the individual sovereigns were as different as it is possible to imagine. Some were great kings with wide dominions; some bore great titles upon only a few square miles of territory. By and large, at least in theory, they were all autocrats with none to say them nay. Their territories, large or small, were their personal property. They taxed at will and spent the taxes as they pleased. Occasionally the central government at Delhi, using the paramount sovereignty of the British Crown, would intervene in some state or other and depose the ruler when he abused his powers too much. This did not often happen; as a rule the separate sovereigns had a free hand. They were Hindu, Muslim or Sikh by religion, and so far as the Sikhs in the Punjab were concerned the princes and their subjects were largely of the same faith. But through the long centuries of Indian history the Hindu and the Muslim had become so mixed up that in many cases the ruling house might be of one faith and the majority of its subjects of another.

These inconsistencies were bad enough, and were added to by the inconveniences of geography. But actually in their performance as governments the independent states exhibited the most striking differences of quality and result. There were some, as we have seen in speaking of Kashmir, in which government consisted of the unmitigated whim of the ruler. There were others such as Mysore where generations of enlightened and benevolent princes had endowed the country with roads, schools, irrigation and electricity well in advance of most districts in British India. I know of no dynasty in any country which has more legitimate reason for pride than that of the ancient house of Mysore. It should be proud (and I know the Maharajah is, in his personally modest manner) because what it did for the people of that country could so easily have been sidestepped, avoided altogether or done in a desultory and half-hearted way. The princes could have spent their money entirely on diamonds and elephants, as other princes did. They did not lack for gems or beasts, either (I saw more elephants there than anywhere else), but they were decades ahead of their contemporaries in the intelligent effort to increase the welfare of their subjects.

However, Mysore is a glowing exception. So is Baroda in one way, because of a single enlightened and energetic prince in the nineteenth century, and so is Travancore in another. In Travancore, as we have observed, accessibility to the sea brought in a very early and continuous missionary activity which gave a fillip to education, and the princely house had only to encourage and extend it. Cochin is much the same. These are very large countries with, relatively speaking, large incomes. But when we come to Hyderabad, the largest of all, with the largest income, we see the precise opposite! The Muslim princes of that dynasty, with a Hindu majority among their subjects, gave to jewels and palaces the vast treasures that should have been spent upon schools and roads and water supply and public services in general. They embellished their capital, it is true, just as they did their numerous palaces, but the villages of the land were left to toil and starve. In the recent reorganization of the states of India, certain administrative lines were redrawn and some minor parts of Hyderabad went to Mysore, just as some parts of Bombay province went to Hyderabad. In the new additions to Mysore (the Hyderabad districts) it was found that every material condition in the villages was far below Mysore standards. It will take years to bring these new additions up to the level of their Mysore neighbors in such simple matters as water supply and communications. Such it is to be governed by "the richest man in the world," as the Nizam of Hyderabad always used to be called.

And if there can be such differences between great states like Mysore and Hyderabad, it is easy enough to imagine what the whimsies and anomalies were among small, irresponsible and vainglorious princes of lesser territories. There were many among them who could farm out whole clusters of villages to the nefarious middleman for years at a time so as to get one big emerald to wear in a hat. The absurd cruelty of such arrangements in the middle of the twentieth century often aroused Nehru to bursts of wrath. It seems strange now that the British permitted the system to endure for so long. They did so, it seems, chiefly because they assumed for about a century that the Indian princes were their best and most loyal friends in the country. They always had plenty of trouble with British India but the princely states were stagnant backwaters; it was easier to let them be.

The new India and the new Pakistan could not let them be. For Pakistan there was not much trouble; a few states only were involved. India inherited the greater part of the problem, of which Hyderabad was the biggest anomaly of all, claiming its independence right in the center of the Indian Union. Every state was supposed to adhere to one or the other of the new countries and most of them did during the spring and summer of 1947. In so doing they brought their headaches with them, their unbalanced budgets and tangle of debts, their backward populations and spoiled, luxurious rulers.

There was really only one way to deal with this situation but the astonishing thing is that it was taken. It worked and it has been a resounding success. If you face such a hodgepodge of disparate structure and have to take over responsibility for it the only thing you can intelligibly do is to wipe it all out and start over again. That was done. It was done to a very great extent within one year of the independence of India and the process was complete by the time of the proclamation of the Republic (1950). You might say that it was a species of slum clearance. The ramshackle principalities were merged into bigger units, their rulers were pensioned off, all their public services came under organized control and their people were admitted at last into the equal citizenship of the Indian Union, exposed to the novelties of the vote and the regularized tax, the free press and right of assembly which characterize democracies.

Credit for the first and most decisive stage of integration, that which merged hundreds of states into large units and made them equal parts of India, must go to Sardar Vallabhbhai Patel. This old friend and adherent of Gandhi, who had come to him as a volunteer in early days, was an astute and successful lawyer. He adopted the Gandhi rules and wore homespun, was a vegetarian, recited the *Gita*, etc., etc., all during the great Gandhian revolution in India. Before that he had been as clever a lawyer as, for example, Mohammed Ali Jinnah, the founder of Pakistan. Patel organized the Congress Party as it had never been organized before, and when independence came he was a past master in the manipulations of local politics. Very often he has been compared to a "boss of Tammany Hall," the Democratic Party machine in New York City, because his way of rewarding ambitions, conciliating factions and soliciting votes was not dissimilar. He "paid off" or punished, as the case might be, in accordance with the standards of party loyalty. But he was also a very sincere adherent of Gandhi's, and although his notions of Gandhian principles permitted him to favor capitalist development —whereas Nehru's notion of the same principles allowed for socialist development—there never has been any doubt in my mind that Patel was a sincere patriot, devoted to the national interest above all things.

I knew him a little, lunched in his house and talked with him at length, during the period which followed Mahatma's assassination. When I returned to India the next year, the first anniversary of the assassination, he greeted me as an old friend. His remarkable intelligence was utterly different from Nehru's, was aimed in a different direction and contained different elements from the start, but they were united in a concern for the freedom of India. Together they constituted a complementary force or combination of forces, and although they were often at loggerheads on specific issues, they supported each other on the vital necessities for India.

Thus when Patel, as Minister for the States, undertook the immense task of reorganizing the Indian princely states, he had Nehru's support at every step. He had also the advantage of a notably alert and vigorous chief of staff in this enterprise, Mr. V. P. Menon, who has since published two volumes of reminiscence (with documentation) covering the critical period. And, ahead of all of them, the last British Viceroy, Earl Mountbatten of Burma, made it plain to the Indian Chamber of Princes that the independence of India was going to be absolute, so far as Great Britain was concerned—that "paramountcy" would automatically lapse, that they would then no longer have any relationship to the British Crown, that they could expect no British assistance in any attempt to impede these arrangements, and that they must therefore either "go it alone" or adhere to one of the two new countries before August 15, 1947.

Almost all of them made their choice in good time and negotiated the terms of union within a few months. These negotiations, so far as India was concerned, were in the hands of Patel and his lieutenant, V. P. Menon.

Patel combined them geographically, at first, with some thought for communal (religious) differences. What seemed rather drastic in 1948 seems ordinary common sense today. In some parts of the country there were almost innumerable small states, forming a patchwork on the land: such were the little principalities in the Gujerat regions north of Bombay. They could all be lumped together with no loss of local pride. In the Punjab there were Sikh states like Kapurthala, Patiala and the rest, which could most reasonably be combined into one unit. Elsewhere a princely state could be added on to this province or that, and of course the very largest princely states could be left, for the time being, as units, although submitting their administration to the central control.

This involved some complicated financial arrangements: the princes had to be pensioned, their debts assumed, their treasuries and tax systems absorbed by the central authority. A batch of new, unfamiliar names sprang up to indicate some new states thus brought into being: Rajasthan, Vindhya Pradesh, Madhya Bharat and P.E.P.S.U. They were geographic combinations for the most part, contiguous territory, although P.E.P.S.U. (Patiala and East Punjab States Union), for the brief period of its existence, was also considered under the communal aspect as a predominantly Sikh state.

That Patel brought all this about within a year without public disorder or rebellion in the greater part of princely India was a dazzling achievement. It had not been foreseen; indeed many wise and great men, including Winston Churchill, had long declared the problem of the sovereign princes to be an insuperable obstacle to Indian union and freedom. Patel settled all that. With the single exception of Hyderabad, which had to be integrated by force, the main body of the Indian Union came into being easily, quickly, as if by nature. Kashmir, a very special case, remains special to this day: we have seen how it differs from all others.

Patel died in December, 1950, three years minus a month after the assassination of Gandhi. The states he so brilliantly combined out of the outworn feudalisms did not long survive him, but not because of anything invalid in their original creation. They succumbed and were rearranged in accordance with a new principle which grew up after independence and involved all the twenty-six states of free India, old and new, in a tumultuous debate. The new principle, which has brought about a redrawing of frontiers in the general equilibration of claims, is that of language.

2

The princely states were pretty artificial, after all; many were relatively recent; some existed merely as rewards for service to the British Crown. They were personal, feudal and transitory. Language, however, is a fundamental element in any society, and many or most great nations in history have found it their principal element of union. It is far more vital than race, ancestry or religion in the Western world: France is a country inhabited by Frenchmen, who are French mainly because French is their mother tongue. They may be of all origins, all anthropological measurements and all religions; the language makes them French.

In India this is not so and never has been. There are hundreds of languages in the vast peninsula, and twenty-six of them are recognized as the chief languages of the country. Race and religion have proved to be elements of union more powerful than language. A Hindu knows his fellow Hindu not by language—often they may have none in common; often they may have only English, the language imported by the temporary ruler—and yet Hinduism is a tremendous bond. So is Islam. The Indian national revolution depended for its success on such bonds as these, in addition to the natural desire of all peoples for independence: the nation, so to speak, felt itself to be a nation for other reasons, and the national revolution was brought about with English as its principal linguistic instrument.

It almost seems as if the language difficulty had not been fully realized during the Gandhian years from 1919 to 1947. All thoughtful men were aware of it; much was written and spoken on the subject; but it is only in recent years that it has become obsessive. Gandhi himself tried to learn something of the main Indian languages. His own mother tongue was Gujerati, from which it was not difficult to pass to a simplified Hindi, or Hindustani-Urdu, understood throughout most of the north. He had considerable trouble with southern languages, however, since they are totally different, and only made a little headway with Tamil, the language of Madras. With this as with other subjects (such as yoga exercises) he found that he had not time enough to go thoroughly into the matter and so resolutely abandoned the effort; he had no use for smatterings. He was content —had to be content—with English as the linguistic base of his life's work.

Rajaji, whose ideas we have discussed earlier, was of course a Tamil-speaker; Tamil is the mother tongue of the old province of Madras and of the new Tamil state of Madras. This meant that he relied upon English in his communications, written or spoken, with his colleagues from other parts of India: his endless talks with Gandhi, through the three decades of utmost significance, were in English.

As for Nehru, we have already related that he talks English in his sleep: we have it on the testimony of his fellow prisoners, chiefly the late Maulana Sahib and also Mahadev Desai. His mother tongue is Hindustani-Urdu in its purest form, as it is spoken in Allahabad, his birthplace. It was the great language of north India and was rapidly spreading when partition came: now it is diverging into two separate languages, since in Pakistan they try to Persianize or Arabize it as much as possible, and in India they endeavor to Sanskritize it, to make it "purer."

Thus, to take only the three highest examples of the national leadership, they had three different mother tongues: Gandhi's, Nehru's, Rajaji's. They had one *lingua franca*, if you choose to employ that rather denigratory term, which was English.

However, English was by no means a *lingua franca* to that generation. It seems to be becoming a *lingua franca* nowadays because a larger and larger number of people speak it more and more badly. Moreover, most of the English-speaking people of India nowadays use the language only with each other: they no longer have to deal with English people very much, and certainly not in government, parliament, courts or civil service.

In Gandhi's generation and those just after it (such as Nehru's) a perfectly free and easy, natural English, an unreflecting English, was the rule. Gandhiji himself had no trace of any particular regional or national accent, although his way of talking was all his own. In his deliberate, thoughtful manner, choosing each word, he talked English as his natural tongue: not his mother tongue but the language he had most occasion to use throughout his life. Nehru, of course, talks like an Englishman. Rajaji never had a moment's hesitation with syntax or vocabulary, and writes singularly clear, almost classical English, but he does possess a slight south-Indian accent in speaking.

In linguistics it is most important to differentiate between the layers of consciousness to which the language applies and within which it functions. The United Nations, in facing this problem —for example in Trieste—adopted a rather useful set of distinctions. In their testings of that multilingual area they classified the results in three groups: the mother tongue, the language of the school, the language of the market place.

For example, in certain areas of Trieste, the city and its environs, we may find that the language of the school is standard or classical Italian (roughly speaking, the language of Dante). We may find that the language of the market place is a Triestino dialect which is a cross between Italian and Croatian. We may find that the mother tongue is the standard or current version of Serbo-Croat. All these are very different and a person speaking only one of them could not understand the other two. Persons in Trieste, subjected to this pattern of linguistics, are obliged to communicate in all three, which means that their mastery of any one is thereby limited.

The psychological effect of two-language instruction in schools, such as obtained in India and still does, has not been studied in any scientific manner. Gandhi found it very inhibiting in his childhood; it vastly increased his shyness and his fear of school. He started in Gujerati and then moved on to English. In those days they started English very early, generally at the age of seven, and the proportion of instruction in English increased as the pupil advanced, until in the secondary schools it became predominant. In colleges and universities English was, and still is, the language of instruction in all subjects. When I went to the Hindu University of Benares some years ago I found that even Sanskrit language and literature, as well as Hindu philosophy, were taught in English, that is, with English as the medium of instruction.

What all this does to the psychological aptitudes of the student at different stages must be guessed; we do not know. But we can say with some assurance that the United Nations classifications, languages of the mother, the school and the market place, do not weigh in India as they weigh in even the most mixed-up areas of Europe. In Europe the language of the mother tends to prevail, not only in childhood but throughout life, and is recognized as determining nationality. In India the language of the mother, although important to the child, often fades into disuse later on, especially if it is a strictly regional tongue. Its place is taken by the market languages (Urdu being the most widespread) or the school language which is, for India at large, English.

This has been the situation for many decades, with individual variations. There were a considerable number of eminent Indians during the Gandhian generation who had used English so constantly, and had so thoroughly forgotten their particular mother tongue or market tongue, that they really had no other language. They were as English, linguistically, as it is possible to be, using that language in their most intimate discourse, in the family for instance, or in personal and private papers such as diaries. Mohammed Ali Jinnah, the founder of Pakistan, was an extreme example. He knew very little Urdu and none of the other languages of the country he had created. Once he was compelled to pray publicly in a mosque and had no choice but to do so in English.

Bombay, the city and the province (now state), speaks Gujerati or Mahratti as mother tongues and market tongues. The vast agglomeration of Calcutta speaks Bengali. These languages all have their different scripts and their distinctive syntax. It is not at all surprising that the many leaders of India who came from those two cities were compelled to rely on English for their whole public careers: and among them were Tilak and Jinnah, on one side, and Tagore and Das on the other.

This bilingual leadership of a multilingual nation did very well for fifty or sixty years, and although there were advocates of a single national language, there seemed no great urgency in the matter until independence came. Then, with gathering impetus, and particularly in the last five or six years, the question of all these tongues became important to pride, to prestige, and to politics. And, as seems natural enough in retrospect, the neglected mother tongue asserted itself over both market tongue and the language of the school.

It may be seen that the movement for the independence of the mother tongues, followed by the demand for statehood based on mother tongues, would follow freedom. Freedom must, by any definition, imply the use of one's own language in public life. But it might not have caught the Indian imagination so swiftly, we think, if freedom had not been accompanied by a well-nourished and organized movement to make Hindi the supreme national language. (The official guidebooks, by the way, issued for the use of tourists, still say that Hindi is "the" national language, whereas there are twenty-six.)

Hindi is a swept and garnished version of the old Hindustani-Urdu which was once the language of the whole north and some of the central areas. Up to the time of partition and independence it was making great headway, just by its own natural momentum, and was spreading outside its earlier boundaries. The moment it acquired so many eager adherents, wishing to substitute it for all others, it also acquired a great many opponents. The movement for the separate mother tongues got its start in the south, but there were similar movements in west and east, with Bombay and Calcutta as the centers. Indeed Bengal had always been a linguistic unit and its distinct language was never really threatened; but it had great influence to bring, in a sympathetic manner, on the demands of other linguistic areas for unity.

Thus the 1950's saw a rising demand for new states based on language—the language, mind you, of the mother: the traditional, historic language of an area as taught by mother to child. If the great regions had been impervious to the movements of population for the past century this might have seemed simple enough, but actually no linguistic area today is without large minorities which came from elsewhere and use (from mother to child) a different tongue from that traditional in the region. Even if you granted language as the basis for statehood you had to consider where it began and where it ended. Where does Tamil begin and where does it end, for instance? There are

Tamils all over India, with large concentrations in industrial areas. And Bombay—well, what a mixture!

The practical difficulties of drawing state lines on linguistic considerations are obvious enough, but the theoretical ones are worse. In Gandhi's generation anything which tended to divide India was regarded as retrogressive and undesirable. Now certainly language, considered as the basis for a political state of semisovereign powers, is a "fissiparous" force in the earlier Gandhian sense. It tends to emphasize division and difference. As such it was theoretically undesirable, but it has come to pass just the same because in recent years it has been shown that the people of south, east and west want it. Nehru himself, who has no wish to encourage "fissiparous" tendencies, yielded to it as being the will of the democracy.

3

So the States Reorganization Commission made its final report to Nehru in 1955 and he submitted it to the people of the various states for debate. It set off a period of the liveliest dispute on languages and state frontiers. In some areas, as may be remembered, there were actual riots on the language question (riots in which the Communists delighted to aid the disorder, although what they care about language one cannot imagine). In the end, the frontiers were redrawn and the new India consists of only fourteen states and seven special territories administered from the center at Delhi. The centrally administered territories are frontier and tribal regions not yet equipped to govern themselves; the fourteen states have been created out of all the old provinces and regions, with geography and economics in mind but, on the whole, with language as the primary determinant. These states are Andhra, Assam, Bihar, Bombay, Jammu-Kashmir, Kerala, Madhya Pradesh, Madras, Mysore, Orissa, Punjab, Rajasthan, Uttar Pradesh and West Bengal. Each of them has a constitutional governor—that is, a sort of viceroy, above the political battle although often an old member of the Congress Party—and a working chief minister and cabinet responsible to the legislature. That is, each state reproduces the constitutional apparatus of the center at Delhi, which in turn reproduces that of the sovereign and prime minister in London: it is the system inherited from England. In all of these states the only prince who acts as constitutional governor is the Maharajah of Mysore (Sir Jaya Chamaraja Wadiyar), whose personal popularity in his large kingdom is an element of stability. His family, the house of Wadiyar, originated in remote antiquity; in modern times it has been distinguished for benevolence and public spirit; thus the Maharajah, himself a very exceptional person, has proved to be the only sovereign left in India who fits into the new scheme of things.

There was considerable turmoil over this reorganization of states both before and after it went into effect on November 1, 1956. The redrawn frontiers transferred some areas from one old province to another new state, chiefly on the basis of language, and some jealousies ensued. There were more serious troubles in the State of Bombay, with its rival languages (Gujerati in the north and Mahratti in the south). Some historic units vanished into larger classifications with new and unfamiliar names. There was considerable administrative readjustment, although not so much as you might expect because English was, and remains, the chief administrative language for all the states. And, of course, there were some who declared themselves dissatisfied with the settlement.

Now, to me the odd thing is that none of this seems to have made much difference. That is, language may be "fissiparous" but at this present moment it does not seem to have created any fissures. India is more united today than it was when I did my first fairly extensive traveling there in 1948-1950. The disturbances over language were chiefly in Bombay, which, as we know, is bilingual at the base and trilingual at the top. Even in Bombay the excitement has all died down. In the other states an easy accommodation has been made between the mother tongues and English. The only loser has been Hindi, which, under the present arrangements, is not likely to become the national language for many decades, if ever.

What I found in the southern states, the focus of the language agitation, was that English continued to be very much the language of government. In the legislatures English is commonly used, and in most state capitals I was told that the proportion of legislators using it for ordinary debating purposes was about two-thirds. The other third employs the state language, whatever it may be. Kerala reverses the proportion; Malayalam, its state and regional language, predominates. Madras uses more Tamil than English but both are current. In other words, once the linguistic state or linguistic unit is accepted, things go on just about as before.

The four main southern languages are Tamil, Telugu, Kanarese and Malayalam. There are others, but these are the old mother tongues sanctioned by many centuries of usage. They are, as we have often remarked, quite different from the northern languages based on Sanskrit. Their script is totally different and so is their sound; a foreigner can perceive little more than that; he must take the scholars' word for the rest. The scholars say that these non-Sanskrit languages, "Dravidian" in origin (that is, native to India before the Aryans brought Sanskrit with them from Central Asia), are as alien to the northern tongues as they are to English or French.

I have pondered over their scripts in an ignorant way, traveling through the whole south last year. It so happened that a Madras publisher (on a grant from the Ford Foundation) was putting out a number of foreign books in these languages just as I was there. A book of mine, a small life of Gandhi in a biographical series originating in New York, came out in all four of the chief southern languages at that time. I was given copies and tried to compare the characteristics of their identical text. It seemed to me that the four scripts, Tamil, Telugu, Kanarese and Malayalam, were quite distinct. A main difference visible to any eye was the degree of circularity or angularity in the letters: one of them (Malayalam) looks like scroll writing. Obviously the demand for independence in language on the part of these states is based on script as much as sound: if a schoolboy must learn one of these scripts, as well as English, he does not want to be saddled with another as well. And yet some of the scripts come rather close to each other even in appearance, so that the suggestion given by an examination of them is that someday they might cohere into one. In actual sound the gulf between three of the languages (Tamil, Telugu and Kanarese) is not so great. Beyond mere sound, a foreigner must rely upon what he is told, which depends, very often, upon who does the telling. Language enthusiasts tend to emphasize the differences, but some judicious informants have told me that these may be diminished with time and the intermingling of populations.

Certainly English comes out the winner in all this conflict of language. There are supposed to be something like four million English-speaking persons in India. My impulse, on hearing this figure for the first time, was rather like Mark Twain's when he was told that there were fifteen million Jews in the world. "Nonsense!" said Mark Twain, "I personally know more than that." Of course the various levels of English spoken in India must be taken into account, and no reasonable person would expect the same *kind* of English from a roomboy in Kashmir as from an editor or teacher in Bombay. But the fact remains that a vast number of persons do speak, read and write English; an even vaster number speak it to some extent, and even understand it, without reading or writing. The principal newspapers in all the great states are in English; the central government, perforce, is operated almost entirely in English; the courts and universities cannot do without English. In local government, as I discovered this past year, many persons prefer to use English rather than the local language, the mother tongue, and this in spite of the fact that both are known.

In other words, the central government at Delhi is compelled to use English because it is the only language common to representatives from all parts of India, the only one that has a chance of general comprehension. This is obvious.

What was not obvious until it happened was that even in government at the state level, where as the result of a great debate the mother tongues have been made not only official (which they always were) but the actual basis of the state, English still wins. In other words, if you are a representative in the state legislature of Mysore you can talk Kanarese, which is the language of the state; you can talk English, or you can talk any other recognized Indian language at the risk of not being understood. In fact most representatives talk English.

Put it another way: English wins at the center (Delhi) because there are too many Indian languages, too many representatives who understand only their own mother tongue *and* English, but no other Indian tongue.

English wins at the state level for quite a different reason: here there are really only two languages to choose from, the local mother tongue and English, both of which are understood, and yet English is chosen as being more suited to public affairs and parliamentary procedure.

What it comes to, I think, is that English is no longer really a "foreign language" in India. For many generations the entire educated class has depended upon the English language for its commerce with the world at large. It was a foreign language a century ago, and was learned originally as a means of entering government service or dealing with the British government. It has gone far beyond that now. There has evolved a rather distinct Indian version of English, as distinct in accent and terminology as the languages of Australia, New Zealand and the United States, but still English. This is the language spoken in innumerable government offices, schools and law courts throughout the land. The actual files for generations back are all in English. The millions who use this language, which we may call Indo-English, have never been in England and many of them may never have spoken to an Englishman, but their daily linguistic instrument is English just the same.

Among well-to-do people, who send their children to expensive English schools either in India or in England, a much more European accent and vocabulary may be heard; often the language they speak is indistinguishable from that spoken in England. I know a considerable number of cases in which English actually becomes the mother tongue. My own acquaintance is not enormous but affords many examples of husband and wife who speak to each other always in English and whose children are brought up with English as the mother tongue. This occurs especially when husband and wife have different Indian mother tongues: when the girl from Madras marries the boy from Delhi, for instance.

In the existing situation I do not see that English will be superseded; it is more likely to be extended. We may look in vain for any parallel to this obstinacy of fact over theory, of practice over desire. Sometimes the linguistic situation of China is brought into comparison, but quite falsely: the many dialects of China, sometimes mutually incomprehensible, were always united by the common ideograph or picture script. All have the same roots and all are susceptible of amalgamation to the official Mandarin language (itself a dialect of classical Chinese). English was used in China, too, for practical communication between people with no other language in common; I have no doubt that it still is; but Chinese can be welded into one language in time because it possesses a common origin and a similarity of structure in all its variants. This is not true in India.

In other cases, Ireland and Israel being two, a determined effort has revived ancient, ancestral languages as the alternative to English. In still others, particularly in Africa, English has remained in government after independence, but only for the sake of official convenience: it is likely to diminish or even disappear in time, except as a diplomatic accomplishment. Wherever there is one established mother tongue, a natural national language, English must have that fate, it would seem in common sense. It must become what French is to us, a second language, one we enjoy and appreciate to the utmost, but in which we do not conduct our ordinary daily affairs of commerce, industry or state.

One more false parallel must be cited to show how unique the Indian case really is. In history we are familiar with a number of states where the ruling classes habitually spoke a language different from that of the people. Such was Russia under the Czars for a good many decades, before the Slavophile movement made the Russian language popular even among aristocrats. The language of the court and aristocracy was French. Many of these people spoke only French to their children and to each other; they wrote letters and diaries in French. But never, at any moment, was French the language of the schools or the law courts. It was a class language but a private one, not public. We know from Tolstoy that a good many Russian aristocrats could hardly speak Russian at all, and yet if they were haled before a court of law they had to do the best they could at it.

A class language is hardly more than a "fashionable" language. When I went to Warsaw years ago I discovered that French was the language of the "fashionable" people there, even with each other. Before the unification of Italy French was the language of the aristocracy, as it was also in Germany. Not so long ago French was the usual language of the upper class throughout the Middle East. But never, in any of these cases, did it become the language of the state. In India it may be said that English is the language of the state.

No other country is in this situation. Switzerland is trilingual, of course, but no one of the three languages is supreme, and a larger nation would find it very difficult to conduct all its business in so many tongues. Ireland uses both Gaelic and English, the Philippines use English and Tagalog. But India is a multilingual nation employing English as the medium of public affairs, and as such is unique.

4

To hear some Indians talk you would think that this special condition was a grave danger to all and sundry, a peril to unity, a cloud across the future. A good many heated speeches have been made in parliament on the subject as well as in the provincial legislatures. Those who get so excited in the matter are forgetting that in fact India has existed on a multilingual basis for some dozens of centuries already, and still possesses one of the most distinct national characters to be seen on earth. Evidently the Indian nation does not depend on language and probably never will.

It is a relief to find that Nehru is quite philosophical about this. He would prefer a single national language, of course, and Hindi is the candidate because it is spoken by more people than any other; but he knows a fact when he sees one, and he believes that the people's will should be carried out whenever it can be ascertained.

"We at the center," he says equably, "were perfectly willing to let the states have their own way in this matter, but we wanted to be quite sure what it was that they wanted."

This is his way of referring to the procedure after 1955, when he submitted the States Reorganization program to public debate and vote. It was a glowing example of his deference to the popular will, even though at the time he was under criticism for not carrying out his own.

And in general it is plain that since the Constitution of India came into effect in 1950 Nehru has been scrupulous in sustaining it. There have been a fair number of amendments to the Constitution (six in five years); to get the land reform enacted, for instance, required an amendment. But so far as the separate states are concerned Nehru and his central government have been anxious not to infringe upon their rights or privileges. This was out of a natural concern for the establishment: if a nation has a new constitution of a federal nature, that nation wants to give it time to grow, to become solidified, to become a part of the consciousness of the citizen. Interference with the states would not serve these purposes.

The state structure went through the two great phases we have indicated: first, the amalgamation and integration of all the princely states into the Indian Republic, and second, the redrawing of frontiers in the States Reorganization plan, largely on the linguistics basis. Once the result was achieved Nehru did his best to see it maintained without interference.

Sometimes it has not been easy. In previous chapters I have tried to show how Kashmir, in its anomalous position, with Indian troops occupying most of the state, has been given something approaching autonomy. This may be a case of leaning over backward. Kerala in recent years, with its Communist administration, invited special attention from the central government as well as from foreigners; its state rights were not infringed upon, and its only genuine clash with Delhi has been with the Supreme Court over the constitutionality of the education bills. By and large every state has made its own way under the law, dependent on the center for a great deal of assistance in public works and food supplies, but locally self-governing, speaking the language of choice and maintaining all the regional or inherited distinctions. It makes a pattern the world has not seen before but it is nonetheless valid for that.

VII *Critics, Colleagues, Friends*

OF THE ORIGINAL Indian cabinet as it took office in 1947, only two men remain—Nehru himself and the Minister of Railroads, Mr. Jagjivan, who is an untouchable. Numerous reorganizations and individual changes have been made through the years with the result that the main constant factor appears to be the Prime Minister—that and the fact that all these cabinets belong to the Congress Party and are based on its large majority in the country and in parliament.

Many changes were the result of critical outbursts in parliament and in the country. Nehru is not immune from the storms which occasionally assail all democratic leaders, and he must yield to them. Such a storm was that which unseated his Finance Minister, T. T. Krishnamachari, in 1958, on the ground that he had not been vigilant enough about the investments of the new All-India Insurance Trust, controlled by his ministry. "T.T.K.," as he was called, was not held personally responsible for any wrongdoing but had to go just the same, and was succeeded by Mr. Morarji Desai.

Such a storm is remarkable for the freedom with which all politicians speak at its height: they seem to have neither fear nor caution. They are many in number and take comfort from that fact. Between storms they are not anxious, individually, to put forward any very trenchant critique of Nehru. All of them more or less belong to his party and his parliamentary majority.

Whatever they may say in private, they are always aware of this fact in public—and perhaps of the party discipline to which they might be subjected.

There are a few general remarks to be made about all the critics, first and most important being that none of them seems to want Nehru to quit his office. Their object has been to influence his thinking or to deflect his course, but not to displace him. Another notable generality is that most of the criticism which has any force, body or penetration is made in private. Hardly anybody except a Communist would care to get up in public and make a fundamental attack on Nehru. Other men in public life feel, with reason, that his popularity is unassailable; an attack on him would rebound upon the attacker. A third generality is that no Indian critic to whom I have listened in all these years questions Nehru's good will or intentions; they direct their attacks upon what they call his mistakes, the things which they themselves would have done differently. They perceive deficiencies in his intellect or character; they say he does not understand this or that; but they never imply or suggest that he is not expending his best effort for the country.

There are some broad categories of these critics: the Communists are at one extreme and the Hindu traditionalists at the other. Aside from Hindu traditionalists there are a good many modern Hindus who dislike Nehru's patience with Pakistan and his benevolence toward the Muslims at large. Many distrust his friendliness toward England and the United States; many more are afraid of his friendliness toward Russia and China. I know of one high-minded and well-intentioned person—he comes to see me every time I go to Delhi—who honestly believes that Nehru's course has encouraged the Communists and made possible their recent successes at the polls. When I look back upon the years I have known him, it seems to me that Mr. Nehru has been about as lavishly criticized by his own people as any democratic leader of whom I have knowledge. The fact that most of these adverse observations are made in private talk does not alter the fact that they are extremely numerous. He does not take a single decisive action without arousing a ground swell of opposition.

Public opposition is another matter. Rajaji may speak adversely on certain subjects—language and military expenditure, for two—but he does not oppose the Prime Minister or suggest that he depart; he only attacks definite strands of policy. Most Congress Party members do not wish, or do not dare, to say so much. So far as loyal opposition is concerned, the main voice is that of Jayaprakash Narayan, the leader of the Socialist Party. He speaks up without the slightest hesitation and, oddly enough, his voice is heard. Perhaps because there are so few in his position—undoubted loyalty to India combined with unceasing opposition to the government—everything Jayaprakash says is widely reported in the press and arouses comment.

Jayaprakash has had a career of considerable interest and it is far from finished. He was educated in America (at three Midwestern universities in succession) and on his return to India became a member, and then a leader, of the Socialists inside the Congress Party. At independence he took his group out of the Congress and has been in opposition ever since, although his actual part in politics is rather nebulous. He more or less renounced political life for some years to follow Vinoba Bhave, the saintly Gandhian who roams India asking landlords to give part of their land to the poor peasants. This, Vinobaji's own land reform, is known as the Bhoodan movement, and the word "Bhoodan" means literally gift land. Millions of acres (up to now, I think, about seven) have been collected in this manner but it has been seen that a great deal of organization would be needed to make use of it. Such things as fertilizer, tools, irrigation and houses are not part of the gift, and often the land itself is not choice. It was hoped that Jayaprakash, in his devotion to the movement, might provide the necessary organization to make these gifts economically significant. He has of late, however, returned to public life, and his voice is heard on critical issues. In the spring of 1959 he has spoken boldly on Tibet and other questions; he feels that Nehru's government is too cautious in its responses to the Tibetan situation.

One could never guess at Jayaprakash Narayan's future. In 1948 I thought he was destined to be the next prime minister of India. The dwindling of the Socialist Party and his own frequent withdrawals from politics make this seem unlikely now, but it would be a rash man who hazarded a firm prediction.

Jayaprakash has a singularly noble appearance, voice and manner; he is large and calm, very calm; I think it would be possible to tell that he was a follower of Gandhi just by looking at him. Nehru has thought highly of him in the past and still does. I have seen a correspondence between them in which Jayaprakash asks the Prime Minister to encourage the building up of a loyal opposition, and the Prime Minister refuses on the ground that this is no part of his duty but rather of those who belong to that opposition. The correspondence, shown me by a third person, may not be authentic, but it sounds like both of them. And I could have little doubt of Nehru's esteem for Jayaprakash because he (the Prime Minister) sent for me in 1948 to introduce me to him; having done so, he left the room.

Press attacks on Nehru are frequent, but again they are on strands of policy rather than on policy as a whole. I do not remember having seen any press comment which demanded the Prime Minister's resignation, a thing most common in other democracies. On the contrary, the whole press was up in arms against it when Nehru wanted to have a trial resignation of only three months! Some humorists and cartoonists, such as those in *Shankar's Weekly*, keep up a running crackle of gibes, sometimes quite funny, which do not lack serious effect. Those who write editorials are certainly not afraid of the Prime Minister—they can be very sharp at times, as during the T.T.K. affair, the scandal in the Insurance Trust—but they draw the line at anything too fundamental, anything that might suggest his departure.

When I think of the critics I am most constantly reminded of the late Dr. B. R. Ambedkar, who was Minister of Law from 1947 to 1951. Ambedkar was an untouchable—aggressively so—and perhaps for this reason, perhaps by temperament, was an inveterate critic of all Indian society. I think I may be entitled to say that he was my friend. I always saw him when I went to India in just those years when he was Law Minister, and we had long talks—or rather, he had long talks and I had long listenings. He was bristling with barbed wire from the inside out, was no respecter of persons and at times used sweeping terms to describe what he disliked. On one occasion we journeyed together on a train to Sanchi and back to Delhi—a long journey

—and spent our days at the Buddhist shrine down there, the great *stupa* where the relics of the disciples now lie. Even then (1950) Ambedkar knew a great deal about Buddhism and lectured me upon it at inexhaustible length; in the end he himself became a Buddhist.

A big, brusque fellow with a most belligerent manner, he delighted me by his utter difference from any other Hindu of my acquaintance. It is a form of genius to be so individual, and it is not much use explaining it by untouchability—I have known a fair number of other untouchables, but nobody at all like Ambedkar. He enjoyed attacking me for what he considered my undue affection for India.

"If you like our Brahmin government so much, Sheean, why don't you pack it up and carry it off to America? We don't need it and maybe you do."

"We have Brahmins of our own, sir," I would tell him.

"Ah, but not like ours . . . !"

And off he would go on one of his hour-long diatribes about Brahminism and the caste system and all the evils therein involved. He was perfectly capable of talking for three hours at a stretch on this and related subjects. He was highly irreverent about Mahatma Gandhi, to whom I believe he was (underneath this irreverence) genuinely attached. He was so obsessed by the caste system, and untouchability in particular, that he could not possibly be fair to the government of India, of which he formed a part. His diatribes were a healthy corrective, just the same, and there was always something in what he said no matter how much he exaggerated. Few cabinet ministers I have ever seen could distribute such tongue lashings to his own associates.

Ambedkar put into his biography in *Who's Who* the startling phrase, "Untouchable by caste." Indians whose biographies appear in that sturdy volume never mention caste, but Ambedkar would have no misunderstanding about it. He then mentions his marriage, in 1948, to Dr. Sharda Kabir of Bombay and says she is "Brahmin by caste."

Dr. Sharda Kabir, a charming woman of great intelligence, had disregarded her own caste rules by becoming a doctor of medicine; she cared for Ambedkar through a serious illness and then married him. It was my impression, especially during that long journey to Sanchi and back, that she loved and revered him inordinately, and I have no doubt she thought him a very great man indeed. Nothing else could account for her humor and patience while he went on and on, hour after hour, about the misdeeds of the Brahmins throughout history. When I asked her how she could, she laughed happily. "I don't listen after a while," she confessed. The whole government turned out for their wedding—Brahmins included, and headed by the Brahmin Nehru—but nothing ever seemed to soften the edge of Ambedkar's resentments.

This extraordinary man claimed to be the one acknowledged head of all Indian untouchables—a point in great dispute—but when they gathered along the way stations between Delhi and Sanchi, waiting for a glimpse of him, if he happened to be asleep or resting he did not appear. It was his Brahmin wife who stood dutifully on the platform of their private car, bowing with folded hands before the poor people outside. I saw this happen often, and at the most inconvenient hours. In his robust way Ambedkar would probably have called this sentimental, but I greatly admired her for it.

He was prodigiously educated, that man. He had degrees from Columbia University and the University of London, had studied at the Sorbonne and was a barrister of Grey's Inn. His degrees were M.A., Ph.D., D.Sc. and LL.D. Degrees do not mean so much, perhaps, but in the torrential flood of his talk there came up great chunks and whirling avatars of learning. He may not have been the greatest of Sanskrit scholars but he could plaster a text with dozens of references to early Hindu authorities. His treatise on *The Origins of Untouchability* was thus embellished with Sanskrit erudition, but its central theme was a rather daring theory, and one which, I imagine, could never be proved. He thought that untouchability arose through the breaking up of tribes in the ancient wars; when a tribe no longer had enough members to be a tribe, its remnants were "broken men" and were compelled to live outside the walls of the town or village, doing unclean work and enduring the insults of the unbroken. This hypothesis reposes upon analogy chiefly; "broken men" from such shattered tribes did exist in ancient times in Wales and perhaps elsewhere. Ambedkar never convinced me, in print or in talk, that such was the case in India.

Perhaps I make him sound unsympathetic, but I assure you he was the best possible company for anybody who was really interested in these subjects. He had no inhibitions whatever; he would say anything that came into his head; if you discounted his unfairness to the Brahmin caste and the government of India —discounted it pretty heavily—there was verve and acumen in everything he had to say. He could not criticize the Constitution of India because he was in fact its principal author—or, as he said, its "architect." As Minister of Law he supervised the entire work, borrowing at will from the constitutions of the United States, England, France and Switzerland; he wrote the actual text in many passages; and he had to see it through parliament to its final adoption. He told me that the doctrine of the separation of powers, as expressed in the Constitution of the United States (and entailing the august independence of a Supreme Court for constitutional debate), was one of his main contributions to the Indian Constitution. I have understood elsewhere that he made many.

But Ambedkar is no more, and critics of his caliber, so brilliant and merciless, are not to be found in public life today. Few politicians can possibly harp on the evils of the caste system as he did, because the sober fact is that an overwhelming proportion of them belong to the higher castes. Many are indeed Brahmins. Even E. M. S. Namboodiripad, Chief Minister of Kerala and a very able leader for the Communists all over India, is a Brahmin. If the caste system is the chief hindrance to progress, as Ambedkar believed, it badly needs another inveterate enemy of low caste or untouchable origin who can fight it with all the unquenchable bitterness of personal experience.

Nehru had long acquaintance with Ambedkar's thorns; so had Gandhi. As long ago as 1932 Gandhi felt obliged, under the compulsion of his inner voice, to begin a fast unto death so as to prevent the untouchables of India being made into a separate electorate, as Ramsay MacDonald wished. That fast aroused India and the world; Ambedkar as head of the untouchables came to an agreement with Gandhi in prison, the fast ended and the separate electorate was abandoned—but on terms which were a victory for Ambedkar. Nehru had been aghast at all this, particularly at the implication that it was being done by the express instructions of God. When the solution came Nehru sent Gandhi a famous telegram, the last phrases of which were: "Am unable to judge from religious viewpoint. Danger your methods being exploited by others but how can I presume to advise a magician. Love. Jawahar."

Both for Nehru and for Gandhi there was the same quizzical, often scornful and skeptical, but somehow affectionate, attitude on the part of Ambedkar. That same remark he made to me about "our Brahmin government" was made on another occasion, also in private, about Gandhi.

"You Americans all love Gandhi," he said. "I never have understood why you didn't import him to America long ago so that we should have been rid of him."

He never could see any resemblance or connection between Gandhi and Buddha, at least in our prolonged conversations. He ended as a Buddhist, and perhaps in his last days he understood more than his combative nature had permitted while he was in the thick of the battle.

2

A fellow member of the government of India is by definition a colleague of Mr. Nehru's. As I have tried to show by the example of Ambedkar, he may at the same time be a severe and unremitting critic. I have also indicated that Rajaji, in his far gentler way, does not refrain from criticism when he feels it necessary. By and large, however, the colleagues of Nehru have ceased to criticize him in public and they do so only by indirection in private. You may say that they are afraid of him, which is partly true, but also they have a feeling that even when they disagree with him they may be wrong and he ultimately right. It is the kind of feeling Nehru himself often had about Gandhi and expressed freely in his autobiography; it is shown in that telegram of 1932 which I have just quoted. "How can I presume to advise a magician," are the words.

Nehru's colleagues in government do not go along with him in everything but they have learned, as he did with Gandhi, that it is best to keep quiet, to wait and see, since the Prime Minister seems to have the magic touch and they do not. I have some fairly shrewd ideas about what the disagreements are between the colleagues, and in what salient respects some of the ministers would "correct" Nehru's course if they could; but they did not tell me so point-blank. After a certain amount of experience in India one can guess these things, and the public debates in parliament generally show the tendencies anyhow. Thus in the early years of independence we all knew that Sardar Patel and Pundit Nehru were at loggerheads on many elements of social and economic policy as well as on the general question of an attitude toward Pakistan. Their debates were in private, and neither one of them ever attacked the other in public. Their divergences were in ideas or perhaps convictions, and did not affect their sincere, well-founded esteem for each other. I had some long talks with both of them at that period and cannot remember a single remark of a denigrating or even critical nature by one about the other.

Among the leading members of the government today the same is true. They all have their ideas, convictions, tendencies and desires; under the existing circumstances, they have mostly velleities, that is, desires which are not quite formulable and cannot be pronounced; but anyhow they are individuals, no two of them alike. It is not a rubber-stamp cabinet by any means, and although Nehru can practically always carry them with him when he tries, it seems that they provide him with some lively debates now and then. These do not transpire to public notice, but anybody slightly acquainted with these personages knows that they must take place.

The Prime Minister's cabinet consists of thirteen full members, heads of the great departments, and there are ministers of state without portfolio, undersecretaries, etc., besides.

(1) The Prime Minister combines that office, with its general supervisory function and responsibilities, and two others: the Ministry of External Affairs, which includes Commonwealth relations, and Atomic Energy.

(2) The Home Secretary, or Home Minister as they say in India, is Govind Ballabh Pant, whom we generally call Pundit Pant, the ranking cabinet minister after Nehru.

(3) The Minister of Finance is at the present moment Mr. Morarji Desai.

(4) Jagjivan Ram has the railways, and we have already observed that he is the only member of the cabinet, aside from the Prime Minister, who has been there since 1947.

Next in rank come (5) Labor, (6) Commerce and Industry, (7) Steel, Mines and Fuel, (8) Works, Housing and Supply, (9) Food and Agriculture, (10) Defense, (11) Transport and Communications, (12) Irrigation and Power, and (13) Law. The names of most of these men would mean nothing to a Western reader and there is no reason why they should be detailed. It may be enough to say that so far as I know they are all faithful and even eager coadjutors of Nehru in the Five Year Plan and the general attempt to raise India's living standards. Mr. K. C. Reddy, Minister of Works, Housing and Supply, is that very lively and positive young Chief Minister of whom I spoke earlier, with respect to Hyderabad; he has lately been summoned to the center; he is good.

The chief colleagues of the Prime Minister are those whose ranks and departments indicate it. They are Pundit Pant (Home Office), Mr. Desai (Finance) and Mr. V. K. Krishna Menon (Defense).

Pundit Pant is by way of being a monument in himself. He is a vast creature who has long enjoyed the confidence of the entire Hindu electorate in the United Provinces, now called Uttar Pradesh, the biggest, richest, most highly developed part of the old British India, and therefore of the Indian Union today. He is five or six years older than Nehru and has the authority of a long, energetic participation in the national revolution, as well as a number of jail sentences. His loyalty and devotion to the nationalist cause are quite beyond question. The species of palsy from which he suffers (and I call it that because nobody offered me a different explanation—it might be what we call Parkinson's disease) makes it quite difficult for him even to sign his name, and yet he does so innumerable times every day. His administration, which we would call the "interior" in many countries, concerns the public order, the individual states and the vast horizontal body of the civil service. He carries out the duties of this office with severe regularity and imperious discipline. I doubt if the Prime Minister himself would dare to intervene in any matter which Pundit Pant had already decided. This huge man, who signifies a great deal to the United Provinces and not so much to India as a whole, is somehow or other a symbol of the old Hindu verities. A colossal Hindu majority stands behind him. He is irrefragably convinced about the cow, for example—"cow protection"—which means that the age-old system of diseased and famine-stricken cattle must still obtain in India. Pundit Nehru opposed him on this in the United Provinces and lost. Pundit Pant is very nearly invulnerable when it comes to anything connected with the Hindu past or the Hindu heritage. He has this peculiar supremacy because he was always an unimpeachable Gandhian nationalist but at the same time never gave up the old Hindu beliefs.

The first time I ever saw Pundit Pant was actually at Mahatma Gandhi's immersion into the Ganges, or into the three rivers which form the Ganges. He descended from a platform outside Allahabad immediately behind our beloved Mrs. Naidu (Sarojini Naidu, the poet and orator whom we shall never forget). Pundit Pant was the Chief Minister and she was the constitutional Governor of the United Provinces. I did not realize—and did not know until she told me weeks later—that she had then suffered a heart attack, from which, as it turned out, she never really recovered. But I did see in Pundit Pant's face, as in hers, the traces of an almost superhuman suffering. I could forgive him a great deal, if there were anything to forgive, for the tears he shed that day.

One must be honest, just the same, and say that Pundit Pant's views of the national polity are not at all those of Mr. Nehru. If we could define them in Western terms, Pundit Pant's views are almost wholly reactionary. He wishes to conserve a form of Hinduism which anybody can see is now outworn. He believes in a wide variety of traditional practices. He would use the club, not the soft or persuasive word, in many instances we have mentioned in this book. I am not allowed to quote a word he said to me—he forbade it in his first sentence, just as Mohammed Ali Jinnah did years ago—but I derived, just the same, an impression which I may convey: that this is the representative of the reactionary and retrogressive Hindu elements in the government of India.

The Prime Minister summoned him to Delhi three years ago, I must assume, because he felt that a "strong" man was needed in the Home Office, and also because the right-wing elements must be conciliated. Pundit Pant is a "strong" man, as nobody can deny; if he had his way he would probably fill the jails with dissidents; but I do not truly believe that he would know what to do with them afterward. That is the weakness of all "strong" men, especially when they are seventy-five years old and more.

Mr. Morarji Desai, Minister of Finance, is all charm and persuasion. There is hardly a man I have met in India who seemed to me more open, direct, sincere and incontrovertible in his main lines of argument. His personality does contain a contradiction which he may himself resolve—indeed we talked about it for some two hours one Sunday afternoon last summer —but I have not resolved it in my own head. It is that between the nonviolence of Gandhi, to which he adheres, and the use of police or other force to quell a disturbance. I have been through all this with Nehru, too, years ago, and he says quite simply, "I must maintain order." Mr. Morarji Desai does not make it as plain as that. He puts it into strictly Gandhian terms and then, if I may say so, into Einsteinian terms—he asks himself, which is the greater violence, which the lesser?

Mr. Desai was for a long time a minister in the Bombay province and afterward Chief Minister of Bombay State. I shall never forget the first time I talked to him (he has forgotten, as he told me last summer, naturally enough). It was in 1950 in Bombay. I arrived rather wan and sad and a little bit late to my appointment with him and he instantly asked me what was the matter. I related my symptoms, which included a little diarrhea and some general lassitude. He pounced on it at once: "What *water* have you had to drink?" I was rather amused at this because Mr. Desai was one of the leading prohibitionists of India and I thought that at least water might be safe from his severities. I confessed that I had drunk some water from the sacred fountain of the great god Shiva out on Elephanta Island, in the bay. He flew into a tizzy of efficiency and told me that this fountain had been contaminated and that he had given orders to have a sign put on it to say so; and when I said I had seen no such sign he pounced on the telephone and gave the orders again, in all languages.

He is like that—prompt, efficient, downright. One likes him instantly because there is really nothing at all to dislike, and everything that can be seen or heard is pleasing. He is wonderfully clean in all his linen, for instance—and how this can be done in Indian heat is incomprehensible: the whitest and sheerest cloth wilts in ten minutes. He looks as if he had just had a bath, no matter when you see him. He has an irresistible candor in his eyes and in his speech. Yet one cannot help wondering how a fundamentally religious personality (that is, both metaphysical and ethical), which is what I consider him to be, can deal with the harsh necessities of government. He had, in the past, not only to order the police out, but to order violence if necessary, including actual firing on the population. I could never have done it myself and I do not really understand how he could do so, although he spent a long time explaining it to me.

Mr. Morarji Desai is supposed to be much liked by "the Americans," whoever they may be. It is almost automatic that he must be disliked by "the Russians," if the foregoing be true. I have never heard any American say anything about him; but, speaking as one individual American, I may state that I like and admire him very much. If he should become the successor to Mr. Nehru, as any of the persons here mentioned may be, I should not feel distressed. I do not for one moment believe that he would, if he were ever Prime Minister, depart from the main lines of Nehru's policy at home and abroad. Of all the cabinet ministers I have met in India, including a fair number who are no longer in the cabinet, this is the one who seems to me to have the greatest ideological scrupulosity.

The third of Nehru's principal collaborators is Mr. V. K. Krishna Menon, now Minister of Defense. Mr. Krishna Menon uses both of his names, like Lloyd George, to distinguish himself from the millions of Menons who spring up all over South India. The Menons are a subtribe of the great Nayar clan on the coast of Malabar. The Nayars, members of the Kshatriya or warrior caste, ruled all those regions for many centuries under various kings and priests. They had subtribes and subdivisions of all sorts, corresponding to various necessary functions, and the Menons were evidently scribes and bookkeepers for the main tribe. (The Nayars have a goodly number of subnames, such as Pillai and Panikkar and others: all are Nayars and until twenty years ago were subject to the matriarchal laws of inheritance.) The Menons have spread all over South India and have so invaded the government services that there are, as I remember, a couple of pages of them in the slender telephone directory of New Delhi.

Now, one of the many remarkable things about Mr. Krishna Menon is that although he comes from such an extremely numerous clan, he seems to have no relations. He has never married and is also devoid of nephews or cousins, at least of the job-hunting variety. One is reminded of Abraham Lincoln and his high regard for a certain member of his government. "The man has no nephews," said Lincoln. In a capital swarming with nephews, all of whom urgently require some lucrative government job, this is a treasurable distinction.

Krishna Menon has many such. He is a perfect demon for work, requires hardly any sleep or food, has proved his patriotism by lifelong devotion to India even in exile, and, what is more, he has brains. According to my own view, which may well be erroneous, the lucidity of his intellect is sometimes clouded by passions and resentments. Its penetration, however, and its ready grasp of almost any problem set before him are beyond question. His likes and dislikes are stronger than would seem quite safe for a man in his position, since they may deflect judgment at times. They also tend to divide those with whom he has to deal, both Indians and foreigners, into friend and foe, which is a positive handicap. The amount of heated debate this man has engendered in the past six or eight years among his own associates and subordinates, not to speak of the public, is exceptional, and the most exceptional thing about it is that it centers upon his personality rather than upon his work. You can throw his name into a conversation any day in Delhi, London or Washington and find yourself in an uproar of argument. It seems strange that a man who carries such a storm around with him should have been used for delicate diplomatic missions.

Krishna Menon was born in Malabar in 1897. After getting his degree at Madras he went to London to the School of Economics and afterward to University College; his degrees are from London University; later on he became a barrister of the Middle Temple. The greater part of his adult life was spent in London, where he joined the Labor Party and was active in it for over twenty years. He was a borough councilor for St. Pancras from 1927 to 1947 and was the Labor Party candidate for the House of Commons in 1938-1941. The constituency was Dundee, now John Strachey's. There was a moment when he drew the Labor Party's censure upon him for disobeying a party directive: he sat on the same platform with the Communist Tom Pollitt after this was no longer permitted.

Throughout this prolonged absence from India Krishna Menon was serving his own country by every means in his power. He was secretary of the India League from 1927 to 1947 and, having joined the Congress Party, became something like a representative of Indian nationalism in the imperial capital. His activity in London was so valued at home that when independence came his return was welcome and his advice valued. Not long afterward he became the first High Commissioner of India in London and organized the establishment, which is bigger than most embassies.

Mr. Krishna Menon's influence in international affairs and on the policies of India has been curiously ambivalent. On the one hand he has shown a strong anti-Western cast of thought and feeling, rising at times to what looks like open hatred. On the other hand he was from the very beginning, and remains today, a firm believer in the advantages of the British connection for India. His support in this matter was valuable to Nehru at a time when so many nationalists wanted to cut all ties with the Commonwealth, and his part in working out the eventual formula (the sovereign Republic associated to the Commonwealth) must have been vital. To this day he looks upon this as the most successful arrangement India has been able to make in international politics. He puts it higher than the contributions made to other settlements—Korea, Indo-China, etc.

As Indian representative at the United Nations during some important sessions of the Assembly and the Security Council, and as Nehru's roving ambassador during some critical years of the past decade, Mr. Krishna Menon has become familiar to a large public abroad. This was easier, really, than becoming familiar to any considerable public in India. He had been away all his life and cannot speak any of the great languages of India, except, one must suppose, the remains of his mother tongue, Malayalam. He relies upon English for all his communications, and although this is the government language, the mass of the people cannot understand it. Nevertheless, he was elected to the upper house of parliament, the Council of States, in 1953 and became Minister of Defense in 1957. In this office, indefatigable as always, he mastered his job in short order and has been notably appreciated by the staffs of the three armed services, whose requests he has granted, and defended in parliament, rather more spontaneously than other civilian ministers. It appears to me that he has been, by and large, a great success as Defense Minister, although one might not have foreseen that he would be; his personality has always given an effect of the barrister-civilian to a degree that made his appointment a surprise. In this case, again, Nehru showed himself more astute than his critics. He knew Krishna Menon, of course, far better than most people in India do; he realized the sheer efficiency and relentless drive that were in the man. Moreover, the Army, Navy and Air Force are themselves so exclusively English in their daily work that Mr. Krishna Menon's lack of Indian languages could not be felt as it might be in some other departments.

The principal enigma about Menon remains, just the same. It is, briefly, this: what would he do if he had his own way? Left to himself, that is without Nehru's guiding hand, what would be his course at home and abroad?

He is said to be ambitious, and he has something of an ambitious look in his thin, troubled face. A year or so ago it used to be said quite often in various capitals that he was set upon becoming Mr. Nehru's successor. It is difficult to imagine a prime minister who could not even speak to the people in any of their own languages, but presumably it is possible. Graver difficulties would arise in Mr. Krishna Menon's isolation from party support, party politics and local realities. If all these things were to be surmounted and he actually came to power, how would he man the helm?

Most observers think and say that he would turn it to the left. I rather doubt it myself; many and many a politician of the Left has kept an even keel when he came to power. Supreme power makes even stupid men reflect, and Menon is not stupid. His dislike for the Western powers in their various arrangements (NATO and SEATO and the rest) is obvious enough, and he has never made an attempt to conceal it. He can be as venomous as any cobra toward what he dislikes. He has also been friendlier than was strictly necessary toward the Soviet Union and Communist China on a number of occasions—up to the point of voting on the Soviet side at the United Nations, without instructions from Delhi, on the Hungarian uprising. But whether these indications of his thought would be continued if he actually came to power is something nobody can say; it is probable that he could not be too sure of the answer himself.

It has been alleged many times that he is, or may be, a crypto-Communist, a secret member of the party. I do not believe it for one simple reason, that he could never deceive Jawaharlal Nehru to that extent. Moreover, he does not sound like a Communist to me—he is nowhere near impersonal enough; he has not the mask. If he were a Communist at all he would be a Trotskyist, it seems to me. At least that is his temperament. In such a matter the accusation is easy and the proof difficult. It is true that the Communists seldom have anything to say about him, although they are lavish in attacks on all other leading government figures. They are also supposed to have supported him in the last elections on "secret orders," which again is a charge unsupportable by proof. What everybody knows, on the public record, is that he is a Socialist of the Left, that he has shown great animosity against the Western powers in some of their policies but that he has sturdily advocated India's association with the British Commonwealth of Nations. This last, on the face of it, is a non-Communist or even anti-Communist attitude, and ought to be enough by itself to dispel the notion that he has secret bonds.

Such murky hypotheses aside—and how distasteful they are

anyhow!—I have one suggestion to make about Mr. Krishna Menon which may shed a little light. I think he instinctively and naturally dislikes Americans. This is not at all unusual and nobody could hold it against him if he would leave it at that. Everybody has likes and dislikes and for many persons they are quite uncontrollable. The emotional revulsion against the United States since its vertiginous rise to power in the last decades has been perceptible in many countries, including some to which we are most closely attached. It has not been mitigated by a tendency on the part of some of us to "throw our weight about," as the English say. Menon has a perfect right to dislike us, but it is astonishing how many grounds he can find for doing so. I honestly believe he blames us for practically everything that has gone wrong in the world in the past decade—or such is the impression he gives. This amounts to prejudice, no less, and prejudice is a very poor instrument in diplomacy. Furthermore it startles one to the point of laughter when he makes an exception—as he constantly does—for Mr. Henry Cabot Lodge. It almost seems that he considers our entire nation of a hundred and sixty million people as being imperialist warmongers and villains, with the single exception of Mr. Lodge. It is difficult to keep a straight face.

At present Menon's work does not touch upon international affairs except indirectly. There is one respect in which it does, however: it is the arming of Pakistan by the United States. The Indian Army, Navy and Air Force must be keyed to the Pakistan threat at all times. It is very bad for Menon's adrenalin glands to discover, as he constantly does, that the modern weapons used by guerrilla assailants in Kashmir come straight from America. A number of bridges were blown up last summer in Kashmir by a species of American bomb which the Indian Army itself does not yet possess. This puts Menon into a rage, but in his place any of us would probably feel the same. The American people do not consciously pay taxes in order to blow up bridges in Kashmir, and I, for example, would not willingly destroy a bamboo footpath or a rope ladder, but it is not much use saying so.

I cannot leave the subject of this most controversial figure without saying one thing more, which is that his intensity, his pride and passion and prejudice, hurt him more than they do anybody else. He has a look of suffering in his face even at the most peaceful moments. He has felt deeply and long; he must have been dreadfully insulted or maltreated at some time or other; there is a look of ancient and remembered wrongs in his eyes. The tempest of his wrath arises from oceanic depths. It might be well to remember this the next time we see him give way to an ungovernable fury in the United Nations Assembly or at the Security Council—if he ever does.

3

Aside from the potent trio, Pant, Desai and Krishna Menon, Nehru's other colleagues have not taken strong individual positions and none has been mentioned, so far as I know, as a possible prime minister. S. K. Patil, Minister of Transport and Communications, is an extremely able party politician; Hafiz Mohammad Ibrahim, the Muslim who is Minister of Irrigation and Power, has wide repute as an organizer and administrator. By and large, all of them are Nehru's followers and ardent supporters of the Five Year Plan; some of them are also his personal friends for years past in the party.

His other friends, in or out of government, are becoming fewer with the passage of time. The greatest of his life were his own father and Mahatma Gandhi—his two fathers, as many have said. There were scores of others with whom he fought the long battle for freedom, with whom he shared jail sentences and organizational work, setbacks and successes, through three decades. A large number of these have gone now; one whose departure affected Nehru deeply this past year was the Maulana Sahib, as Gandhi always called him—Abul Kalam Azad, the Muslim scholar and national leader. The Maulana had great independence of character; as I have said, he was the only person who habitually smoked cigarettes in the presence of Gandhi, for instance. He never hesitated to speak his own mind to either Gandhi or Nehru, right up to the end. His great prestige was unique among Indian Muslims and his death leaves them bereft of any really authoritative leader known to the whole nation.

First among Mr. Nehru's friends should be named, of course, his own family: his fragile wife Kamala Devi, who died in 1936 and was greatly mourned; their daughter Indira (Mrs. Feroze Gandhi), who is now President of the Congress Party; his two sisters, Vijayalakshmi Pandit and Krishna Hutheesing; and his brother-in-law Ranjit Pandit (Mrs. Pandit's husband) who died in 1944.

They are a remarkable family by any standards—remarkable for looks and wit and assorted capacities for work. All of them took part in the national movement, even the frail little Kamala, Mrs. Nehru, who was to die of tuberculosis in Switzerland. Ranjit Pandit was a scholar, fond of Indian literature, history and art, with a special affection for the secular Sanskrit works (Kalidasa, for instance, the playwright of the ancient language). His long friendship with Nehru brought about that return to Indian studies which is expressed in the book *The Discovery of India* (published in 1946).

Mrs. Pandit is the best known of them all outside of India, since she has held three of the most important foreign posts (Ambassador in Moscow, then Washington, then High Commissioner in London). She has also spoken with great effect in the United Nations, to which she led a delegation at the moment of independence. For one year she was President of the Assembly of the United Nations; as such she was known, at least by sight, to an immense American public (television and newspapers). This prolonged tour of duty abroad has kept her out of India for a long time, except on visits, but she was already widely known there through the nationalist movement and as a cabinet minister (the first woman to hold such a post) in the United Provinces. When I first went to India her photographs were sold in many of the city shops, along with those of other leaders; they are still being sold there, twelve years later, and usually the same photographs.

Mrs. Pandit's grace, charm and wit are indeed famous; there is no need to expatiate upon them. She has a natural gift for making friends and has a multitude of them around the world. What is not always fully realized is that her judgment of character and situation, the fundament of diplomacy, is generally about as good as one can find in high places. Of course, her course is directed from Delhi; so is that of every ambassador; Nehru has a firm grasp of the Ministry of External Affairs. But in all the daily effort of representation and negotiation, the directives from Delhi, although firmly borne in mind, cannot meet every need. There is a constant demand upon qualities of heart and head in applying these directives to the situations the ambassador meets. It is in such matters—which no directive could supply—that I have had occasion to admire Mrs. Pandit's skill. She is, I think, about the best I have observed; you might say she was an ambassador born—a natural phenomenon in her adaptation to that special work. Possibly she might never have had a chance to use these gifts if she had not been Nehru's sister; who knows? (The chicken or the egg?) In the result it matters little, because India has had the benefit anyhow.

Indira Nehru, Mrs. Gandhi, carries into a new generation the characteristics of her family. She, too, has grace, skill and judgment, a liking for politics, the ability to make a good speech. She has recently become President of the Congress Party, which, as the Prime Minister said in a press interview, was "not a good thing for the country in principle." He meant, of course, that the choice of his only child for the most important party position was bound to arouse surprise and criticism; it savored of some hereditary principle, it could be attacked on several grounds, especially since Indira is the third generation to hold that same office. But if she could do the job and was the right person for it, should her relationship to him get in the way?

As a matter of fact, Mrs. Gandhi has been active in the party for years, and her knowledge of its organization has grown steadily. Many visitors to Delhi in recent times have taken their troubles to her; this applies to Congress Party workers from all over India; Mr. Dhebar, as President of the Congress, consulted her often; she has her father's confidence. Furthermore, she is the one person who is constantly in touch with the Prime Minister, since she lives in his house. All of these circumstances have fitted her to be the party chieftain, as things stand today in India, quite aside from her undoubted ability and her interest in political work.

Nehru himself entered the Congress as his father's son and rapidly became a leader of the youthful elements in it, as Indira is today. Such a transmission of capacities and interests is not at all rare in political families; we have a number of them in America (the Roosevelts, for instance) and England has burgeoned with them for three or four centuries. A child brought up in a political household, hearing political discussion at all times, seems likely to take a more natural attitude toward that element (like a fish in water) than those who are thrown into it. We have seen rebellions against the paternal interests, too—it works both ways—but the development of Indira Gandhi's political activity has been constant and steady. It is not surprising when we consider that it was to her that Nehru wrote those numerous lesson-letters from prison—the letters which were afterward collected as *Glimpses of World History*—when the child was in her teens. When she grew up she married a politician, too: Feroze Gandhi, a member of parliament and a particularly active one. When, at the age of forty-one, she became the head of the huge political machine, she was perhaps fulfilling a destiny, or beginning one; at all events we see it now as a natural, perhaps an inevitable, evolution.

Nehru's younger sister, Krishna, although she took part in the national movement and went to jail for it, has not been in public life since independence, but she seems an exception in that family. There are other public servants in the clan (not all bearing the name Nehru); and there is one cousin, B. K. Nehru, who is at present head of the economic mission to Washington with the personal rank of ambassador. His qualities are such that he, too, is likely to have a prolonged and distinguished career.

Aside from the family itself Nehru has firm friendships in many quarters, not least in England. The Mountbattens are among these; the last Viceroy and his wife, themselves very exceptional persons, appreciated Nehru's quality at their first meeting. It was fortunate that this was so, since the period of preparation for independence was filled with danger and difficulty. The comprehension, esteem and confidence which could be felt between the Mountbattens, Nehru and Gandhi was of immeasurable help in pulling India through dark days. The Mountbattens' friendship is unchanging; Mr. Nehru often stays in their house when he goes to England; Lady Mountbatten visits India on her trips for the order of St. John of Jerusalem.

In India the Naidu family, mother and two daughters, were lifelong friends. Sarojini Naidu was a Bengali by birth (of the celebrated Chattopadhyaya clan) and her daughter Padmaja is now constitutional Governor of West Bengal. The other daughter, Leilamani, an Oxford woman with a keen mind, used to be in charge of Arab concerns in the Ministry of External Affairs; she died only this past spring. The gradual elimination of so many familiars of the past has saddened Nehru, as it does everybody, and has still further restricted the small circle of his intimates.

It was never a big circle. It is often called "the court" in Delhi, by way of badinage, but there was nothing courtly about it. It was a high-spirited and talkative collection of relatives and friends who enjoyed a joke and were interested in a wide range of subjects. The tone was generally light, or was whenever I caught a bit of it, and if there were any prerequisite—anything common to every member—it was the sense of humor. Nehru himself has recalled in his autobiography how his family and friends made fun of him at the breakfast table. "O Star of India," they would say, "O Light of the East, have some marmalade," echoing the high-flown salutations that used to be commoner some decades ago than they are now. (It must have been good for him!)

With all its power and glory, the prime ministership is not a position in which new friends are likely to be made; most of those who come have some interest at stake, and moreover there is little time to spare from work. That is why Nehru's circle grows smaller and his life, crowded though it is, grows lonelier. His absorption in government and foreign affairs tends, gradually, to take the place of all those who have gone, but it is certainly still true, today as a decade ago, that he can abandon all care and laugh at a joke, tell a story or play games with the children when he gets a chance.

He has, in fact, something approaching a special gift for friendship with those who have nothing to ask from him—as I have suggested before, it works most spontaneously with children, peasants and members of the armed services, just to name a few enormous categories. I do not know into which of these categories one might put my own friends, Dr. Bosiswar Sen and his wife. Mrs. Sen was born American, Gertrude Emerson by name, a known and valued writer; Dr. Sen, addressed as Boshi by a wide acquaintance, is one of the best plant physiologists in the world, a pupil of the late J. C. Bose. They live at Almora, in the Himalayan foothills, where Boshi also has his laboratory and works strange wizardries upon sheaves of wheat and other innocent growths.

The Sens are among Nehru's many nonofficial friends and have been so counted for many years. It was at Almora, their mountain retreat, that he served his last term in jail shortly before the evolution of circumstance called him to power. When he was released from prison he went to the Sens' house for his first hours and his first night of freedom. It was there that he bestowed his remaining stock of mangoes (sent him to jail from home) on an Englishwoman who had chanced to call that day. Their view of him is not at all that which obtains in the jungles of Delhi officialdom: they see him with steady affection, clearly, with a sort of unclouded and imperturbable loyalty.

In 1948, after the assassination of Gandhi, I went to Almora to stay with Boshi and Gertrude Sen for a week or more—a week of such tranquillity as could seldom be found elsewhere. From the terrace of their house can be seen some of the highest peaks of the Himalaya. Kashmir, China and Tibet are the remote highlands visible on a clear day, filling the semicircle of the unimaginable white horizon. I had read in Nehru's autobiography that the clouds came into his cell in that jail at Almora, every evening at about the same time. I expressed the desire to visit the jail, and his cell, and the Sens arranged it with the governor.

"You may depend upon it," Gertrude said to me, "that if he says the clouds come into the cell, they do."

We traipsed across the town, downhill and then up on the other side, to a rather elaborate tea with the jail officials. I saw the regular cells and talked to some of the ordinary prisoners. We were taken afterward up to the long, narrow cell, plain and now empty, where Nehru had spent his last months of political imprisonment. There was nothing to be seen but walls, floor and ceiling. I think the prison officials were a little puzzled about why I wanted to linger on there after the first glimpse. And then—yes—just as I had begun to think we must go, the wisps of cloud came in at the windows on both ends of the room, ghostly witnesses, drifting with the slow, irresistible fragility of a thought. When they met in the middle we went away.

VIII *The Man Nehru*

JAWAHARLAL NEHRU reached his seventieth birthday in a state of health which many a man half his age would envy. He is capable of great fatigues and long hours of work; he still likes to ride a horse and climb a mountain when he gets the chance; he beams and glows with well-being on most occasions, although all who know him have seen him in darker moods. And, like other great blessings, his physical solidity is almost taken for granted. He has occasional medical examinations for the sake of the office he holds, and comes through them with the good marks (blood pressure and the like) of a man twenty years younger. For the work he has done and still has to do in this world the natural advantage of physique and constitution must be counted as very nearly primary, or second only to the vigor and elasticity of the mind.

Not so long ago, seeing him again after a year's absence from India, I was struck afresh by this aura of well-being and said to him, "You never have illnesses, do you?"

He laughed and answered, "It's been a long time now since I've had a really first-class illness."

It would be difficult to find any particular reason in diet, habit or daily custom to account for this. It must be due in the first place to a very sound constitution from birth and before. He follows no particular regime and in fact pays little attention to ideas of health. In this he is utterly different from Mahatma

Gandhi, who, to the end of his life, was eager to hear about any new notion of diet or exercise and to read of it in print. Nehru became a vegetarian under Gandhi's influence, it is true, but a vegetarian who pays practically no attention to the matter—that is, he eats the vegetables but he does not talk about them or make them a main concern of his life. It does not matter much to him and if I am not mistaken he occasionally relaxes the dietary rules (to the extent anyhow of chicken or fish) when he is on his travels. During his school and college years in England he ate meat, like everybody else, and never has had any prejudice against meat-eating. He is vegetarian merely because most of his countrymen are, and because Gandhi emphasized "innocent" food so much. There are Hindus who can hardly endure the sight or smell of cooked meat, even when it is for the consumption of others; Nehru never belonged to this category.

He loved to ride in his youth and still does. He grew up in a household where the stables were very important, and his father, Motilal, kept many good mounts as well as carriage horses. Mountain climbing is another exercise he took to as if by nature, and it has remained a favorite diversion for him. He has recorded in his autobiography how nearly he came to an untimely end, once in Norway on holiday from Cambridge, by his fondness for the rocky slopes. Occasionally, even now, he gets some opportunity to indulge these predilections and does so eagerly.

His only regular exercise is a bit of hatha-yoga, the ancient body-training system of India, which he picked up from a little book that came his way long ago during one of his early jail sentences. He only learned a few of these exercises. They are simple, very slow exertions in stretching and bending, quite unlike the sharp physical jerks known to Western schools and armies. (The Chinese have a similar system of slow exercise.) Nehru did a few of them in jail—they are not difficult to learn from the diagrams and description in books; I did them for some years myself—but later on he dropped all but one, which is standing on his head. This, too, is a slow exercise, not a violent one, but by the time you have assumed the correct position every part of your body has undergone a certain amount of stretching or flexing. It is one of the best early-morning exercises in the yoga system, developed by trial and error over many centuries, and almost any doctor even in the West would recommend it. It has remained Nehru's one regular tribute to bodily health, rendered every morning no matter what happens. The whole business, including the slow lifting of the entire body until it rises arrow-straight above the head, some immobile minutes and then the equally slow descent, does not take more than ten minutes at most. Many persons who do this exercise poise the weight of the body on the shoulders (I always did), and some do it against a wall for security; but I believe Mr. Nehru does it with the weight poised on the cranium and with no external support.

Yoga exercises, by the way, are not in the least violent, or should not be: they are so easy and natural to those who are used to them that they are performed by men of the most advanced ages, eighty and beyond. Neither do they leave any sense of fatigue; if they do, they have not been properly performed.

The routine of life for Nehru is, of course, arduous, because a day contains only twenty-four hours, but when he is in Delhi it is at least very regular. He is up, usually at seven, and always used to breakfast with his family downstairs. He still does when there is any family, but they are pretty well scattered now. I remember one occasion when I breakfasted with them all in his house in York Road. That was in 1948, in his own house, before he moved to the imposing Prime Minister's House where he now lives. (It is an official residence, like the White House, belonging to the nation.) There were his nieces, the Pandit children, and his daughter Indira and at least one grandchild, along with the Sheikh Abdullah and me—I shall refer to that breakfast in another connection—and it was a merry meal, like a family party almost anywhere, but rather more English, perhaps, than anything else. Mr. Nehru enjoys that kind of gathering but it is no longer a daily occurrence: those who met that day are in many different places or even countries now.

He works, of course, at almost any hour, even at breakfast, and there is no time when a dispatch may not be given to him if it is important. But nine o'clock is the normal time for him to arrive in his office and start dealing with the affairs of the day.

He has a well-staffed and well-run secretariat, part of which remains on duty at the Prime Minister's House and part of which goes with him to his office in the Ministry of External Affairs. This office, commodious and rather bare, has one very big angular desk in the corner, where the Prime Minister sits; it has an enviable expanse of space for papers, but I have never seen it even partially covered by them, much less cluttered. Obviously the Prime Minister's own efficiency, in addition to that of his secretaries, keeps the papers on the move; they do not pause long on top of his desk, anyhow. There is a telephone there, but I have never seen it used or heard it ring. (There are not many persons in Delhi who would be put through to the Prime Minister if they tried.) When the Prime Minister wants anything he touches a buzzer which is heard in the equally large office and waiting room outside.

But also Mr. Nehru gets up and goes after what he wants from time to time. It is not in his nature to sit behind his big desk all day long and receive persons and papers as they come, or ask for what he wants through secretaries. Ever and anon he will take to his agile feet and pop around the corner to some nearby office to ask a question or look at a paper or give an instruction. In this he differs from any chief of government or chief of state I have ever seen—he would always much rather go and do a thing himself than wait for it to be done for him. Time has softened most of his asperities, including impatience, but he still gets bored when he has to sit still and wait. This, of course, increases the alert, attentive manner of everybody who works in that section of the Foreign Office. None of them, from the highest official to the least important, knows when the Prime Minister might come swiftly through the door to ask a question. They all have to be prepared at any moment.

Oddly enough, Mr. Nehru is casual and very easy in his manners; it is not his fault if others get a trifle tense in his presence. At the White House, or at Number 10 Downing Street, the casual and easy manners belong to the outer offices. They do not in the Prime Minister's office at External Affairs in Delhi.

He has another office which he uses while Parliament is in session. It is in the Council House, the great circular building by Sir Herbert Baker which either completes or distorts the great designs of Sir Edwin Lutyens (depending upon your aesthetic judgment). External Affairs is in the South Block of the Secretariat, right at the end toward the palace (the Rashtrapati Bhavan, built as a viceregal palace). Mr. Nehru's office in External Affairs is at the extreme corner of the Ministry, with big windows on two sides. It is cool enough with big fans from the ceiling and he has never wanted it to be air-conditioned. Those buildings (the palace and the Secretariat) form in their combined magnificence one of the proudest architectural creations for centuries past; they are all by Sir Edwin Lutyens and show his susceptibility to the baroque and the neo-classic, to Mogul forms and colors and materials and to the shape of the land. Parliament House (we always used to call it the Council House) is, by contrast, heavy rather than splendid, and squat rather than solid, even though it is built of the same red sandstone as the Lutyens buildings. (No doubt what we see is the difference between architects of the first and of some lesser rank.)

In the Parliament House Mr. Nehru's offices are between the immense circular corridor and the open courtyard in the middle of the structure. He can conduct his work there and still be in touch at all times with what is going on in either of the two Houses of Parliament. There are loud-speakers bringing the debates to his desk; he can turn them on or off; if he finds that his presence is required, he can dart along to the House in a minute or two. The inconvenience of two offices is, chiefly, that papers which are needed in one may often be found only in the other, but Nehru puts up with it for the sake of constitutional propriety. He would rather undergo any amount of such minor inconvenience than falter in respect to the House (the Lok Sabha, lower house) to which he was elected and to which his government is responsible.

The smooth, quiet and competent operation of these offices has always impressed me. No voices are raised; there never seems to be any kind of altercation of the sort which is so very usual elsewhere in Delhi; nobody ever seems to be too late or too early or in too much of a rush. It is done, of course, by skill in management. Some species of straining or screening or selection has taken place before we even reach these offices, although it is done so unobtrusively that I have scarcely ever noticed. There also must be some security arrangements, too, but they never have been visible to me. Many or most offices in Delhi—or ministers' houses, for that matter—give an impression of considerable confusion; many applicants sit waiting for hours to be received; there is a certain amount of din and a perpetual crackle of dispute.

Nothing like that can be perceived at Nehru's two main offices or in the Prime Minister's House. We enter a zone of quiet, where the voice of reason can be heard, and although we are well aware that time is rationed out carefully, drop by drop, nothing forces the fact upon our attention. This was so even in the worst days of 1947-1948, when a certain amount of disturbance might have been expected. In spite of utterly different architecture and surroundings, the Executive Offices in Washington have something of the same quality, as of the still point, the central silence, at the heart of a cyclone: the quietest place is the President's room.

The Prime Minister's House, on the south side of the great Lutyens structures, is outside the viceregal or presidential enclave in rather spacious lawns and gardens. It is the former Commander-in-Chief's House and was also designed by Lutyens, although not in the red sandstone he used for the palace and Secretariat. Mr. Nehru's staff works on the ground floor here, to the left of the entrance, and he has his own study and library on the floor above. One office on this floor is air-conditioned; so is Mr. Nehru's study upstairs, as is his bedroom; but the house in general is kept cool by fans and by its own thick walls.

Apart from all that goes on in the two offices (Parliament House and External Affairs) there is a huge amount of work done here. Mr. Nehru always takes papers home with him. He is in the office, except for the luncheon interval, until half past five or six every evening, but he often has time to see private friends or obtain a little rest before dinner. After dinner he works on papers; before he moved into this official residence he used to take them to bed with him. He tries, of course, to keep up with the dispatches from all the Indian embassies abroad, as well as those innumerable papers from other ministries, or the Planning Commission or the scientific institutes, which come to his desk. He does not often get to sleep, I am told, until about two in the morning, which leaves only five hours until he has to get up again. His relatives and friends have complained for years that he did not sleep enough, but their protests never made much impression on him and he appears to thrive on disregarding them.

The round of duties thus described is broken into by visits to hospitals, playgrounds, scientific institutions, schools or any other enterprise which, by being new or in need of support or by obtaining novel results, has aroused Nehru's interest. As I have often remarked for years past, nearly every new building of consequence anywhere in India seems to have had its cornerstone laid by him. In the past week in Delhi, rather an average week, the Prime Minister visited a new hospital for children's diseases and went all through it, speaking to many of the small patients; he attended a recital of the Hungarian pianist Földes, given in aid of the Prime Minister's Relief Fund; he made a couple of nonpolitical speeches. Engagements of a purely social nature, dinner parties and the like, grow rarer with him, but he never ceases to find time to visit and encourage undertakings of a kind which seem to him desirable.

This part of his activity has, as I mentioned in the section on politics, drawn considerable criticism. "Why does he waste time on children's art shows and all these things?" Delhi inquires. "He hasn't enough time for his work as it is." I have never seen the validity of such criticism: on the contrary, Nehru's constant interest in every legitimate Indian activity, the very breadth and variety of his good will toward any effort, combined with his travels and the fact that so many of the people can see and hear him, seem to me to form, in the aggregate, a valuable part of his contribution to national unity, confidence and hope. He would not be half the man he is for India's present and future if he stayed all the time in his office, plowing through papers.

At the same time the diversity of enterprises claiming his support, encouragement or physical presence may help to keep him alert and youthful. He is a man who is quite literally interested in almost any creative or fruitful activity, and to see it operate constitutes a refreshment of mind and spirit for him. As Frank Moraes has said, his mind in this respect is broad or wide rather than deep: that is, its range of interest is vast and he knows at least something about a vast number of things. For such a mind the spectacle of a new undertaking, whether it is a children's hospital or a miniature model of water-power projects, a park or a school, provides unfailing stimulus. He can be bored by aimless talk or long speeches, and sometimes it is difficult for him to conceal the fact; but he cannot be bored by a surgical operation.

Then, too, Delhi does not offer much in the way of organized entertainment, to which most persons in the Western countries turn for relaxation. There are no theaters except for films; plays are few and far between; music is rare except on the radio; there are infrequent visits to the capital, now and then, by Indian classical dancers from the south. The attention Nehru constantly pays to scientific or social undertakings, to meetings with a purpose, to art shows or to prize-givings and the like, may take the place of all that organized relaxation which plays such a part in Western life. He gets something restorative out of meeting all these varieties of men and women and seeing the work they do; they derive great advantages, even material ones, from his interest. It is a transaction of mutual benefit. Often it is difficult for him to squeeze out the extra half-hour needed for such visits but my own feeling is that he will never cease to do so.

As for taste and preferences, they cannot influence his conduct or the allotment of his time as much as they did in private life. That is, he may naturally like one kind of thing better than another, but his duty as Prime Minister obliges him to give equal attention to equal efforts. I happen to know, for example, how keenly he enjoys folk dancing done by actual villagers from every part of India; it refreshes and delights him; it is not only beautiful in itself for the most part, but it affords a kind of panorama of his beloved country in its simplest, least self-conscious forms. By contrast, Indian classical dancing, the *Bharata Natya*, so tremendously stylized and complicated in its choreographic language, gives him nothing like the same keen pleasure and, moreover, it is invariably presented at enormous length. A full program of classical dancing takes up more time than any evening in a Western theater (even Wagner). In spite of this,

Nehru never fails to attend and support the efforts of the classical dancers and their musicians.

It is so with a considerable range of other interests. For example, one of the keenest pleasures of Nehru's life for about fifty years was certainly reading. He always used to read a great deal, mainly in history, philosophy and poetry, but also in pretty much every other realm. During his long years in jail reading was his principal occupation; except writing, there was no other.

As Prime Minister he is obliged to read dispatches and other documents for such a large part of every twenty-four hours that the old pleasure has been very nearly obliterated. That is, eyes and mind and the faculties of attention are all so battered by the day's work that they cannot pass on, with the old acuity and delight, to the books that accumulate, even if there were time for them. It is one of the penalties of the position, and although I have not heard him mention it for years, I know that at one time he regretted it deeply.

Moraes has said, in his *Jawaharlal Nehru,* that the Prime Minister is a lonely man. This, of course, must be true in one sense, because so many of his old associates have died and others have dispersed, and one does not make friends with any ease from high pinnacles. This is not to say that Jawaharlal is "Olympian"—the word is a cliché for all of our eminent elders, it seems to me, whether true or not. He is as down-to-earth as you may choose, and never loses his firm grasp of common sense. But the position he holds is certainly Olympian and discourages all but the most respectful approach. There lies the clue, I should say, to whatever loneliness he may occasionally feel: it is in the position and not in the man. He, too, regards his own position with respect, and would not do anything to take away from what is due the office. We have all seen a gradual diminution in his visible or external zest, a dampening of impetuosity, of the impulsive word or gesture. It is not only the passage of time which does this; it is also *where* the time has been passed, which in his case has been, for more than twelve years now, at a great elevation over the generality of mankind.

The old impetuosity is still there, governed but not extinguished. He can take a garland of marigolds from his own neck and throw it with a gesture of abandon to a pretty girl in a crowd: he always used to do it and he would do it again any day if the impulse struck him. His extremely expressive countenance, always changing, never still, reveals the play of mind and temperament over any subject presented to his attention. Control has come—yes; and perhaps this is not to be deplored—but the play and interplay of impulse and feeling can be discerned beneath it.

Temperament, sensibility and emotional response are not far beneath the surface, and those who know him well can tell at one glance what his state of mind is at any moment. This is most uncommon among men of power, used to command, holding in their hands the instruments of fate over many other mortals. Power atrophies or brutalizes the sensitive elements in most men, as we have repeatedly seen in many countries, and there is no cause for wonder at it: when you can make or break others by a word, when almost everybody you ever see comes with a petition, when bestowal and rejection hang upon the lift of your eyebrow, you must harden or perish. Nehru has, I think, hardened very considerably, in that he can say no and close his ears as well as the next one, but he never has lost his uncanny sensitivity to currents of thought and feeling in the air, even when he must in self-defense repel them. He has had to be decisive but he has never become a brute, which must, I should think, make the burden of power weigh more heavily than it does upon the unimaginative.

And yet this man of imagination and sensibility, whose capacity for suffering through others—through and for the masses, the unfortunate and the disinherited—is manifestly great, says in so many words that he has had almost everything he really wanted in life and has made no untoward sacrifices. He has said that on the whole he has known happiness; he does not feel his own "loneliness," if it exists; he does not believe he ever had to give up anything he fundamentally valued. The surrender of the family wealth, which took place when his father and he began to follow Gandhi, made little impression on him; he has never missed it. He never took the drastic vows which Gandhi demanded of those who freely chose to live in his own small community; Gandhi would never have asked such a thing, nor did Nehru ever attempt to live the monastic life of the Gandhian village. He has always been free, except for such bonds as he himself assumes toward the country or for other purposes; he has kept the peace with his own conscience; and in most of the matters which go to make up normal existence he has had a full, good life. This is on his own recognizance; and it would be a waste of time to sympathize with him for a "loneliness" he does not feel or sacrifices that never cost a pang.

Among the penalties of such an office as his—certainly one of the chief, for almost anybody—must be boredom. The number of pompous and meaningless speeches to which such persons have to listen, the quantity of inflated nonsense they have to read, would quell me to a coma in only a day or so; and these things used to be quite difficult for Jawaharlal, too. He never has suffered fools gladly, and when he has to sit still for half an hour or so while some self-important nincompoop tells him a long tale of imagined woe—well, I have seen what a crushing effect it sometimes has. He smells that rose he keeps at hand, and he looks out the window, and very often he thinks of something else. But on the whole he has conquered his former impatience in these respects and does not betray, except to those who know him well, how weary and depressed such things make him feel. In an ideal world everybody who has an appointment with an enormously busy man would say precisely what he had to say and then get out. Such is not the case anywhere on earth, and least of all in Delhi.

The ungoverned phrase, the flash of temper, the glitter of uncontrollable impatience—all these are still in Nehru's armory, I suppose, although I have not seen them for some years now. His famous "tantrums," as they are called in Moraes' book and as they are usually called in Delhi conversation, never came my way but once, and although I was in the immediate neighborhood of such a disturbance at the Bandung Conference, I was never aware of it. (Nehru is supposed to have had a series of "tantrums" at Bandung, but he was all sweetness and light whenever I saw him there.)

I may as well narrate the one and only occasion when I experienced an outburst of Nehru's wrath. It is probably a fair example of these storms which by now have created a sort of legend in India. It was in early 1948 and concerned the Sheikh Abdullah, the "Lion of Kashmir," who was then in the highest favor with Nehru and was a guest in his house in Delhi.

From Karachi, acting upon information which seemed to me good, I had sent the *Herald-Tribune* in New York a sort of general résumé of the Karachi point of view on Kashmir, with some statements about the Sheikh Abdullah which were, as I know now, very wide of the mark. My informant had told me of some "mysterious absences" of the Sheikh from his state; during these vanishments he was supposed to have visited Moscow. In point of fact he was in jail until he became Prime Minister of Kashmir, and his time was accounted for all through the period in question. The mere mention of a visit to Moscow in that period was slightly sinister for any controversial figure. The whole tone of my article, which I had sent by mail from Karachi, was unfair to the Sheikh and not very good for India. It appeared in the *Herald-Tribune* on the very day when the Kashmir debate opened, for the first time, in the United Nations at Lake Success. It was cabled back to Delhi in full by the Indian delegation.

I had been in Delhi for a week or ten days already, and had almost forgotten that air-mailed article. I had had two or three very friendly conversations with Mr. Nehru during this time. One evening I was summoned to York Road, where he lived then, by one of his secretaries, and when I went into the room the Prime Minister used there he had the cable from New York in his hand.

He tore the article to pieces, as might have been expected. He showed me how impossible it was for the Sheikh Abdullah to have visited Moscow during this critical period, and turned some other statements in the wretched composition completely inside out. But as he was doing so he got angrier and angrier. The usual even pallor of his face turned quite red and he seemed to have some trouble with his breath; at times it was difficult for him to get the words out; the tendons in his neck, I remember, stood out as I never have seen before or since. He was considering not only my Karachi lucubrations but also, in a general way, the wrong-headedness and unfairness of a press which would pick up an untruth to "make a story." The fact that I did not know it was an untruth made no difference; I should have found out. This session, which was by no means brief, made a most painful impression on me. I was not only distressed at being the cause of such a storm but I felt that I ought not to be present at it—that I had no right to see the Prime Minister out of control. There was, in fact, something from the depths about it—something elemental. It is perhaps the recollection of this episode which has made me think, as I have thought for years and still do, that it was Gandhi, and not Mother Nature, who made Mr. Nehru nonviolent.

However, when such things occur it is my belief that Nehru regrets them. Certainly within a day or so after the occasion described I was asked to York Road for breakfast one morning, in the family scene I have already mentioned. After breakfast was over Mr. Nehru took me with the Sheikh Abdullah out onto a balcony at the side of the house, on the ground floor overlooking the garden. "Talk, you two," he said, and shut the door on us and left us.

I had a long talk with the Sheikh and had to revise my very second-hand notions of his personality. From that time onward, for at least a few years, I met him again on visits to India, and never without pleasure. I should have gone to see him in Kashmir last spring and had arranged to do so on a certain morning, but he was arrested at midnight the night before.

On one other occasion Mr. Nehru lost his temper with me, to my knowledge (there may have been others of which I know nothing). This was about a year later when he was going to Hyderabad and had consented to take me along—his first trip to the Nizam's dominions since the "police action" there and its absorption into the Indian Union. There were other guests and the plane was taking off at eight in the morning from Palam Airport, rather far from Delhi; I was late and arrived to see the aircraft climbing over the field, just gaining altitude. As I was told, Mr. Nehru was furious with me for this indefensible tardiness and I really thought for a few days that I might never see him again. It was Christmas Eve when this happened, and Christmas was a dismal day. Not long afterward, however, one of the secretaries telephoned to invite me to go with him to Calcutta on a three-day visit, previously described, to receive the relics of the Buddhist disciples Mogallana and Sariputta, sent home from England in the heavy cruiser *India*. That journey in all its wealth of incident proved to be one of the most memorable I have ever made. My participation in it, I have always thought, was due to the fact that Mr. Nehru regretted having lost his temper on the earlier occasion.

Now, of course, a really fiery temper requires the utmost determination to overcome. I believe it is quite true that Mr. Nehru has such a temper by nature but has fought a serious battle to subdue it—a long battle in which it is my impression that he almost always wins. There was one episode we heard about, during the private meetings of the conference in Bandung, in which a moment of anger caused Nehru to say something which could be construed as derogatory to the sovereign status, or anyhow the sovereign dignity, of Pakistan. If we heard the story correctly, he began the next session by expressing his regret for that remark, whatever it was. In other words, when he cannot altogether keep down the leap of the flame, he regrets it and makes up for it, frankly and sincerely. The long story of his relationship with Gandhi contains some incidents of the kind, and provides, also, an explanation of how he came through the years to achieve the iron will with which he now almost always subdues impulses to anger.

Along with his temper, Mr. Nehru's "vanity" comes in for much castigation in India and is often mentioned in print. His younger sister, Mrs. Hutheesing, wrote a whole book some years ago in which these temperamental defects, temper and vanity and the like, were well canvassed. The only contribution I can make to the momentous debate over his "vanity" is to say that I have never seen it, at least in any form recognizable to me. Only a week or so ago somebody was saying to me, "When he's talking to you does he show you his right profile or his left profile?" I was obliged to reply that I had no idea. My impression is that for the past twelve years he has usually talked to me full-face, but I really do not know. He is very mobile and his face itself changes constantly; it would be surprising if he did not turn this way and that, from time to time; but as for "showing his profile," I never saw him do such a thing and cannot imagine what the operation might be like.

Some of this "vanity," therefore, must be in the eye of the beholder, because with rather extensive opportunities to do so, I have still never seen it. The theory that he has a "favorite profile," either left or right as the case may be, seems to me utter nonsense. He does not seem to me to pay any more attention to his appearance, clothing and suchlike, than a decent respect for his high office requires. And as for posing, in the sense of striking an attitude, it seems to me quite alien to his nature. I have seen him make many an impetuous gesture, especially in crowds, but these are natural, quick and fleeting expressions of the general excitement—rejuvenation, which he always seems to get when he is surrounded by a seething mob. I have seen no evidence of pose at all. Among members of the Government of India, Mr. Nehru's colleagues, there are several who strike poses both in public and in private, and deliberately arrange the position of head, arms and hands; Mr. Krishna Menon is famous throughout the world for it. One glances away from him instinctively to see where the photographers are, even when none are present. Never once have I been conscious of such a thing with Nehru.

It is possible that a good many instances of what I call sensitivity, and among them the susceptibility to praise or blame, the desire to be liked, the wish for as wide a measure of approval as can be obtained, would classify as "vanity" in the eyes of some observers. I do not see it thus. To me it appears that Nehru's nature obliges him to seek approval, but not because he is vain; on the contrary, it is because he is humble. He very much wants to be liked and I dare say for a large part of his life he wanted to be loved. This appeal arises from an essentially childlike wonder at his own quite staggering success in this world: "Why am I chosen?" is the gist of it. I cannot see the connection between this kind of reaching out toward others and the plain, vulgar disease called vanity, which flourishes in the higher levels of many contemporary societies. It would be quite easy to name chiefs of government in our time who have lived in their own vanity as the fish live in the sea. Without even going back to Mussolini and Hitler, our own Western democratic systems have afforded several examples. That kind of vanity is as obvious as red hair or big feet, and I have never seen a suggestion of it in Nehru.

There are Indians of my acquaintance who will laugh immoderately at the idea of the word "humble" as applied to their resplendent Prime Minister. They think of him as blazing away in temperament, intellect and success, replete with the intuitions of genius and wearing only lightly, with a really sovereign grace, the panoply of fulfillment. That is one vision, and rather a common one, of Nehru's personality. It goes along with all sorts of glittering, rubbishy notions about his life in general, as if half a dozen Shakespearian heroes (notably Romeo, Julius Caesar and Mark Antony among them) had combined to form him. For such beglamoured observers there will be something absurd or even unseemly in the word "humble" as applied to him.

Still I must use it, and in doing so must distinguish sharply between its meaning and that of the word "modest." Nehru is not in the least modest; he is far too intelligent. He knows what he can do and has long since precisely appraised those great gifts which came to him by nature or at birth. No man who has had so much could be modest. What he can accurately do is perceive his own limitations, and he does so with better results than his critics can show.

Humility arises from the secret places of the heart, not from calculation or design; it is not learned and cannot be acquired; it is there or it is not. I have perceived it in Nehru when it was not intended to be perceived—indeed, those are the only times to catch so rare a bird. It differs rather sharply from the all-pervading humility of Gandhi, which was, by the time I saw him, woven into the texture of every moment in every day. Nehru is humble toward great ideas, toward protagonists and exemplars, toward history itself; he reveals by a turn of the most ordinary phrase, or sometimes by a glance or a slight shrug, how far he is from claiming a kinship with them. If he is a man of destiny, as many now believe, he is surely the one of that species who most consistently rejects the hypothesis. He has no mission; India has no mission; he says, "What right have we?" And essentially what he says is what he remarked to me last year, "We go on, a step at a time, and do the best we can."

Most of all, as I tried to indicate in the first section of this book, he is humble toward Mahatma Gandhi and toward the idea of Gandhi. That idea is partly memory, of course, in his case, but I think it has come to be more than just memory. It is the hindsight of years, the reflection upon many crowding events, the accumulation of perspective. Events which happen today or tomorrow may well confirm to him (and I think they do) the true grandeur of that wise and good old man who formed his mature life. They were at odds upon many things which seemed more important to Nehru at the time than they do now, and it is almost certain that Gandhi foresaw the progression. Theoretical disagreement, as Gandhi always knew and as Nehru knows now, cannot disguise fundamental unity.

There would be little purpose in dwelling upon these debated and debatable strands of Mr. Nehru's complex character if they were merely the small talk of a talkative capital. Their significance arises from the position our protagonist occupies in India and in the world. If his temper were not well governed, for example, or if his vanity were such as the ill-disposed say, there might be serious impairment of judgment at critical moments. A hot-headed or impetuous chief of government is a danger in any country, particularly if he is misled by some element of vain self-righteousness and self-approval, some sense of being superior to all other men. Nehru would conceivably be more dangerous than any other if he really had the shortcomings which have been attributed to him—more dangerous because of the extent and depth of the influence he and India, or India and he, have exerted over the whole world since Gandhi's death.

No such dangers exist, I am convinced, and not only because this is the result of my own direct observation, but because the public record fails to show any result of these supposed temperamental defects, any instance of harm done or action taken under their sway. My observation suggests that a great deal of Nehru's youthful impetuosity has been burned away in the crucible of time; without loss of vigor, he has become altogether a quieter person since I first met him in January of 1948. His will power has had as much to do with it as all the innumerable external events which have been packed into these years. He knows that to govern India he must first govern himself (a Gandhian lesson) and he has done so.

2

One comes up, just the same, against the fact that this is an extremely powerful personality which affects others near and far. In his own immediate circle, official or personal, jealousy is rampant—jealousy of or for his favor originally, but growing into sincere hatreds and dislikes which never fail to complicate any given situation. Nehru seems unaware of all this but I have a shrewd suspicion that he learned long ago to ignore it; it is not a thing he can curb or control in any way, and the best treatment is not to see it. Excessive devotion, amounting almost to worship, is perhaps commoner in India than in the West. Certainly it bothered Gandhi a good deal, and in his immediate circle, too, there were many jealousies, do what he would to overcome them. I have heard Nehru referred to as "our Buddha" by two lifelong intimates, and the expression does convey something of their concentration upon him.

Outside this intimate circle, which has dwindled in recent years, the effect of his personality is felt in concentric circles through officialdom, parliament and the capital in general, growing somewhat less as one leaves the epicenter. The most vocal of the critics are, so to speak, around the edges.

But then—going on farther—we come to the great masses of India as a whole, and I have described the ardor of their manifestations. Here the accretion of his immense legend, which began very early in his life, determines a crowd behavior verging upon chaos. No police force can control the mob when it is determined to get a good look at "Jawaharlal," as they call him. I have seen the police linked arm in arm all down a long street, only to be broken up like a paper ribbon when the vast crowd suddenly began to surge. This is all enthusiasm, of course, and no doubt as much for the legend as for the reality, but there is no other person in India who so evokes it. He confesses freely that contact with the masses, any contact, refreshes and encourages him. Once in Calcutta the car I was in, following his, was stopped for quite a while by the coagulation of humanity, and during the time I heard a young boy on top of a telephone pole screeching out the same words, over and over again, in Bengali. I asked the security officer sitting with me what these words were and he translated: "I have also seen! I have also seen!" Evidently the strength Jawaharlal gets from them is also passed back to them, in some peculiarly Indian transaction.

His effect upon others, near and far, cannot but have some influence on him—it must at least rebound upon him like an echo. Of course he has been used to it since his first return from England, long ago. Every powerful personality gets used to these electrical results of its own presence; Mr. Roosevelt's experience was not dissimilar, in American terms. Under such circumstances it would be difficult for anybody not to become egocentric and perhaps also selfish for at least part of the time, since there is such a convergence of forces to encourage it. And yet—differing again from Nehru's younger sister and others who have written on the matter—I cannot see any untoward effect on Nehru. He enjoys all these manifestations frankly and simply. They put him into excellent spirits, but I must testify that they do not seem to go to his head; in fact he is never gayer or more natural, more completely unpretentious, than after such an outburst. He could never be pompous under any conditions, but after he has been through one of these tremendous popular demonstrations he is as merry as a grig. Such, at any rate, has been my experience.

What is more, the public speeches of Nehru exhibit no trace of pomp or ceremony, no egocentric parade or search for melodramatic effect. He is not an orator at all. On the very rarest occasions, such as the day of India's liberation (August 17, 1947) and the death of Gandhi some months later, obviously under the strain of overwhelming emotion, he has spoken in the vein of great historic moments. "We have a tryst with destiny," he said when India became independent. (And is it not true?) When Gandhi died he said, "The light of our life has gone out."

As a rule he speaks good, plain English without any striving for effect, and he does not prepare what he is going to say except in his own head. Almost all of his speechmaking, which is incessant, shows a tendency to digression, as is normal to human beings. In other words, he gets up and talks: he does not prepare and deliver literary or oratorical efforts. In matters of consequence to the historical record—on a debate in parliament, for example, where he has to sum up in the knowledge that his words will be quoted for quite a time—he does prepare a written text and reads from it, but I believe I have only seen this about twice. His talks in public are as natural and unpretentious as his talk in private, and are in exactly the same language.

This is so rare as to be practically unique in the history of our time. Gandhi had only one way of talking, it is true, on public or private occasions, but then Gandhi never faced a parliament or an international conference. His influence, just the same, may have helped to bring about Nehru's simplicity of utterance, which, at least in his maturity, does not distinguish between an audience of one or of any other number.

Most prime ministers and politicians have one language for the public and quite another for their private moments. With the single exception of Winston Churchill, there is not one I can call to mind whose full rhetoric and vocabulary could be poured out over a luncheon table as easily as in the House of Commons. Winston used a public language in private; Jawaharlal uses a private language in public; that is a salient difference. But of the more usual phenomenon, the politician with two languages, any experienced observer must have collected many examples.

During my earliest days in journalism, in the 1920's, I was sometimes exposed to the eloquence of M. Aristide Briand in Paris and Geneva. M. Briand was a truly wonderful speaker with a resonant, musical voice. They used to say he "had a violoncello in his stomach." He used the French language resourcefully, on a high level and with strong emotional effect, although sometimes the intellectual content of what he had to say was rather tenuous. Imagine the astonishment of a very young reporter in discovering that when M. Briand was not speaking from a platform, he used downright gutter French, Paris slang and all the rest of it, the language of the newsboy! This may have been partly an affectation, but I was always assured that it was his natural language—the other was his professional disguise.

In less extreme form we have observed the same thing all round the globe. Mr. Roosevelt's private talk had nothing like the polish and drive of his public speeches and was not really in the same language, although it never lacked pith and moment. More recent examples will occur to everybody. It is taken for granted in our time that statesmen must talk in an artificial way, partly because they seldom write their own speeches and partly because they cannot let the public into the secret of how they really talk and think.

If Nehru ever had a public manner and language he sloughed it off long ago—long before I knew him. The Gandhian ideas of truth precluded any such artifice, which, I imagine, was not in his nature anyhow. In the result we have a singularly harmonious, continuous and natural expression which in itself indicates, taken all together and over the years, a singular sincerity.

The powerful personality must in itself produce—I have tried to show—disturbances in others, and most of the charges made against Nehru arise, I think, from those disturbances. Egocentric vanity, "tantrums" and various other prima donna characteristics which are attributed to him may be, often are, the names given by an injured and resentful person to aspects which could quite easily bear another interpretation. A disappointed office seeker may quite naturally say, and believe, that Nehru has poor judgment in making appointments. A person who, for whatever reason, is no longer urged to come to the Prime Minister's house may say that Nehru forgets old friends. In the aggregate what we come to is, really, that Nehru is a human being like anybody else, and has offended or disappointed a certain number of persons whether he wanted to do so or not. They will exaggerate any weakness they may perceive, and so far as my own observation tells me anything, it is that they have exaggerated beyond measure.

All of which does not mean that he is without defects; he is neither monk nor saint, but a man among men, bearing quite a sizable burden, getting impatient and bored and weary from time to time. He certainly must not have been, at any period, "easy to live with," as the saying goes. His concentration is too great for him even to notice half of the small domestic details which make up ordinary life. It was always so: for a long time he was completely engrossed in the national revolution, struggling to set India free, and it involved his entire being. He had no other life. We are not surprised to learn that everybody in his family went to jail during the freedom struggle; not to do so would have been to put a barrier between him and them. His two sisters, his young daughter Indira and even his fragile wife, Kamala, thus defied the laws and took their turns in prison. They must have grown used to the sort of abstraction which has been a lifelong refuge of his, and also—as I know from them—to the peculiar kind of reckoning which especially prevails among politicians, journalists, and persons involved in some collective moment. It is this kind of reckoning:

"When did we get that horse (or piano, or cow)?"

"It was shortly before the Round Table Conference."

Or, another imaginary example which might well be true:

"When can we take the family to the hills?"

"Not until we know what Hitler means by that last speech."

Such ways of thinking, since they relentlessly mix up public events with private life, are often the despair of the nonpolitical. They depersonalize the personal existence to a degree which most women and some men find cold, hard, almost beyond endurance. If I am not greatly mistaken Nehru's entire existence since his return to India has exhibited this confluence and intermingling of the personal and the impersonal, with the inevitable result, of course, that the personal does in time tend to get pushed to the wall.

And another consequence of the powerful personality, wrapped up in public affairs, is a certain reluctance to delegate authority—a feeling that Benjamin Franklin expressed in one of his aphorisms. "If you want a thing well done," said he, "do it yourself." The characteristic is well known in the West; again we refer to F. D. Roosevelt as an example of it. With Nehru we can see it in all things great and small. At the proclamation of the Republic of India (January 26, 1950), which was an immensely solemn occasion in the great throne room of the viceregal palace, cabinet, diplomatic corps and guests assembled to see Rajaji, as the last British Governor-General, leave the throne and Dr. Prasad, as first President of the Republic, take his place. There was thereafter a salute of twenty-one guns, a prolonged and thunderous salute to the new nation, while the whole population rejoiced in the streets. Well . . . On this occasion those who came early to the throne room were privileged to see the Prime Minister darting about, rearranging chairs, verifying the place cards for the ambassadors, and otherwise performing the useful functions of a chief usher.

In the preceding year, at the Second Asian Conference, I arrived early one morning and, from my place in a press balcony, watched the Prime Minister going from desk to desk of the foreign delegates, making sure that there were pens, pencils, paper and—yes—ink. He looked into every inkwell.

The extent to which he keeps track of departmental activities in his own government, the influence he exerts over many of them and the likelihood (which many high officers feel) that he may descend upon them at any moment, can be seen to be examples, on the larger stage, of this desire to do everything himself. Of course there are gradations in his interest and its direction. So far as I know he does not concern himself too much about detail in the economic ministries (finance, commerce and industry, etc.) although he does lay down the general principles to be followed. In his own ministry, which is External Affairs (including Commonwealth Relations) and Atomic Energy, in the Prime Minister's office and in the Planning Commission, he is vitally concerned and holds all the reins in his hands.

In fact one of the reasons why he seems, to most Indians, utterly irreplaceable is that he does so much and has done so much in the government as a whole during his lengthy administration. One often hears it said that whenever he leaves his office it will require several men to do the work he now does, and I think it is true. They will, severally, be excellent, and there is no lack of them, but the single direction must, perforce, be missed. Perhaps Nehru could have made it easier in this past decade by delegating authority, but easier for what? Easier, that is, for his successors: for in sober fact I know of nobody in India who does not regard his incessant, pervasive activity as one of the galvanic forces in the birth of the nation. What he has done, in being everywhere at once, has been invaluable, but it will only make the absence more painful when he is gone. The choice he made (if he had a choice) was perhaps as much determined by his own nature as by the objective necessity. They often work together.

3

The fundamental dogma of communism, that human history is determined by the means of economic production, is alien to Nehru's nature. He is very well aware of those nonmaterial forces, such as love, art and patriotism (to name only a few), which decisively affect the behavior of men and its objective historical results. He hardly ever speaks of material progress without conditioning it by the inclusion of other elements. This being so, it seems odd to a good many observers that his public expressions about communism seldom or never go to the root of the matter. What he says, in one form or another, is that communism may have desirable ends in view, such as the abolition of poverty, the fully classless state, and so on, but that its means have involved so much violence, deceit and all-round wickedness that it cannot achieve these purposes. It is the Gandhian identification of means and ends: no good end can be attained by evil means, and violence is evil.

If I may hazard an opinion in this matter, it is that Nehru has deliberately chosen not to go beyond the Gandhian analysis for a number of reasons which I shall name. First of all, Gandhi's language is native to India and is understood by everybody; it has that ethical basis and religious coloration to which India is accustomed; it carries far more weight than any purely intellectual argument.

But second, it must also be said that Mr. Nehru's acquaintance with Communist theory and dialectic is limited. He says so himself. He read Marx when he was in prison. (The Mahatma, by the way, tried to read Marx and did not like it enough to finish —this in the very late part of his life.) He is acquainted with Lenin's development of dialectical materialism. But he has never really had time to explore that mass of argumentation which constitutes the Russian Communist structure, and he has made no attempt to do so. He will not, therefore, engage in the argument *à fond:* he will not say, or at any rate never has said, that this is an erroneous theory of human society and history, that it does not fit the facts and that it cannot permanently prevail. Even though his own instinct tells him that economic materialism is an inadequate thesis for the human complex, he does not feel *qualified,* it seems to me, to make such a declaration. It would seem to him pontifical, to say the least, and perhaps also wrong. He prefers the Socratic answer: "I do not know, but I know that I do not know."

And third, as everybody knows, India's two neighbors to the north are the most powerful of Communist states, and India's primary necessity is to keep the peace. The "five principles of co-existence" to which Nehru has had recourse, more in hope than in confidence, represent the admission of this fact. They are not the creation of naïveté or ignorance, as so many bumptious editorialists in the United States have assumed, but they are a postulate of super-realism, which, very often indeed in human affairs, may bring about that condition which they postulate.

Nehru's celebrated letter to Congress Party friends, published last year, is printed as an appendix to this book so as to show, in his own words, how he wishes his followers to approach their own consideration of communism.

But when all this is said, as it could be said upon the public record, there remains a fact of very considerable significance to be noted. It is that Nehru, the man, the human being, never for one moment talks or acts like a Communist or even like a person who has imbibed some shreds of Communist theory. He has not a hint of the doctrinaire rigidity, the all-knowing and intolerant certainty, the ready-made sufficiency for all questions, which are the prime characteristics of a Communist. In discussion he is above all humane, trying to find human reasons for human behavior and never judging too harshly where he thinks a motive, rather than its result, can be respected. Communists and those influenced by communism, including a great many Socialists of the leftward sections, never stop judging all men and all happenings by their own rule-of-thumb. Nehru is far too civilized, too acquainted with humanity, to imagine that a slide rule can serve such purposes.

"I am far more a man of the people than my father was," he said to me last year. Certainly for a long time this was true: he went among the oppressed or landless peasants of his own region, the United Provinces, and worked with them to improve their lot, lived with them, knew them, retains to this day his sympathy with them. *But*—to help them, not to use them; as a friend, not as a theory-ridden Communist organizer. He has only recently seen, with a sense of shock, that the Communists in many districts have gone into the field not to help the farmer, but to use him for Communist Party purposes, availing themselves of every weapon, particularly of caste, for their own ends. It was not thus that he went to the farmers in his youth.

Nehru's native refinement of instinct, his detestation of vulgarity and pretense, and even his well-developed sense of humor, are exceedingly non-Communist or anti-Communist characteristics, it seems to me. Of course there are plenty of Communists with a sense of humor—Khrushchev first of all—but it is a weapon, not an instrument of civilized pleasure, and it is never directed upon themselves or their own doings. Nehru's applies to everything, including himself. His fastidiousness, perhaps a family characteristic, can be overcome when he wills, but it is never absent. He gives a sort of *grand seigneur* impression to many persons, and always did, long before he became Prime Minister. It would be impossible to imagine any Communist or Fascist regime, any society given over to the dictatorship of the loud-mouthed few, where he could conceivably feel at home or even live. Freedom of thought and speech have always been the lifeblood of his intellect, and he is as ready to claim them for others as for himself.

During the latter half of 1959 an event of some consequence took place: Mr. Rajagopalachari, whose misgivings have been treated earlier in this book, came into the open with a call for the formation of a "conservative" party of opposition to Nehru's government. The word "conservative" is disliked by various elements which may go into this opposition, and Rajaji has expressed himself as willing to accept some other name, perhaps an Indian word. It is all in the formative stage; organizing is going on right now; it may be some time before the new party can get itself in order and put candidates into the field. Jayaprakash Narayan, the gifted Socialist leader whom I have also discussed earlier, was present at the opening meeting of the "conservatives," by invitation, but took no part in it. Rajaji is an astute and experienced politician, although no longer young, and if he has decided to come out into the streets with a new party we may feel fairly sure that the plans are already well advanced.

What will be Nehru's attitude?

Well, without asking him, I am sure he will always say that every opinion must be heard, every party has a right to organize, every Indian citizen should speak his mind. He will always express reverence for Rajaji as one of the great figures of the Indian national revolution for many decades. (He did this only recently—knowing well what was afoot.) He will also assert his own point of view, which involves industrialization and successive Five Year Plans leading to something called "a socialist pattern of society." Thus he will say—must say—that Rajaji and his "conservatives" are wrong, but that he welcomes the chance to argue it out with them. This is the democratic way of doing things, in which he firmly and deeply believes. And even with a conservative oposition on the Right and a Communist opposition on the Left, certainly the chances are that he will continue to carry things his own way for as long as he wishes to do so.

Many of us outside of India find a very positive element of hope in Nehru's existence, his ideas and his adherence to his own principles, both at home and abroad. He would appear to be the only chief of government anywhere at present who has a genuine world view, along with an extraordinary intuition about the relations of the forces. His work is not done; there is much to come. I have attempted to show what he has done since independence, and to indicate the qualities which have made this possible, along with the effort and aspiration he evokes from India. There is one word I have rarely used in connection with him, but it imposes itself in the end, since he is one upon whom experience is not wasted. Nehru not only knew wisdom once and remembers it, but he has himself become a man of wisdom.

Appendix

The Basic Approach
by JAWAHARLAL NEHRU

(NOTE: *This document was written for private circulation, for the guidance of friends and followers, but the All-India Congress Committee obtained permission to reprint it later in its fortnightly publication, the* Economic Review. *The text used here is that of the* Economic Review. *It has also appeared in other countries and languages during the past year.*)

We have many grave internal problems to face. But even a consideration of these internal problems inevitably leads to a wider range of thought. Unless we have some clarity of vision or, at any rate, are clear as to the questions posed to us, we shall not get out of the confusion that afflicts the world today. I do not pretend to have that clarity of thinking or to have any answers to our major questions. All I can say, in all humility, is that I am constantly thinking about these questions. In a sense, I might say that I rather envy those who have got fixed ideas and, therefore, need not take the trouble to look deeper into the problems of today. Whether it is from the point of view of some religion or ideology, they are not troubled with the mental conflicts which are always the accompaniment of the great ages of transition.

2. And yet, even though it may be more comfortable to have fixed ideas and be complacent, surely that is not to be commended, and that can only lead to stagnation and decay. The basic fact of today is the tremendous pace of change in human life. In my own life, I have seen amazing changes, and I am sure that, in the course of the life of the next generation, these changes will be even greater, if humanity is not overwhelmed and annihilated by an atomic war.

3. Nothing is so remarkable as the progressive conquest or understanding of the physical world by the mind of man today,

and this process is continuing at a terrific pace. Man need no longer be a victim of external circumstances, at any rate, to a very large extent. While there has been this conquest of external conditions, there is at the same time the strange spectacle of a lack of moral fibre and of self-control in man as a whole. Conquering the physical world, he fails to conquer himself.

4. That is the tragic paradox of this Atomic and Sputnik Age. The fact that nuclear tests continue, even though it is well recognised that they are very harmful in the present and in the future; the fact that all kinds of weapons of mass destruction are being produced and piled up, even though it is universally recognised that their use may well exterminate the human race, brings out this paradox with startling clarity. Science is advancing far beyond the comprehension of a very great part of the human race, and posing problems which most of us are incapable of understanding, much less of solving. Hence, the inner conflict and tumult of our times. On the one side, there is this great and overpowering progress in science and technology and of their manifold consequences, on the other, a certain mental exhaustion of civilisation itself.

5. Religion comes into conflict with rationalism. The disciplines of religion and social usage fade away without giving place to other disciplines, moral or spiritual. Religion, as practised, either deals with matters rather unrelated to our normal lives and thus adopts an ivory tower attitude, or is allied to certain social usages which do not fit in with the present age. Rationalism, on the other hand, with all its virtues, somehow appears to deal with the surface of things, without uncovering the inner core. Science itself has arrived at a stage when vast new possibilities and mysteries loom ahead. Matter and energy and spirit seem to overlap.

6. In the ancient days, life was simpler and more in contact with nature. Now it becomes more and more complex and more and more hurried, without time for reflection or even of questioning. Scientific developments have produced an enormous surplus of power and energy which are often used for wrong purposes.

7. The old question still faces us, as it has faced humanity for ages past: what is the meaning of life? The old days of faith do

not appear to be adequate, unless they can answer the questions of today. In a changing world, living should be a continuous adjustment to these changes and happenings. It is the lack of this adjustment that creates conflicts.

8. The old civilisations with the many virtues that they possess, have obviously proved inadequate. The new Western civilisation, with all its triumphs and achievements and also with its atomic bombs, also appears inadequate and, therefore, the feeling grows that there is something wrong with our civilisation. Indeed, essentially our problems are those of civilisation itself. Religion gave a certain moral and spiritual discipline; it also tried to perpetuate superstition and social usages. Indeed, those superstitions and social usages enmeshed and overwhelmed the real spirit of religion. Disillusionment followed. Communism comes in the wake of this disillusionment and offers some kind of faith and some kind of discipline. To some extent it fills a vacuum. It succeeds in some measure by giving a content to man's life. But in spite of its apparent success, it fails, partly because of its rigidity, but, even more so, because it ignores certain essential needs of human nature. There is much talk in Communism of the contradictions of capitalist society and there is truth in that analysis. But we see the growing contradictions within the rigid framework of Communism itself. Its suppression of individual freedom brings about powerful reactions. Its contempt for what might be called the moral and spiritual side of life not only ignores something that is basic in man, but also deprives human behaviour of standards and values. Its unfortunate association with violence encourages a certain evil tendency in human beings.

9. I have the greatest admiration for many of the achievements of the Soviet Union. Among these great achievements is the value attached to the child and the common man. Their systems of education and health are probably the best in the world. But it is said, and rightly, that there is suppression of individual freedom there. And yet the spread of education in all its forms is itself a tremendous liberating force which ultimately will not tolerate that suppression of freedom. This again is another contradiction. Unfortunately, Communism became too closely associated with the necessity for violence and thus the idea which

it placed before the world became a tainted one. Means distorted ends. We see here the powerful influence of wrong means and methods.

10. Communism charges the capitalist structure of society with being based on violence and class conflict. I think this is essentially correct, though that capitalist structure itself has undergone and is continually undergoing a change because of democratic and other struggles and inequality. The question is how to get rid of this and have a classless society with equal opportunities for all. Can this be achieved through methods of violence, or can it be possible to bring about those changes through peaceful methods? Communism has definitely allied itself to the approach of violence. Even if it does not indulge normally in physical violence, its language is of violence, its thought is violent and it does not seek to change by persuasion or peaceful democratic pressures, but by coercion and indeed by destruction and extermination. Fascism has all these evil aspects of violence and extermination in their grossest forms and, at the same time, has no acceptable ideal.

11. This is completely opposed to the peaceful approach which Gandhiji taught us. Communists as well as anti-Communists, both seem to imagine that a principle can only be stoutly defended by language of violence, and by condemning those who do not accept it. For both of them there are no shades, there is only black and white. This is the old approach of the bigoted aspects of some religions. It is not the approach of tolerance of feeling that perhaps others might have some share of the truth also. Speaking for myself, I find this approach wholly unscientific, unreasonable and uncivilised, whether it is applied in the realm of religion or economic theory or anything else. I prefer the old pagan approach of tolerance, apart from its religious aspects. But, whatever we may think about it, we have arrived at a stage in the modern world when an attempt at forcible imposition of ideas on any large section of people is bound ultimately to fail. In present circumstances this will lead to war and tremendous destruction. There will be no victory, only defeat for everyone. Even thus, we have seen, in the last year or two, that it is not easy for even great Powers to reintroduce colonial control over territories which have recently become independ-

ent. This was exemplified by the Suez incident in 1956. Also what happened in Hungary demonstrated that the desire for national freedom is stronger even than any ideology and cannot ultimately be suppressed. What happened in Hungary was not essentially a conflict between Communism and anti-Communism. It represented nationalism striving for freedom from foreign control.

12. Thus, violence cannot possibly lead today to a solution of any major problem because violence has become much too terrible and destructive. The moral approach to this question has now been powerfully reinforced by the practical aspect.

13. If the society we aim at cannot be brought about by big scale violence, will small scale violence help? Surely not, partly because that itself may lead to the big scale violence and partly because it produces an atmosphere of conflict and of disruption. It is absurd to imagine that out of conflict the social progressive forces are bound to win. In Germany both the Communist Party and the Social Democratic Party were swept away by Hitler. This may well happen in other countries too. In India any appeal to violence is particularly dangerous because of its inherent disruptive character. We have too many fissiparous tendencies for us to take risks. But all these are relatively minor considerations. The basic thing, I believe, is that wrong means will not lead to right results and that is no longer merely an ethical doctrine but a practical proposition.

14. Some of us have been discussing this general background and, more especially, conditions in India. It is often said that there is a sense of frustration and depression in India and the old buoyancy of spirit is not to be found at a time when enthusiasm and hard work are most needed. This is not merely in evidence in our country. It is in a sense a world phenomenon. An old and valued colleague said that this is due to our not having a philosophy of life and indeed the world also is suffering from this lack of a philosophical approach. In our efforts to ensure the material prosperity of the country, we have not paid any attention to the spiritual element in human nature. Therefore, in order to give the individual and the nation a sense of purpose, something to live for and, if necessary, to die for, we have to revive some philosophy of life and give, in the wider sense of the word, a

spiritual background to our thinking. We talk of a Welfare State and of democracy and socialism. They are good concepts but they hardly convey a clear and unambiguous meaning. This was the argument and then the question arose as to what our ultimate objective should be. Democracy and socialism are means to an end, not the end itself. We talk of the good of society. Is this something apart from and transcending the good of the individuals composing it? If the individual is ignored and sacrificed for what is considered the good of the society, is that the right objective to have?

15. It was agreed that the individual should not be so sacrificed and indeed that real social progress will come only when opportunity is given to the individual to develop, provided the individual is not a selected group, but comprises the whole community. The touchstone, therefore, should be how far any political or social theory enables the individual to rise above his petty self and thus think in terms of the good of all. The law of life should not be competition or acquisitiveness but co-operation, the good of each contributing to the good of all. In such a society the emphasis will be on duties, not on rights; the rights will follow the performance of the duties. We have to give a new direction to education and evolve a new type of humanity.

16. This argument led to the old Vedantic conception that everything, whether sentient or insentient, finds a place in the organic whole; that everything has a spark of what might be called the Divine impulse or the basic energy or life force which pervades the Universe. This leads to metaphysical regions which tend to take us away from the problems of life which face us. I suppose that any line of thought, sufficiently pursued, leads us in some measure to metaphysics. Even science today is almost on the verge of all manner of imponderables. I do not propose to discuss these metaphysical aspects, but this very argument indicates how the mind searches for something basic underlying the physical world. If we really believed in this all-pervading concept of the principle of life, it might help us to get rid of some of our narrowness of race, caste or class and make us more tolerant and understanding in our approaches to life's problems.

17. But obviously it does not solve any of these problems and,

in a sense, we remain where we were. In India we talk of the Welfare State and Socialism. In a sense, every country, whether it is Capitalist, Socialist or Communist, accepts the ideal of the Welfare State. Capitalism, in a few countries at least, has achieved this common welfare to a very large extent, though it has far from solved its own problems and there is a basic lack of something vital. Democracy allied to Capitalism has undoubtedly toned down many of its evils and in fact is different now from what it was a generation or two ago. In industrially advanced countries there has been a continuous and steady upward trend of economic development. Even the terrible losses of World Wars have not prevented this trend, in so far as these highly developed countries are concerned. Further, this economic development has spread, though in varying degrees, to all classes. This does not apply to countries which are not industrially developed. Indeed, in those countries the struggle for development is very difficult and sometimes, in spite of efforts, not only do economic inequalities remain, but tend to become worse. Normally speaking, it may be said that the forces of a capitalist society, if left unchecked, tend to make the rich richer and the poor poorer and thus increase the gap between them. This applies to countries as well as groups or regions or classes within the countries. Various democratic processes interfere with these normal trends. Capitalism itself has, therefore, developed some socialistic features even though its major aspects remain.

18. Socialism, of course, deliberately wants to interfere with the normal processes and thus not only adds to the productive forces but lessens inequalities. But, what is socialism? It is difficult to give a precise answer and there are innumerable definitions of it. Some people probably think of socialism vaguely just as something which does good and which aims at equality. That does not take us very far. Socialism is basically a different approach from that of capitalism, though I think it is true that the wide gap between them tends to lessen because many of the ideas of socialism are gradually incorporated even in the capitalist structure. Socialism is after all not only a way of life but a certain scientific approach to social and economic problems. If so-

cialism is introduced in a backward and under-developed country, it does not suddenly make it any less backward. In fact we then have a backward and poverty-stricken socialism.

19. Unfortunately many of the political aspects of Communism have tended to distort our vision of socialism. Also the technique of struggle evolved by Communism has given violence a predominant part. Socialism should, therefore, be considered apart from these political elements or the inevitability of violence. It tells us that the general character of social, political and intellectual life in a society is governed by its productive resources. As those productive resources change and develop, so the life and thinking of the community changes.

20. Imperialism or colonialism suppressed and suppresses the progressive social forces. Inevitably it aligns itself with certain privileged groups or classes because it is interested in preserving the social and economic status quo. Even after a country has become independent, it may continue to be economically dependent on other countries. This kind of thing is euphemistically called having close cultural and economic ties.

21. We discuss sometimes the self-sufficiency of the village. This should not be mixed up with the idea of decentralisation though it may be a part of it. While decentralisation is, I think, desirable to the largest possible extent, if it leads to odd and rather primitive methods of production, then it simply means that we do not utilise modern methods which have brought great material advance to some countries of the West. That is, we remain poor and, what is more, tend to become poorer because of the pressure of an increasing population. I do not see any way out of our vicious circle of poverty except by utilising the new sources of power which science has placed at our disposal. Being poor, we have no surplus to invest and we sink lower and lower.

22. We have to break through this barrier by profiting by the new sources of power and modern techniques. But, in doing so, we should not forget the basic human element and the fact that our objective is individual improvement and the lessening of inequalities; and we must not forget the ethical and spiritual aspects of life which are ultimately the basis of culture and civilisation and which have given some meaning to life.

23. It has to be remembered that it is not by some magic

adoption of socialist or capitalist method that poverty suddenly leads to riches. The only way is through hard work and increasing the productivity of the nation and organising an equitable distribution of its products. It is a lengthy and difficult process. In a poorly developed country, the capitalist method offers no chance. It is only through a planned approach on socialistic lines that steady progress can be attained though even that will take time. As this process continues, the texture of our life and thinking gradually changes.

24. Planning is essential for this because otherwise we waste our resources which are very limited. Planning does not mean a mere collection of projects or schemes, but a thought-out approach of how to strengthen the base and pace of progress so that the community advances on all fronts. In India we have a terrible problem of extreme poverty in certain large regions, apart from the general poverty of the country. We have always a difficult choice before us; whether to concentrate on production by itself in selected and favourable areas, and thus for the moment rather ignoring the poor areas, or try to develop the backward areas at the same time, so as to lessen the inequalities between regions. A balance has to be struck and an integrated national plan evolved. That national plan need not and indeed should not have rigidity. It need not be based on any dogma; but should rather take the existing facts into consideration. It may and, I think, in present-day India, it should encourage private enterprise in many fields, though even that private enterprise must necessarily fit in with the national plan and have such controls as are considered necessary.

25. Land reforms have a peculiar significance because without them, more especially in a highly congested country like India, there can be no radical improvement in productivity in agriculture. But the main object of land reforms is a deeper one. They are meant to break up the old class structure of a society that is stagnant.

26. We want social security, but we have to recognise that social security only comes when a certain stage of development has been reached. Otherwise we shall have neither social security nor any development.

27. It is clear that, in the final analysis, it is the quality of the

human beings that counts. It is man that builds up the wealth of a nation, as well as its cultural progress. Hence education and health are of high importance so as to produce that quality in the human beings. We have to suffer here also from the lack of resources, but still we have always to remember that it is right education and good health that will give the foundation for economic as well as cultural and spiritual progress.

28. A national plan has thus both a short-term objective and a long-term one. The long-term objective gives a true perspective. Without it short-term planning is of little avail and will lead us into blind alleys. Planning will thus always be perspective planning and hard in view of the physical achievements for which we strive. In other words, it has to be physical planning, though it is obviously limited and conditioned by financial resources and economic conditions.

29. The problems that India faces are to some extent common to other countries, but much more so, there are new problems for which we have not got parallels or historical precedents elsewhere. What has happened in the past in the industrially advanced countries has little bearing on us today. As a matter of fact, the countries that are advanced today were economically better off than India today, in terms of per capita income, before their industrialisation began. Western economics, therefore, though helpful, have little bearing on our present-day problems. So also have Marxist economics which are in many ways out of date, even though they throw a considerable light on economic processes. We have thus to do our own thinking, profiting by the example of others, but essentially trying to find a path for ourselves suited to our own conditions.

30. In considering these economic aspects of our problems, we have always to remember the basic approach of peaceful means; and perhaps we might also keep in view the old Vedantic ideal of the life force which is the inner base of everything that exists.

Index

ABOUT THE AUTHOR

VINCENT SHEEAN has been a free-lance news correspondent for thirty-five years, tracing world history in places like North Africa, China, Palestine, Spain and India. His early adventures are described in *Personal History*, that classic of the roving reporter which set a trend for news memoirs in this country and became the basis for a Hitchcock movie thriller, *Foreign Correspondent*. One of his most hazardous jobs, covering the North African Riff War, also inspired the famed operetta *Desert Song*. His uncanny time-sense carried him into many areas of crisis both before and during the Second World War. In its later stages he served as intelligence officer with the Air Force.

In 1945 he covered the San Francisco Conference organizing the UN, and three years later was present in the garden at Birla House when Gandhi was assassinated. These two events merged in his mind, producing an unusual study of the Indian leader, *Lead, Kindly Light: Gandhi and the Way to Peace*. Last spring the Westinghouse Broadcasting Company sent him to Asia to do some television and radio interviews and documentaries. Some of these were made in India with Prime Minister Nehru.

Sheean's news career began on Midwest papers after graduation from the University of Chicago. He has written more than twenty books, fiction and nonfiction. He is married to Diana Forbes-Robertson, youngest daughter of Sir Johnston Forbes-Robertson, the late English actor and manager. They have two daughters.